Stars in My Eyes

Photographer: Jay Thompson - from Tony Charmoli Photo Archives

Stars in My Eyes

Adventures in Show Business

Tony Charmoli

TurningPointPress LLC

TurningPointPress 2015
PO Box 81, Teaneck, NJ 07666
turningpointpress@gmail.com
www.turningpointpressllc.com

Copyright © 2015 Tony Charmoli
Foreword © 2015 Mitzi Gaynor

All rights reserved. No part of this book may be reproduced, scanned, or distributed in any printed or electronic form without permission of the publisher and/or owners of the copyrighted material. Please do not participate in or encourage piracy of copyrighted materials in violation of the author's or creator's rights. Purchase only authorized editions.

ISBN 978-0-9973829-0-7

Photos not otherwise credited are from the author's collection or photographers unknown.

**Edited and designed
by Paul Manchester**

First Edition

The cover photo by Zachary Freyman
(with Virginia Conwell's legs)

Will and Tony

This book is dedicated to my dear friend,

Wilford R. Sanders

TonyCharmoli.com has a variety of videos of the dances and shows that you'll read about in the following pages - take the time to explore and I think you'll enjoy yourself. They will add to your experience of this book.

CHAPTERS

Foreword by **Mitzi Gaynor** 09

Chapter 1   **Early Years** 12

Chapter 2   **New York & Broadway** 41

Chapter 3   **Early TV (1949-56)** 56

Chapter 4   **Dinah Shore** 88

Chapter 5   **Some TV Specials (1960-66)** 110

Chapter 6   **Danny Kaye** 120

Chapter 7   **European Adventures** 129

Chapter 8   **Some Night Club Acts (1955-70)** 140

Chapter 9   **Some Variety Shows (1968-90)** 153

Chapter 10 **Juliet Prowse** 183

Chapter 11 **Puppets & Muppets** 190

Chapter 12   **Forays in Film** 197

Chapter 13   **Friends** 202

Chapter 14   **Woman Of The Year** 224

Chapter 15   **Circus Of The Stars** 229

Chapter 16   **Mikhail Baryshnikov** 239

Chapter 17   **Star Search** 242

Chapter 18   **Pageants** 245

Chapter 19   **Mitzi Gaynor** 259

Chapter 20   **The Christmas Party** 269

Thankfulness 281

Index of Names & Shows 287

Foreword by Mitzi Gaynor

"**G**OOOORGEOUS!" He shouted, charging down the stairs from the control booth at NBC's massive Studio 4 in Burbank following a particularly good take of one of the all-singing, all-dancing numbers from the five TV specials he fabulously choreographed and directed for me. I lived for those shouts of "goooorgeous" from Tony, we all did really, because it meant we'd done him proud. And if he was proud, we'd look good, maybe even great.

It seems like I've known Tony all of my life. It's because some of the happiest times of my life are so tied together with him. I think we first met somewhere in the middle-fifties – the 1950's (not the 1850's you b*#tch). I was movie-starring my way through New York (puff-puff) probably on some publicity tour, and Tony was busy triumphing as he always did on *Your Hit Parade*, *The Dinah Shore Chevy Show* or one of the countless other TV classics on which he made gypsies, star-ladies, comics, and trained seals etc., look, well, goooorgeous!

Fast forward a few years to the early 1970's. My husband and producer Jack Bean had a wonderful meeting with Tony that changed our lives. In fact I remember Jack coming home and saying "where has this man been all our lives!" They had clicked, and then we certainly clicked. Tony even clicked with my best-friend-hairdresser-soul mate Tommy Carlino; and if you clicked with Tommy - all was right with the world.

Tony first brought his limitless creativity to my stage show, adding a knock-out troupe of singers and dancers, "the Cast of Thousands" he called them, when we opened the new Superstar Theatre at the Tropicana Hotel in Las Vegas in 1973. Then Tony got busy triumphing for me, and from then on it was an unstoppable, joyous, memory-filled ride.

You see, Tony gets me, and he sees things in me that I don't see in myself. Did I mention he's kind? Some choreographers ask you to try a step, a step you know you can't do well. And when you try it, and fail, they still insist on keeping it in the number. So all through that number you're anticipating and worrying about that one step you know you can't do well. Not Tony. Oh sure, he'll ask you to try the step, and that's great. But here's the difference, when he sees you can't really do it, he says "Well, let's try something else, you don't do that so well." No bruised egos, no thrown clipboards, no wasted time… just fun.

And a fun time we had, through high-kicks at midnight taping *Mitzi…and 100 Guys* or *Mitzi…Roarin' in the 20's*, and years on the road in Las Vegas, the Cave in Vancouver B.C., Miami Beach, the Westbury Music Fair, Norfolk, Portland, Tulsa, Memphis, Cohasset, Paducah, Sandusky and all across these United States and Canada. And we're still doing it, still having great fun.

I'm so proud to know him, so proud that he's my friend, so proud of the fact he shares so much of his great, grand and glorious talent with me, and so proud he's written this wonderful book so that we can all revel in and relive some of the spectacular days of real honest-to-goodness show business through his eyes.

Tony, I adore you. And guess what, you're goooorgeous!!!

Love ya,
Mitzi

Years ago when I was a very young boy, I saw Janet Gaynor in *Tess Of The Storm Country* and I knew I just had to get into show business. This is my story of working my way to Hollywood.

The Charmoli's: Pa, Ma, Butch, Nell, Al, Claire, Art, Mudge, Alfred, & Tony

Chapter 1
Early Years

MT. IRON, MINNESOTA

Having been born and raised in Northern Minnesota, I had to survive many cold winters loaded with snow and freezing temperatures. Now in my grown up years I have to make public appearances and I am often approached with, "For your age, you look great! What's your secret?" My reply is, "I was born in Northern Minnesota and for the first 20 years of my life, I was frozen." After that you can say anything.

In 1890, iron ore was discovered in Minnesota on the Iron Range, so there was a rush for jobs to mine the ore. Arriving from Italy around 1900, my father, Phillip Charmoli, age 18, was in a group of new immigrants that traveled to work in the mines. The job seemed to pay him well enough to send for his bride-to-be Adolorata Minelli, his girlfriend in Montefalcone, Italy. When she finally arrived, he courted her for twenty-eight days before they married in 1902 and had nine children. I was the ninth.

Early on I learned that you have to be tough to grow up the youngest in a family of eight. I say eight as the oldest sister, Minnie, passed away during some kind of epidemic. The children were all born two years apart, but I came along at a little more than three years apart. When I was old enough to know more I'd tease my mother with, "It must have been a cold winter night for you and Pa!" And she'd come back with a gruff, "Oh Tony, you're terrible." And I would counter with, "Ah Ha! I was right!"

When chores are handed out to the oldest, they'd get passed down to the next in line, which eventualy would wind up being me. If I refused, I'd get a boot in the ass from my older brothers. I learned how to work.

For a poor family who was occasionally on relief, there were many hardships. Even with working at the mine, money was tight. We lived near the railroad station and the winter would bring coal deliveries to those who could afford it. During the unloading, there would be spillage and my brother, Alfred, and I would get our buckets and rush over to the railroad tracks and pick up all the fallen coal we could carry. He could always fill his bucket, but a full bucket was too heavy for me. I'd hear my mother complain to my father that it was too much for me, but he'd say, "He has to learn." I didn't get what I had to learn but kept at it till I was able to fill my bucket. It kept us warm in the freezing winters. Once a month or so, Alfred and I took our little wagon out to the Relief Station to pick up our allotment of a hundred pound sack of flour. If we didn't do that we were told we wouldn't get any pasta. Imagine an Italian household without pasta.

Phillip and Adolorata Charmoli's engagement photo.

My father worked in the iron ore mines at night and had to sleep during the day, so that meant we had to pussyfoot around the house while he was in bed. But finally he'd had enough of the mines and he got a job working for the city as a policeman and volunteered as a fireman. He was one of those people that everybody loved. And we loved that he didn't have to work in the mines anymore. One Saturday, he surprised us all when he was elevated to Fire Chief, he drove past the house clanging the bell on the big red fire trunk yelling, "Hey Gram! Look at me; I'm Fire Chief. Come on Tony, jump on I'll give you a ride!" A kid riding a fire truck! WOW! It was heaven.

One day when my dad was on duty somewhere, my sisters Claire and Al decided to take the old

Ma, Claire, Nell, Nell's husband- Camillo, me, & Pa

Chevy for a run. I was just a four year old kid at the time and they asked if I wanted to go along. Of course I did. The ride was great until way out somewhere we ran out of gas and had to walk a long way to town to get gas. We had no container to put the gas in. The station attendant said he would give us a gallon if we could leave some collateral to prove we'd bring the can back and pay him. Nothing seemed to satisfy the attendant until Claire offered me as collateral. That seemed ok with the attendant. I seemed to be worth a gallon of gas. My mother was furious when she found out, but I was too young to understand why.

We were also taught how to make wine. I would accompany my father on his yearly visit to the grape supplier in Hibbing, Minnesota where he would put in his yearly order for a ton of Zinfandel Grapes from California.

Guess one which will be the dancer?

We were poor but he always managed his yearly ton of grapes. Alfred and my sister Mudge and I would get into our rubber boots to stomp and crush the grapes in our individual tubs. I always danced in my tub while crushing my grapes. Then my mother and father would carry the crushed mash to the barrels. We had special rubber mats to stand on while waiting for our tubs to be returned for the next round. When done, the boots were hosed down and hung to dry and put away 'til the next season. Those boots were never used for anything else but stomping grapes.

When the wine was ready for drinking, Pa would go to the cellar each night and draw out a small pitcher full and bring it up for dinner. We each had a wine glass at the table and my father would always go around the table one by one offering wine to each of us but of course none of us drank wine - naturally one could not pour it back in the barrel so he drank the whole pitcher himself each night. After dinner he always seemed a little happier and slightly tipsy. Now that's one way to raise a large family without going crazy in the evenings.

My father was fun and he liked to dance. He would roll up the living room rug and ask my mother to dance but she always refused and said, "Dance with Tony." I was just a little kid, but I loved it and as I grew older, I still loved it and on and on until it blossomed into a full career. My sisters also would join in, but my brothers were always off playing football or something.

We all spoke English among ourselves at table and always to him because he had to speak English in his work as a policeman or fireman. My mother stayed with Italian and we would reply in Italian. It was useful many years later when I directed a couple of shows in Italy.

We also learned about gardening. We had a large garden behind our rented house and another on a lot we rented several blocks away. As a child, my mother always packed a lunch and took me with her to the second garden which was large and full of what wasn't in the one near the house. The part I liked best was when we stopped for lunch. She always made a large frittata of some kind and a few other things. We'd

"Coombar" of C. Charmoli & Co.

sit on the ground and enjoy it in our garden. Incidentally, I did have a small toy hoe and a few other small garden toys so I could garden as well. It was all part of growing up in an Italian household.

My Uncle Leonard had a grocery store and butcher shop. We called him "Coombar" (for Uncle). My father occasionally helped out as a butcher. As a kid there was one rule I had to honor. Whenever I went to the store I was allowed to take one cookie from the cookie bins. I could choose any one but only one. I honored this because I knew my uncle was strict and if I disobeyed he would take this privilege away from me.

Theater was in my blood at an early age. It started when I was in kindergarten and the teacher asked if I would carry a poster across the stage announcing the swimming meet on Saturday. Of course I would, my sister was the diver on the team! When I got home my sisters asked what the teacher wanted and I told them about the poster. Claire said, "You can't just walk in with the poster - you have to do a little dance as you carry it." She taught me the banana split where you wiggle your feet from side to side as you travel across the stage. The next morning the teacher brought me up to the stage and handed me the poster, which turned out to be as big as I was. To see where I was going I had to hold the poster just above my shoes so now all you could see were my feet and my curly hair. She gave me the cue and I started across and soon you could hear giggles from the audience and by the time I reached center stage they we were out and out laughing.

All they could see were my shoes and curly hair so I stopped, lowered the poster and peered over the top to see what they were laughing at, and then they just burst out laughing and applauded even more. I raised the poster back in front of my face and continued the banana split off. They all stood up with wild applause and yells of "Encore! Encore!" The teacher told me to run out and take a bow and when I did they all yelled, "Bravo! Bravo!" Since then the theater has never left my bones.

Once when I was still a little kid my father brought home a little black lamb. I went wild for that little lamb. It went everywhere with me except to school. I couldn't anticipate that I wouldn't have my little lamb forever. That never entered my mind. Then, Easter came and my dear little lamb was nowhere to be found. I asked my Pa and he told me it was on the dinner table. I was shocked. I cried and cried and wouldn't eat lamb for years. But, eventually I got over it and must confess that now I rather like lamb.

On the summer holiday, my mother, sister, brother, and I would go out into the woods and pitch a tent to stay overnight to pick wild blueberries at sunrise the next morning. My mother always told me to stay close to her but once I got so involved with the picking I kept getting closer and closer to the top of the bush when suddenly I came face to face with an Indian. I had never seen an Indian before and screamed bloody murder. My mother and brother, thinking it was a bear attacking me, came running on the double and were gratefully relieved when they saw it was only an Indian. I grew to like Indians and learned their dances and purchased their costumes.

As a kid I often went next door to visit the Minnelli's. There were four sisters and a brother. On one visit I went to visit Rosey, the youngest of the sisters, and all the other sisters also happened to be there. This combination of sisters rarely happened. I was sitting in a chair next to the kitchen stove when a big family argument broke out amongst the sisters. Mrs. Minnelli tried to stop it but was totally ignored. I became frightened and was frozen to my chair. Suddenly Anne reached for a rather large kitchen knife and sailed it across the room full force at Lucy who ducked in time for it to whiz by and lodge into the leg of my chair a hairs breath from my ankle. I was frozen as Mrs. Minnelli screamed and grabbed me. A hair missed disaster. I was instructed never to mention this to anyone and never did until late in life when Molly was gone and there was not much left of the family. Rosey and I talked bout it and it never went farther than that.

Above: Pa, Tony, Claire, & Nell;
Left: My first painting at the age of six.

16

Mr. Minnelli was always very frail and sick in bed. He seemed to like me and I always went into the bedroom to visit with him. One day I got an urgent summons from Mrs. Minnelli and I dashed over and went right in to see him. It wasn't long before he reached up to embrace me and died in my arms. For some strange reason it didn't frighten me and I didn't cry. I must have felt it was inevitable. Thinking back on it I guess this must have been very grown up for a very young boy.

That summer vacation after kindergarten, I used to jump into my bib overalls and go to the house across the street, which was a dirt road, and sit on their front steps with the Minnelli girls and watch the cars drive by. The girls always sat on the lower steps. When the man who lived there saw I was there, he would come out and sit on the top step and straddle me on the step above so I would be between his legs. In the hot humid summer in Minnesota I wouldn't wear a shirt, shoes or underwear and soon he'd slowly slide his big strong hands over my shoulders and along my chest then wander down inside my overalls. We all just kept looking at the cars while this was going on. I didn't know this was considered bad, I just knew it felt good and I shouldn't tell anyone and didn't. This all ended when summer vacation was over.

Late at night around this time, my father was often awakened by the squawking of the chickens. One evening he decided to sit out in the chicken coop to see what was causing the chickens to get so upset. He found out the very next night. When the intruder entered, my father flashed his big light on him and saw it was none other than the guy from across the street. He shouted, "Put that chicken down. Don't you know that when you upset the chickens like this, they won't lay eggs? Now get out of here. When you want a chicken just ask me for one and I'll give it to you, but don't ever let me catch you in the coop again."

The next Christmas, Santa had left a little set of oil paints for me. I had no lessons, I was excited to have it and knew right off what I wanted to paint. I had saved a magazine that had a picture of an Indian on the cover and I just copied that. I had no lessons - I just painted. I still have that painting. One of my sisters had it until she passed away and now I have it hanging in my house. Painting seemed to come naturally and I'm still doing it.

While still in grade school we could take piano lessons free of charge. My schoolmate at the time was Eugene Nelson and his family had a piano. The major problem was we didn't have a piano and never did get one. I had some piano keys on a cardboard strip and I would practice the fingering but obviously there was no sound. Eugene Nelson said I could come over to his house and practice with him. But, he lived way across town, so I mostly just practiced on my cardboard strip. Miss Perala was our teacher and seemed to enjoy having Eugene and me in her class. We were very dedicated to taking the lessons and Eugene's parents were very good about letting me practice with him every Saturday.

When Miss Perala thought we were good enough, she talked to the Principal and recommended that we play at one of the high school assemblies. The time came and Miss

Tony on far right with Junior High Puppetry club

17

Tony, his niece Dorothy, and Mickey the wonder dog.

Perala took us up to the Assembly Hall and announced to the packed auditorium that they were in for a treat. Two of her young students, Mr. Charmoli and Mr. Nelson, were going to entertain them with a duet on the piano. Eugene and I walked out to the piano and waited for the applause to die down, and then looked at each other and BANG away we went to a smattering of applause. We were doing pretty well when the sheet music slid to the floor. We both froze with our hands suspended in position ready to strike the next chord. We were holding our breath in this suspended silence and finally Miss Perala walked out, picked up our music and put it into place on the piano and BANG we were off again. Well, the auditorium just shook with laughter and loud applause. We rode it out to the end with no more stops and hit the loudest ending chord our little fingers could muster up. We stood up together to take our bow and immediately a standing ovation mixed with cheers of "More! more!" rocked the hall. We became the talk of the school. I forgot to mention Eugene and I were the same size - short - and so were our fingers.

My oldest brother, Butch, was coaching football at Dupont Manuel High in Louisville, Ky., He sent me a Chow dog called Mickey. Mickey walked me to school every morning and at the school door I would say, "Now Mickey, go home." And he would obey. My mother always kept track of the time for school to let out and then say, "Mickey, go get Tony." and he would always be waiting at the school door for me. The other kids would also wait with me because they just loved to see the jumping, turning, and barking that Mickey did upon seeing me. He was a great escort and protector.

Growing up in a large family means everybody has a bunch of chores. My brothers and I took care of outside stuff and sisters did house chores. My brother Alfred and I fed the rabbits and stacked the woodpile, and I always fed my dog, Mickey. My father fed the pig and chickens, and my mother fed the cat.

While I was still in Jr. High School, my sister Albina had married and given birth to a baby girl she named Dorothy. Al was employed in a factory and couldn't take care of her baby in St. Paul, so she left her in the care of my mother. My sister Nell ran a beauty shop in nearby Eveleth and gave Dorothy a permanent which my Mother couldn't handle, so the task was given to me. Besides getting myself ready for school I had to help dress baby Dorothy and do her hair. Dorothy was too young to comb her hair out and fix it herself. Combing out the snarls often caused screams of "Ouch" - not the most pleasant of chores for an adolescent boy. It was a task I simply detested. Then, I had to dress her and feed Mickey before getting off to school. Mickey slurped up his food, and off we'd go. Having completed all these chores made me feel like I had already done a day's work.

During part of summer vacation, I would go to St. Paul to baby sit Dorothy while her mother and dad were at work - I rather liked being in the big city. The apartment they had was at the top of a steep flight of stairs. One night, when Dorothy's parents were out late I put Dorothy to bed and then went to my bed myself. Later in the night, I had the feeling something was not quite right and went to check on Dorothy and she wasn't in her bed. I rushed out to the hallway and there was Dorothy sleep-walking. She was out in the hallway standing at the top of that huge flight of very steep stairs. I took her by the shoulders and turned her toward the apartment door and guided her back to her bed. She slept through the whole thing. The next morning she didn't remember what she had done. I certainly was a hero when I told her parents. Looking back I can say that in a way I became Dorothy's mother.

Summer vacations always required a little creativity to entertain ourselves on the Iron Range. One famous spot was the open pit mine. When the mine had delivered all its ore, the natural springs were allowed to fill the huge open pit and it became our swimming hole during summer vacation. The water was ice cold which made all our little dicks shrivel up but we played in the water anyway. Some boys had swimming trunks but the rest of us went naked.

There also was a small hill of land that jutted out into the water covered with trees and bushes which made it a great place to visit and explore as it was difficult to reach without swimming. One of the good looking young Scandinavian boys and I often swam to the little forest on the peninsula. We always told the other guys that we were going hunting. But, once on the peninsula after a short rest to catch our breath we went deeper into the foliage till we were hidden from view. Then we always had a fun time discovering what boys could do while naked. Sworn to secrecy and a promise not to tell anyone, we'd swim back to the mainland, dressed and went our merry ways with "I'll see you at school!" This became our routine during summer vacation.

Those little escapades were memorable and on graduation he wrote in my yearbook:

Dear Tony,

"Don't forget all those walks we had— Picking berries, hunting etc. Here's wishing all the success to a swell kid that really has got it."

Best wishes,
(name withheld)

Years later he with his lovely wife and two children came to visit me in California. It was a wonderful visit with a genuinely warm embrace on departure.

There was no movie theater in our town so as a kid I used to hitch a ride on the back of the Greyhound bus to the next town five miles away. The bus had a rack on the back of the bus that held a spare tire, and if you snuck up before the bus took off you could hold on to the rack without the driver seeing you. It was frequently cold hanging on as the bus sped along but as long as you kept your head below the back window the driver never noticed. But that is how I'd get to the next town to see a movie. Sometimes a friend would come with me but not always. Of course I just told my Ma that I hitched a ride as she would not have approved of me hanging onto the back of a bus. In those days, hitching a ride was not like it is now. Everybody knew everyone.

My first heart throb was Janet Gaynor in *Tess of the Storm Country*, but my devotion soon changed when I first saw Eleanor Powell. She became my idol when I was still a junior in high school and made me want to dance.

I earned my money to go to the movies by caddying for Miss Peltier who was our Geography teacher. Every Saturday morning. I would meet her and we would drive to the golf course. For a kid it was tough carrying that heavy bag of clubs but I would do anything to see Eleanor Powell. Miss Peltier paid me twenty-five cents each time she played the nine-hole course. By hitching a ride on the back of the Greyhound Bus my transportation was free, and with my caddy wages I could afford my theater ticket.

I improvised dances and became pretty good at it, besides I was always told I was cute doing my dances. My father brought this to the attention of Mr. Radcliff our local orchestra conductor and he and my father agreed I should perform at one of the local band concerts in the park. When asked what I would like to dance to, I suggested *Valse Bluette*. The band knew it so a date was set. There was no rehearsal I just had to improvise. My oldest sister Nell made my costume. The time came and my father packed my costume and we drove to the bandstand in the park and he helped me get ready.

The park was quite full of spectators when the time came. I was told I could come out and dance at any point in the music. I went out to applause and danced my little butt off and when I got tired I'd leave the stage, then dance back on after a short breather. I did this several times until I became totally fatigued. I had no idea *"Valse Bluette"* was so long. By the end I was a whipped puppy. I don't recall if I got good applause or not. On the drive home my father was silent until I asked, "Pa how was I?" Without hesitation he said, "You were on too long." I couldn't believe my own dad didn't think I was terrific. To this day that still rings in my ears because it's very good advice. "Never Stay On Too Long." My mother who wasn't there (and typical of a mother) assured me I probably was very good and wondered if they liked Nel's costume.

Word got around school that I was interested in dance, and in junior high, the heavens opened up when June Peterson offered to teach me. She said she would teach me if I would team up with her. It made no difference that she was in high school and I was just in junior high. It was joy to my ears and in no time we were a team and got a job dancing in the vaudeville circuit on the Iron Range. We first started with just a regular tap dance, but to make our act seem more difficult we loosely chained our ankles together so the sound of the chains slapping the stage added a rhythm all its own. It drew applause every time.

I learned something else on that circuit. The boy who shared the dressing room with me at a certain time of the year always ate his lunch alone in the dressing room. Once I asked if I could join him. "Okay," he said, "if you like matzo and an apple." He informed me that his religion required that he eat only this diet at certain times of the year. I said, "Well, sure. I'd like to try it." So, I had my first matzo. I thanked him, but went out to lunch after that.

When I was about 15, I saw an ad in the local papers announcing that lessons in ballroom and other forms of dance would be sponsored free by the WPA at the park in Virginia City. The park was only five miles away, so I quickly hitched a ride over and enrolled. Since I was the only boy student, my first dance instructor Ida Canossa decided that I should partner her in her annual recital. I had grave doubts that this would work out because she was so much taller than me. Wouldn't it look funny for a young kid to be dancing a romantic ballroom number with his much older and taller dance teacher? She convinced me we should try and the rehearsals seemed to be okay. The other students watched a rehearsal and gave their

Dancing with June Peterson

approval. On show night I gave it my all. The performance went very well and we got a big hand of approval from the audience. In fact we got a standing ovation. The reaction just proved I had to be a dancer.

This was a good segue during my high school years to other dance teachers who would give me free lessons if I came to join their schools of dance. Ida and I did a show one night in Virginia and a man named Denis McGinty with the WPA was in the audience. When I told Ida I needed a ride home she replied, "I'll have Denis take you home." He took me home all right, but straight to his hotel room first, WOW! I learned a lot that night. Denis McGinty, who was probably in his 30's, traveled around quite a bit developing WPA arts programs.

My dance schooling progressed, and soon a tap dance teacher, Wilhelmina Gardner, suggested that another student, Dolores Vecchi, and I would make a good team. So we began dancing at various events together around the area.

At the same time I was the School Cheerleader. When I graduated into high school I thought to support my

Tony with Jeanette Ruska

brothers on the football field I should have two girls join me in cheering the team on to victory. They became a welcome add and when I asked my brothers if they liked our cheering they all agreed it was a help. By the time we got to be seniors, I had a group of about 14 girls. I choreographed all the movements and we all created the cheers. Little did I anticipate something like this was going to develop into my life's work. Dance and choreography just seemed to pour out of me.

I also developed an early passion for theater and was always involved with the High School theater productions - whether it was on stage or painting sets backstage. Our Drama teacher Ruth Caddy was an enthusiastic teacher.

She directed me in the play *For Whom the Bell Tolls*. I was the court Jester and at the climax of the story, I was to run into the palace and bow before the king and if the bells rang all would be saved. The performance went along quite smoothly until the end when I ran into the palace and knelt before the king. I remained in the bow for a very long time. I could feel the audience getting nervous and then I slowly raised my head and spoke my line. That was the cue for the bells to chime with the happy ending. When the curtain came down Miss Caddy rushed to embrace me with, "Tony, that was magic! How did you think to make that long very dramatic pause?" I said "Miss Caddy, I forgot my line."

When I graduated from high school, Ruth Caddy wrote in my yearbook;

Dear Tony,
I guess words are pretty poor things after all, aren't they? You know teachers are supposed to inspire their students but I feel slightly at a loss when confronted by a student who inspires me. I know you'll do great things Tony, and I hope you remain just the swell person that you are now. With the best wishes in the world.
Ruth Caddy

In addition to all the dance and theater, I was an altar boy and served 6:30 mass every morning before school. Those early torturously cold mornings made it very difficult to leave the house to serve mass at a very empty church. But at least the school was right across the street from the church.

Besides serving daily mass, I taught future altar boys the Latin prayers necessary for the daily ceremony on Saturdays. It was a tedious task but sometimes amusing. Once I noticed that whenever we came upon the word "cogitaccione," the kids always giggled behind their prayer books. One morning I stopped the lesson and asked, "Now what's so funny?" Let me explain, there is a man in town named "Cosmo Baroni" whose nickname was "Coggi" and one of the kids stood up and said, "Well Tony, every time we come to the word "cogitaccione," we say "Coggi shit on Tony." Well, I laughed too and I agreed it was very funny. But, I didn't think Father O'Connell would find it funny, so he never found out about it.

On Easter Sunday, the Gospel was read in Latin and English. Father O'Connell thought it best so as not to hold the congregation too long. He would read the Latin version from the altar while I would read the English to the congregation from the pulpit. Of course we had a race but I said it wasn't fair because he could skip whole passages and nobody would know and I had to stay with the text. Of course he always won.

*In Drama Club, I also played an operations officer in **Ceiling Zero** who sent out the planes- which coincidentally would be my real life role during WW2*

    I missed Father O'Connell years later after I had moved on to college in St. Paul, I was driving through the town to which he had retired and I stopped in to see him. It was summer and the front door was open but the screen door was closed. I rang the doorbell and way out in the garden I could see him get up from a chair and approach the door. When he opened it and saw it was me he threw his hands in the air and exclaimed, "Glory be to God, Tony it's a blessing!" We visited and gabbed for quite a while. That's the last time I saw him.

    It seems everybody in their early stages develops a crush and that happened to Miriam, a young girl in my class. She could play the piano and offered to play for me when I danced. We started rehearsing at her house because her family had a piano but soon it became clear that she wanted more than rehearsals. In the cold winter, her dad built an igloo in the back yard and she invited me to come over and play. It was cold in that igloo but she was hot and wanted to go the full monty and do the nasty. We were so young and at that young age I didn't want the problem of a baby. Growing up with so many siblings I had no confusion about what comes along with hanky-panky. I had other more sensible plans. She kept it up until she realized she was getting nowhere with me.

    Our friends in school didn't know all this was going on and regarded us as the perfect couple. We even made the cover of the yearbook. Graduation finally came and we split because her family moved. No more Miriam. My prayers were answered.

    I walked to school and always had to pass the City Hall on my way. Often I'd drop my father's lunch pail off then continue around the corner past some guys who were always sitting on a bench out front. Every time they'd tease, "There goes Alice!" I got so angry once, I stopped and blurted out, "Now listen you bums, one day I'll amount to something and you'll still be sitting there on your big fat asses!"

    Years later, I'd had a career in New York and was already well established in California, when they showed up at my front door. Of course I knew who they were, one doesn't easily forget that sort of past. We went out into the garden and I offered them a drink.

with Miriam on the yearbook

23

Everything was moving along in a strained fashion when one had the audacity to ask, "Well, when are you going to give a big Hollywood party for us?"

"What? What nerve," I said. "Just put what's left of your drinks down and my houseman will show you to the door. I never ever want to see any of you again."

And I never did.

Long before graduating, in my junior year, my drama teacher Ruth Caddy decided to write to the Ted Shawn School at Jacob's Pillow in Massachusetts and recommend me for a scholarship for the summer of 1938 between my junior and senior years. She saw all the activities I was involved with and saw potential for my future. Jacob's Pillow would introduce me to a whole new world of professional dance.

I'm eternally and gratefully indebted to Miss Caddy. Two scholarships were given out by Mary Washington Ball who was running the Ted Shawn School at the time and I was one of the lucky ones. A girl from Kansas was the other. Despite my mother's concerns about the distance, I knew I had to go. I didn't know how a sixteen year old with no money could afford to get all the way to Massachusetts, but I had to go.

The last trip I made to Mt. Iron was many years later to grant my mother's last wish to be buried next to my father. My sister Nell and I flew her body back to Minnesota and took care of fulfilling her last wish.

JACOB'S PILLOW

As a young student I had no money. But my sister Mudge had a girlfriend who thought it was important that I go and loaned me ninety dollars for a round trip bus fare to Lee, Massachusetts. My parents weren't totally behind this but I knew I just had to go. The bus ride was interminable. I had to hitchhike the final 9.5 miles from Lee up to the school at Jacob's Pillow. Being a cute young boy, I was soon picked up by a young gentleman named Walter Terry who turned out to be the dance critic for the *New York Herald Tribune*. We hit it off immediately.

The summer training was focused and intense, but I loved it. The facilities were rustic but were just fine for a bunch of young dancers. There was one eccentricity at the Pillow, and that was the bathing facilities. The facilities were okay, but there was only one set of outdoor showers, and the time delegated to girls' showers and boys' showers often varied. One day I had to hurry and get dressed to help park cars and as I rushed into the shower area I discovered the scholarship girl from Kansas sitting totally naked shaving her leg while extending high into the air. On seeing me she let out a big scream yet didn't drop her leg or even try to cover up. She just kept on shaving and screaming totally exposed. I just lifted her to her feet and told her to do that later because guests were arriving. I had little time to shower and get dressed so I could go park cars. I rushed and cleaned up just in time for the first guest's arrival. After parking cars, I hurriedly dressed for the show - or rather undressed, as my costume was a tiny flesh color jock strap. Just another day at the Pillow.

At one Saturday concert, the original Shawn dancers were to perform. Johnny Shubert wasn't available so Shawn asked me to take his place that night. It was a big deal for me, an honor really, as just a student, to be picked to perform with the prestigious Shawn Dance Group. Still, I had to help set up the platforms and chairs in the Barn Theatre. The front row of chairs was right on the barn floor and the rest on tiered platforms up to the back of the barn.

Showtime! The theatre was packed with middle-aged to old ladies chattering away in their summer finery in anticipation of seeing a bunch of naked men dancing before their very eyes. They settled down during the overture, then out we came, bounding in our nakedness to applause and cheers from the enthusiastic crowd. After the next few beats we all stopped and held our pose for six counts.

I stopped right in front of a lady who said in a loud whisper which could be heard through the whole barn, "He's new here." It struck us so funny it set all of us laughing to the end of the number. We discovered how difficult it is to perform while you're laughing on the inside. But that concert turned out to be a great farewell to the men's company.

As a scholarship student, I helped in the kitchen, parked cars on show day, and generally made myself useful. One evening handsome Barton Mumaw, Mr. Shawn's chosen one, approached me in the kitchen while I was on KP duty and said, "Tony, Mr. Shawn would like you to bring his pitcher of water up to him tonight." I did that and gave a polite knock. I got a sweet "come in" and entered. Mr. Shawn was lying on his back on his bed in a very provocative position. Bathrobe carefully draped to show

Shawn in his bathrobe

the right amount of flesh and he said, "You can put the water there and come and sit down," indicating the corner of the bed. I was tempted but I thought, if I do a misstep I could be thrown out, so I opted to sit in a chair in the corner. I was aware of his intent, but in my heart I felt I made the right decision. I was never asked to bring his water again. Besides someone else had asked me to visit him at night, which I accepted.

Jess Meeker, the pianist for the school, had a cabin of his own tucked away in the woods. After class, rehearsals and kitchen duty, on my way to the upper farm where I was housed, it was simple to wander into Jess's cabin. It was much more romantic with candles and soft music playing, just the two of us alone in the woods. We'd go over the music he was composing for the two dances I was choreographing for the end of the season. Jess always turned each visit into a simply great Jacob's Pillow experience and also a great way to end a day of intensive dance training. I don't remember if we had a glass of wine or not but Jess succeeded in making these Pillow evenings unforgettable. I said yes to everything. It was heaven.

Mother Derby who lived on her own ranch next door also befriended me and often invited me over for some of her home cooked meals. We would dine on her picnic table outdoors and were always visited by birds and squirrels, sometimes a bunny and sometimes other creatures. At one time she worked the kitchen of the Pillow and for some reason lost favor but wouldn't tell me why. She took good care of me and that's all I had to know. As we say, let sleeping dogs lie.

Ruth St. Denis came to Jacob's Pillow one weekend to teach and perform. During her visit I met her and she proved to be all the exotic things attributed to her.

Barton Mumaw

That weekend, I was using the one and only one ironing board when Miss Ruth arrived carrying a big bundle of chiffon costumes she'd be wearing in the show that day. Seeing I was using the ironing board said, "Mr. Charmoli you're at that ironing board at an unfortunate time. Here press these."

And she threw the huge bundle of chiffon down at my feet. Fortunately for me just at that moment the scholarship girl from Kansas was crossing through when I stopped her, explained the situation and told her to press the mass of costumes because I had to go outside to park the cars of arriving matrons for the afternoon matinee. I squeezed by that one. I enjoyed her performance but I was not overwhelmed. Her show was typical Miss Ruth, exotic, mostly posturing but beautiful and definitely Miss Ruth.

During a break in class one day a reporter from the Boston Globe asked me if he could get an interview with Miss Ruth. I presented this to her and she said, "Tell him I'll see him in the Tea Garden in half an hour."

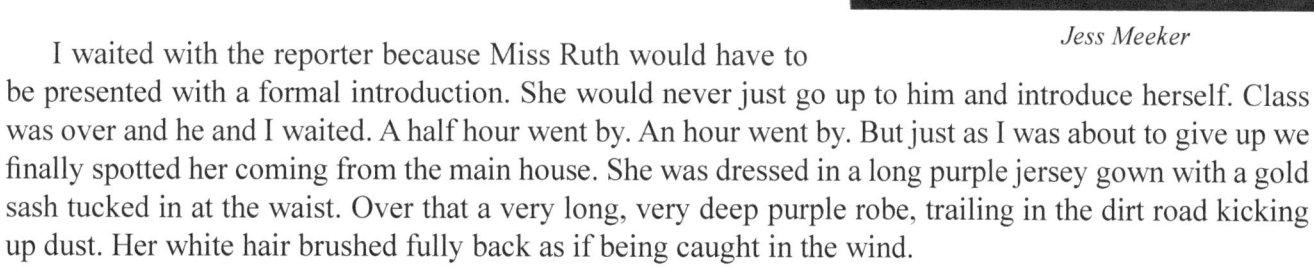

I waited with the reporter because Miss Ruth would have to be presented with a formal introduction. She would never just go up to him and introduce herself. Class was over and he and I waited. A half hour went by. An hour went by. But just as I was about to give up we finally spotted her coming from the main house. She was dressed in a long purple jersey gown with a gold sash tucked in at the waist. Over that a very long, very deep purple robe, trailing in the dirt road kicking up dust. Her white hair brushed fully back as if being caught in the wind.

The reporter was agog staring at this magnificent creature. He was fixed like a deer in headlights, mouth open, not moving a muscle as she walked right past him into the tea garden and up the two steps making sure the robe was properly draped on the steps, then she did a slow turn which tightened the gown to make it seem painted on her body and finally looked like a regal queen.

Then she spoke, "Mr. Charmoli who is it that wishes to see me?"

I said, Miss Ruth, may I present the reporter from the *Boston Globe!*" Then made a mad dash to get cleaned up leaving the two of them together. Unforgettable!

Years later in California I had another meeting with Miss Ruth. I was invited to a party at the Chateau Marmont honoring a dignitary from Japan and would I

Jess Meeker

Miss Ruth making an entrance

27

Photo by John Lindquist

bring Miss Ruth, because he had met her in Japan and asked to see her. I called Miss Ruth and she accepted.

The day came. I picked her up and arrived at the bungalow where the party was being held. Nobody was at the door to greet us so I just opened the door and stepped in. The party was in progress and there were steps leading down to the main ballroom where it was packed with guests having a good time.

I put out my arm to escort Miss Ruth down the steps when she said, "Tony, let's step outside."

I was surprised but did what she requested and I asked, "Don't you want to stay?"

She said "Yes, but will you announce me because I don't remember which one he is."

We re-entered, and at the top of the steps I announced, "Ladies and gentlemen, Miss Ruth St. Denis!"

Wham! The entire party stopped to look. The Japanese dignitary stood and approached her. Now she knew which one he was. The party guests parted and I helped her to regally walk down the steps into the ballroom where he and Miss Ruth met in the center of the floor to tremendous applause as he kissed her hand. That woman was all show, and it did make the party an unforgettable one. Henry Jaffe, the host, thanked me over and over again for bringing her. I had a good time with all the theater guests I knew. It became an unforgettable Chateau Marmont party.

Back to Jacob's Pillow. John Lindquist, a famous photographer from Boston who visited the Pillow on weekends, asked to photograph me on one of his visits. He walked me into a favorite secluded spot of his in the countryside and asked me to take off all my clothes. I thought what have I gotten myself into? Since we were alone, I thought it would be all right, so I proceeded to disrobe. He asked me to climb up on a large rock. Then he directed me to hit various dance poses and continue with some of my own until he told me to stop. He was quite satisfied with the shoot and didn't try any funny stuff. I guess he realized I was too young. But not very long afterward I got a very excited call from him to tell me one of the photos he had taken of me made a full page in Dance Magazine and the cover of another. He thanked me over and over and sent me the silver dragon ring I had admired that he was wearing on the shoot. He came to New York to see me dance in several concerts and to parties at my apartment. Since then I've lost the ring and John is gone too. But, we remained good friends to the end.

At the end of the school season, all the students were asked to create a dance for a final recital. One afternoon, Shawn came into one of my rehearsals to see what I was doing. I had created a piece to be

Photo by John Lindquist

performed as someone read Mother Goose's nursery rhymes. As I rehearsed, I asked Shawn to read the text as I was missing my narrator that day. He liked what he saw so much, he told me to create a second number for the final concert. I was the only one of all the other students asked to create two pieces. That was quite an honor.

My first dance went well, but everybody loved the choreographed nursery rhymes. Our pianist, Jess Meeker, composed original music. I had one of the girls stand next to the piano and recite the nursery rhymes as I performed out on the studio floor. The response was excellent. I was thrilled when Shawn himself picked me up in his arms and embraced me with high praise. It was a lovely gesture. I couldn't have asked for a better way to end my dance training at Jacob's Pillow.

Shawn was genuinely interested in my career and later came to visit me in New York a number of times, quite pleased and proud that I continued in the dance field and seeing success. Walter Terry, the dance critic for the New York Herald Tribune, always joined Shawn on his visits to me in New York. I became quite good friends with Walter and we often went to dance events together but always sat far apart from one another. This was a precaution against being criticized for befriending the dance critic of a prominent newspaper who seemingly would be partial in his reviews of my work.

Walter always stayed at my house on his visits to the West Coast. He lectured at different schools and universities in California. I don't know how he drove to them and did his speech because he always left my house after having drunk half a bottle of Bourbon. I did notice that he drank his own bourbon, which was on the cheap side, and didn't hesitate to empty my good stuff when he ran out. In all the years I think he replaced mine only once, but who's counting? He was a good friend and remained so until the end. When I was a penniless young boy hitchhiking in the Massachusetts countryside he did pick me up and drove me to Jacob's Pillow.

Tony rehearsing.

I did see Barton Mumaw once again. He was such a handsome son-of-a-gun and had always been Mr. Shawn's personal property. He was the star of the Pillow and also an excellent dancer. But though he was the envy of the Pillow, time went on and the men's group disbanded. Barton eventually turned up in New York City and needed work. By then I was a busy choreographer in Manhattan. One day I got a call from Hanya Holm, one of the teachers I had studied with, and she said, "Tony, Barton is in town and having a hard time, do you have any work for him?" I told her I had an opening for a bit part in a TV Production but I'd be ashamed to ask a star like him. "Please do," she said. So I did ask and indeed he took the job and was very good in it. Soon

after that he moved back to his hometown in Florida to teach dance, but I'll always cherish the thought that I got to choreograph something for the star of the Pillow. That was like a period to my Jacob's Pillow experience.

I did return to the Pillow another time to present my ballet Gotham Suite performed by an all-black male dance company sponsored by Aubrey Hutchins. Lena Horne also backed this company. The ballet was performed in the new theater. That was my last visit to the Pillow.

WILL

I returned to Mt Iron after that summer at Jacob's Pillow to begin my final year of High School. I was still leading and choreographing the cheers for the football games and finding dancing gigs around the area. My dance partner Dolores and I were excited to get a gig performing at the Hotel Duluth for Valentine's Day.

Dolores' parents drove us down to Duluth. We had time to rehearse on the stage in the hotel early in the day, and then we had some time to kill. A hotel clerk was making eyes at me while he showed us our dressing rooms, but I was not at all interested in him. While Dolores and her parents checked into the hotel, I decided to surprise my old friend Denis McGinty who happened to live right across the street from the Hotel Duluth. Denis had been up to Mt Iron a number of time since we had met - he was a great favorite of my parents and we'd had a lot of fun over the previous year.

My heart was pounding in anticipation of seeing Denis again and expecting to have another fabulous sexual visit. I dashed across the street to his apartment, knocked and Denis opened the door just a little bit. Seeing me, immediately his mouth dropped to his chest.

I said, "Denis aren't you glad to see me?" He sighed and took a small step to his right, opened the door and sitting on the couch at the far back wall was Wilford R. Sanders who was visiting from Minneapolis. Upon seeing this great hunk of manhood who was Denis' "soul mate," my heart jumped and pounded like never before. Denis had told me about Wilford R. Sanders and of the great sexual encounters they had.

Denis immediately spotted the fireworks between the two of us and said, "I have to drive my sister to the docks to catch a boat for a cruise on Lake Superior. I'll be gone for an hour. You both know where the towels are," and slammed the door shut.

Within seconds Will and I were at each other. Our clothes came flying off and our hearts were about to burst. They were pounding so loudly the climax and explosion compared to the blasts heard in the iron ore mines. Heaven couldn't be better than this.

I quickly got dressed, rushed back to the hotel and into my costume. I was running very late and Dolores was waiting for me. We raced up the steps to the door that led onstage. We waited there as the music started up - ready to make our entrance when I felt a hand groping me from behind. I looked back and saw the hotel clerk just as we were supposed to go on. I pushed him away and jumped out on the stage. I didn't mean to push the guy down the long flight of steps behind us - I didn't hear any more of him.

Dolores and I were a smash hit. The audience response told us that. To top it off the hotel manager came to us and said he wanted both of us back again next year. Music to our ears.

On the drive home I asked Dolores "Weren't you worried when I was gone for so long? She replied, "No, I know the routine without you." I guess that put me in my place.

Though we kept in touch by phone, I didn't see Will for a long time after that.

I graduated from High School in June, 1939, and attended Virginia Junior College for the next two years. There was a free bus that drove us to Virginia City every day. I kept a pretty heavy class load. A teacher with the unfortunate name of Mary Eileen Asseltyne took me under her wing and decided to train me in public speaking. She was grooming me for the National Speech Tournament. On top of my other studies, I had endless meetings and rehearsals with Miss Asseltyne.

She assigned me to write a five minute speech honoring Sir Neville Chamberlain of England. I said, "But Miss Asseltyne nobody likes him - how can I win with that?"

She replied, "I want you to write one speech for and one against him."

I wrote the speeches and rehearsed them many times with Miss Asseltyne as my audience. The Minnesota State competition was first and she chose the speech for Sir Neville. That made me nervous. She assured me that it was the winning speech.

We both went to the first event. There were ten speakers competing in a huge auditorium and while the first speaker was on, the rest of us were in a holding room next door. My turn came and it was pure torture until I hit the stage and started to speak. A calm came over me and I delivered the Champion Speech of the evening.

Miss Asseltyne was very pleased and didn't say "See I told you so."

The Debate Team

After that we won the Pacific Northwest and went on to the National in North Carolina.

Miss Asseltyne and I eagerly boarded a train to go to Charlotte, North Carolina. In those days we were still using ground transportation to any state in the union. The trip took us through southern states and I saw things I had never seen before. All I knew about Negros was from history books. We only had Italians, Austrians, Scandinavians and Indians in Minnesota. This trip was an education for me. We didn't have TV yet so this trip really opened my eyes. The scenery was wonderful and the Southern plantation homes were beautiful. Then passing through another railroad station I saw a sign that read, "BLACKS - WHITES."

I asked Miss Asseltyne what that was about and she explained that blacks were not permitted to use the same toilets as whites. "Why not?" I asked. She said, "That's the law." She also explained that blacks were not to eat in the same restaurants. This appalled me.

We arrived in Charlotte and upon entering the hotel we saw all the trophies in the lobby piled high on a table. Miss Asseltyne pointed to the top trophy and said, "That's yours." I just looked at her.

In addition to Oratory I entered Extempore Speech. In this category you draw subjects out of a hat and are given a short time to prepare a speech of three to five minutes on the subject. I drew "The Negro and the Poll Tax." Here I am, my first visit down south in a country where all are supposed to be created equal and all the judges are white. Naturally I would be against it. How could I possibly win with such a charged question? I couldn't even speak to my coach for advice. My name was called.

I stepped onto the stage, pulled myself together and spoke. "My question is "The Negro and the Poll Tax." I took another deep breath and said. "Rather than offer my opinion on this subject I withdraw my place in this competition!"

You could hear a big gasp from the audience and then they surrounded me with "Bravos" and handshakes. Miss Asseltyne asked, "Well, how did it go? I told her of the question I drew and my reply. She said, "You did the noble thing."

I still had my oratory category to do. I gained strength from the extempore brouhaha and now was my big chance. My name was called and I drew myself up and stepped onto the stage, took a deep breath and delivered my speech as if my life depended on it. Miss Asseltyne's prediction was right on the nose. I took the top prize. This event became the talk of the tournament. Other contestants surrounded and congratulated me with hugs and hand shakes for I took home the top Trophy as the USA National Speech Champion. Next was to be Europe, but because of the war in Europe the event was canceled. But, this win landed me a full 2-year tuition to the College of St. Thomas in Minneapolis.

While going to Junior College I had only seen Will once when I hitchhiked to Minneapolis to see the Shawn Dancers in concert. I stayed overnight with Will. It was very late when we got to bed but we managed a quickie because he had to go to work early and I had to go to school. He drove me to the city limits. I hitched the two hundred mile ride home.

My sisters Claire and Al were living in Minneapolis, so when I started that fall at St. Thomas I rented a room across the street from their apartment. My white haired landlady Mrs Uttamark was quite impressed that I had won the National Speech Championship and was very supportive of my studies. I typically ate with my sisters across the street. My schedule was very busy but being so close to Will I found time to see him from time to time.

Over the course of the year I stayed at Will's house more and more. The college granted me permission to live off campus, so I eventually moved in with Will and his family. The college is on the St. Paul side of the Mississippi River and Will lived just across on the Minneapolis side. He drove right past St Thomas on his way to work each morning. I couldn't ask for anything more perfect.

Living with Will's family worked well in many ways. Will's sister Pat hated schoolwork so I did it for her. She was thrilled and didn't mind my living with them at all. His mother disliked ironing shirts so I did that for her and helped out with other chores around the house. His stepdad was a conductor on a train and loved to "shoot the bull" on his off-duty time. All this made for happy times for me - a stranger living with them. I was accepted in all ways.

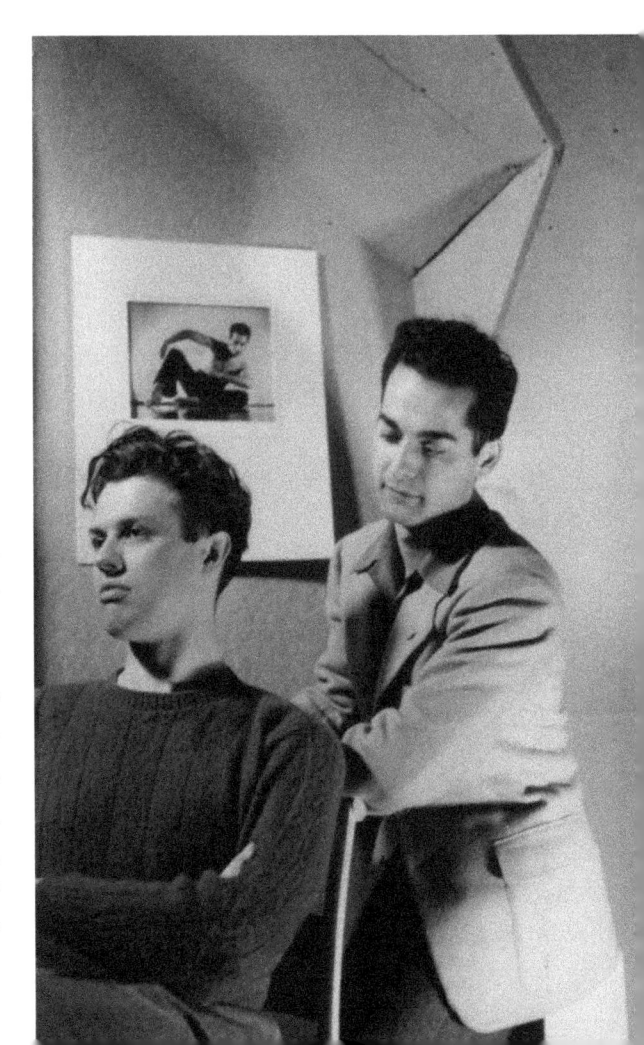

On December 8, 1941, the US entered World War 2. That spring Will told me that he would be joining the Navy the following day. I was very relieved when he came home after with news that he didn't pass the entrance exam because of color-blindness. But my relief was short-lived as instead he joined the Army. I was drafted soon after and was inducted into the 43d Fighter Squadron and after training was sent to the jungles of Panama as an operations officer. Will became a secretary to General Eisenhower in Europe.

We didn't know if we'd ever see each other again.

PANAMA

During the three years we were at war, Will and I had no communication. We had great trust in each other and felt that our friendship was solid. But, people die in wars. We had to just trust Fate would bring us back together again.

I served as operations officer in the 43rd Fighter Squadron Air Force and based in the primitive jungles of Panama. We were there to protect the Canal. I would send pilots out on missions to survey and protect the approaches to the canal. They would report anything suspicious to me, and I would relay the information up the chain of command. I can tell you now that German submarines tried to blow up the Canal several times. I'd relay this information to Washington and they'd give us a go ahead to destroy anything that came too close. Destroying the Panama Canal would have been a major disaster.

Sometimes the pilots had to bed down in Jungle outposts where facilities were primitive. The next day they'd come and report. Lt. Rainwater was a camp with his reports. He'd sit on the corner of my desk, cross his legs and purr, "Well Sgt. Charmoli it was like this. We didn't see nuthin' dangerous but we did play 'drop the soap' in the shower." Of course soap-dropping was not relayed to Washington. Only the important stuff.

In order to protect the Panama Canal, the young pilots had to go through extensive training and exercises at our home base. I could see the planes from my office and one day they were rehearsing steep dive bombing. One pilot after another did their dive successfully, but one wasn't able to pull out of his dive and crashed right into the earth and burst into flames. It was the most difficult thing I ever had to watch and the saddest day of my entire duty in the Air Force. The whole squadron was struck with sadness. He was a favorite among all the guys and the only pilot we lost in the 43rd Fighter Squadron.

Lt. Devlin took me up in a plane with him to show me the defenses we had. He took me up on a flight to observe the Canal and all that we were protecting. When we had reached a certain altitude and leveled off to fly parallel to the Cannel, he said, "Look to your right." I couldn't believe my eyes! The whole long hillside opened up to reveal a row of cannons aiming and following us in their sights. It was scary. Looking down the barrels of a row of cannons is a peculiar feeling. They followed us until we were out of sight. It was really frightening. Fortunately, we had clearance to make this flight or we could have been toast in a second.

I had the feeling Lt. Devlin was of the gay persuasion for he seemed to find a comrade in me. He gave me a lot of attention and made the service a very bearable place to serve.

He also gave me flying lessons. I was okay doing a takeoff and certain maneuvers but landing was out of the question. I would make the approach and start the landing but when getting close to the ground, I would chicken out and pull back and up and away. When I'd see the runway racing towards me I was afraid the landing gear would collapse on setting the plane down and we'd be duck soup. I never got over it. I'm just fine not having to fly airplanes. I never did find out if Lt. Devlin was gay or straight. I guess we both didn't want to run the risk of finding out. Doesn't matter. We won the war either way.

I also found a good friend in a fellow named Zeke who was very straight and with me most of the time. On rare occasions when some of the guys were going into town Zeke always dragged me along and made sure I was having a good time. He always brought me goodies from the PX and would even take care of my laundry. I'm sure whoever he married after the service had a good life.

The jungles of Panama was dangerous because snakes seemed to be everywhere. We were instructed that while walking through the thick brush we should stomp heavily and the earth vibration would cause the snakes to slither away.

Lying face down on his bed one day my buddy, Zeke, let out a wild scream of "HOLY SHIT!" We came running and there he was face to face with a coral snake which had wrapped itself around the leg of his bed and was staring him right in the face. Zeke flew out of bed and out the screen door. We found a whole nest of coral snakes right under the corner of our bunk house. He got to work with a heavy shovel and sent them to heaven and we were never bothered again. We all knew coral snakes are very deadly creatures. Zeke was our hero!

Another day, I was lying on my bunk, when I heard something. I sat up then turned and looked square into the jaws of an iguana inches away from me peering through a thin screen. I screamed, and in a flash Zeke came to the rescue. He ran out and caught it by the tail then dragged it away from our bunkhouse and released it. Coming face to face with an Iguana is not a pretty sight when you just wake up. Their long knife-like tail can whip like a dangerous sword. It happens in a flash and in an instant you could be minus a leg... or a finger... or... who knows what. Snakes and other critters kept life from getting too dull in the tropics.

On leave with buddies

There never was anything romantic between Zeke and me. It was plain and simple. He was a very dear friend who loved taking care of someone who in this case, to my good fortune, happened to me.

The Day Room was a place where guys could go to relax. One day one of the outrageous privates decided it was just too drab so he took it upon himself to decorate it. He got sheets and other stuff from the supply store and any place he could find stuff to fluff up the room. Sheets were used as curtains to drape the windows, and with lots of other fabulous dressing he transformed the room from the plain drab Army Air Corps look.

The Commanding Officer came in one day and screamed, "Who did this?" When he found out, he discharged the mad decorator queen and some of his obvious cronies and sent them back to the states by boat. This didn't stop our friend. He decorated the boat as well, and word got back to us that they all got dressed in handmade drag, and they outrageously partied all the way back to the states where they were immediately discharged. The 43rd Fighter Squadron became rather sedate after that and quite a few of us missed their outrageous shenanigans. Those wild colorful service men often brightened our day.

Though we all were proud to serve our country, life in the Panamanian jungle was monotonous at

With Bitsey performing for the troops in Panama.

times. The men were bored and needed entertainment. So, someone suggested I put together a show to entertain the guys. I was allowed to get out of uniform to stage, direct, and perform in the production.

I found a cute little American girl named Bitsey Gates who was a dancer and lived with her mother nearby, so I asked her to join me in doing exhibition ballroom dancing. Not only that, but her mother was a seamstress and made costumes for us. A local group did the music and the guys cheered to see me dancing with a cute girl. The sight of a cute dancing girl was not something they saw very often. And I also enjoyed getting dressed up in a civilian tux on these occasions. I gathered other talented guys and some locals and put a show together on a regular basis. It was amazing to see how little it takes to entertain a bunch of guys stranded out in a jungle for a long time. I got quite a few volunteers who often stopped the show with their varied, sometimes goofy, amazing talent.

One night I made a big mistake. I saw all the servicemen were way in the back and only a few officers filled the seats in front. Here's my mistake. I called out to all the servicemen and said "Guys come on down closer to the stage. Fill up these empty seats. They didn't move. I was then informed that the enlisted men do not sit with officers. I'm sure that's all changed now.

※

When the war ended in the late summer of 1945, we were honorably discharged and I was sent back to Fort Snelling where I had been inducted. It turned out that Will had been discharged only the week before and he was there to pick me up at the gate. It was a very happy reunion. After almost three years of being separated we had a lot to catch up on. We both felt ours was a friendship made to last. Even a war didn't break it up.

Of course, we started sharing stories about our experiences. Will had worked in General Eisenhower's office. We all read in the news that General Eisenhower sent weekly letters to his wife Mamie in the States.

We all thought that was very thoughtful of him but Will revealed that those intimate letters to his wife were written by the soldier secretary in the outer office and Will would deliver them to the General for signing. Talk about second hand love and we all thought it was such a noble thing for the general to do. Fortunately Mamie never found out.

Renovation of the attic loft in Will's house was completed during the war. That first night back we shook the rafters in our new attic apartment and picked up our lives together once again. Will went back to the Minnesota State Office in the Capitol and I went back to St.Thomas College to finish my degree.

I was anxious to get to New York to get into theater, but I also wanted my college degree, in case New York didn't work out. I went to the Dean and told him I'd like to graduate midterm that upcoming Spring.

The Dean said, "That would be impossible! You'd have to carry too many hours. Nobody has done it before."

I asked "How many hours would that be?"

He replied "At least nine hours."

I said "Try me."

Begrudgingly, he granted me his permission. Not only did I do my regular studies, but I also coached the debate team to their first win ever. I also appeared in a couple of the college theater productions and danced with the Gertrude Lippincott Company in Minneapolis. In addition to all of these extra activities, I completed my studies on time.

The dean graciously made the arrangements for me to get my test leading to a degree. I walked into a room of professors seated at a long table. I was directed to stand on a mark on the floor facing them. They could ask questions on anything I should have learned on the specific subjects they represented. I felt like Joan of Arc at the stake. Nervous at first but in spite of all the stress I was under I pulled myself together and despite a close shave on the subject of *Beowulf* (which I did not read... still haven't), I passed my final oral exam. I was congratulated by my professors. I graduated midterm in early April with a degree in English Literature. I was packed and ready to go to New York two weeks later.

Now, Will and I had to face what we had talked about before. I wanted theater in New York. Was he going with me or was he staying with his job at the State Capital? Will had given me no answer, and I was leaving the next day. The hour was late when we went to bed and cozied up to one another. I asked the question again. He just turned over with his back to me. There was a long silence.

"I'm going in the morning - are you going with me or am I going alone?"

I cuddled up closer behind him and tightened my embrace. Still nothing. "Well are you?" My heart was pounding until I thought it would burst. The silence was killing me? My heart was going to explode.

He quietly said, "I quit my job today." Then he turned and smiled at me.

Hallelujah! I really did explode! "WE'RE GOING TO NEW YORK!" What happened after... let's just say is unprintable? I will say heaven could never be better.

Mountain Iron Army Vet Bids For Fame, Fortune On Broadway Stage In New York

MOUNTAIN IRON—Broadway, fame and fortune beckoned to Tony Charmoli, St. Thomas college graduate, as he boarded a plane this week at Wold-Chamberlain airfield, Minneapolis, Tuesday for the bright lights of New York. Tony is the son of Mrs. Philip Charmoli Mountain Iron.

Having just completed his studies with a B. A. degree and Magna Cum Laude honors, Tony has his heart set on scaling the heights in the legitimate theater. And if the opinions expressed by his dramatic and speech instructors at St. Thomas, Dr. Max L. Schmidt and Robert Rourke, are any criterion, then Tony can't fail.

Tony as a Virginia Junior College student in 1941, won a national collegiate oratorical contest in North Carolina for which he was awarded and accepted a scholarship at St. Thomas.

Charmoli completed a year and a half at St. Thomas before the army claimed his services, but did find time before his departure to study ballet dancing under the famed Ted Shawn.

In his three years in the army Tony produced several plays for his GI mates and received wide acclaim for entertaining soldiers with his dancing, singing and dramatic ability.

Returning to St. Thomas last fall following his discharge, Tony was student director of the Northwest debate tournament, assisted Robert Rourke in the production of "Brother Orchid" and "Best Foot Forward" and was elected president of Pi Kappa Delta, campus forensic fraternity. Recently he turned down an offer ... the renewned Monte Carl... sse to take

Family picnic & going away party - Will's mom on right, my mother in the center.

Photo: Roy Schatt

Chapter 2
New York

ONE YEAR TO MAKE IT

We arrived in New York in the Spring of 1946. I decided I'd give myself a year to get on Broadway. My brother Butch had been hounding me to take a teaching job in Louisville, Kentucky where he worked as a coach at the university. But, I thought I could make it in New York. Will and I had some money saved up from the war. I would give myself a year.

Our first Apartment in New York

Broadway was always a dream of mine as it must have been for anyone interested in theatre. First it was the movies but it seemed the stage was more attainable because I had the taste of theatre in high school plays and more in college. Now in New York, I was within reach of getting into a dream, a Broadway Show.

My little dance partner in Panama, Bitsey, was a big help when I called to tell her I was moving to New York. Bitsey had a brother who owned several properties in Manhattan and after the war everything was tied up and it was impossible to find a room. We needed a place to stay so I called Bitsey, and her call to her brother did the trick. Her brother owned a hotel on 46th St. between 6th and Broadway and he could give us a place adjoining the hotel. It was walking distance to some of the dance studios I'd be going to. It wasn't luxurious but it was homey.

Right after we secured the hotel room, I went to the American Theater Wing to enroll in dance classes. Having served in the Air Force for three years with an honorable discharge, I was entitled to free classes of my choice. I chose the top teachers in New York. Ballet, Helene Platova and Bob Pageant. I chose Modern, with Martha Graham, Hanya Holm, Lucas Hoving, Jose Limon, and Charles Weidman, and Tap with Ernst Carlos and Peter Birch. I had danced with the Gertrude Lippincott company in Minneapolis, had danced with Ida Canossa, Wilhemina Gardner in Virginia, so I already had a strong foundation in dance.

Ballet classes with Helene Platova were excellent and a lot of fun. All the top dancers from the Ballet to Broadway studied with her. Her Russian accent alone was enough to warrant taking her class.

Lessons with Platova were a hoot. One day in class we were doing attitude turns, which is standing on one leg and the other bent to the back and turning. The standing leg should be straight but I preferred to bend it.

Plotsy, as we preferred to call her, kept tapping her cane and correcting "Toni, Toni, zee knee, zee knee!"

I said, "but Plotsy, l think I look better with the knee bent."

She looked at me for a moment then commanded "Everybody ze other leg! One more time straight knee! Tony bend ze knee!" It was her way of agreeing with me.

She was a favorite teacher, in a distinctly different style of dance from Martha Graham. I worked my butt off in Miss Graham's classes, but I enjoyed them at the same time.

One day during a break I asked her, "Miss Graham dance is so tough, why do we put ourselves through this?"

She replied, "Mr. Charmoli, we come into this world with sealed orders."

Sounds like Truth to me.

Soon after we arrived Will went to work for a furniture company on lower Park Avenue as office manager.

The dance world of New York was a small world and I soon reconnected with Charles Tate, a dancer I knew from Jacob's Pillow. He invited Will and me to come see him dancing in *Showboat*. I was excited to see my first Broadway show. Since I had class all day and Will was at work we decided to meet at the theater. I arrived on time - but no Will. I took my seat up in the balcony and started watching the show when I noticed the dark form of someone crawling up the stairs. It was Will - and he was so drunk he couldn't even walk up the stairs. Finally, he fumbled his way through the dark to his seat right next to me. I was so embarrassed and angry I didn't even speak to him. He giggled his way through the show drunk as can be. Of course it was hard to stay mad at Will. He had stopped at

Photo by Fritze Henle

a cocktail party after work and before the show and was not that much of a drinker to begin with. It was something that years later we could laugh about.

Mostly my days were filled with running from one class to the next. One time passing our hotel between classes with a dancer, Jean Hulouse, she said, "You live right here don't you?"

I said I did and she asked to use the bathroom. I took her to the apartment and she ran straight for the john. Jean then stopped in a panic, quickly turned around and said, "But there's no door!" I said, "I'll sing loudly and make lots of noise, what do you want, a brass band?" We got to class on time.

After class we all would pile into a Horn and Hardart Cafeteria across the street for our free lemonade. We discovered there was a table near the windows loaded with wedges of lemon and a container of sugar. We would always be thirsty after a ballet class so we made our own lemonade. What could be better than free cold lemonade? The management soon caught on to this and the table with its contents disappeared. However, broke dancers are good at finding free food. At a party I introduced myself to an attractive young lady and asked what kind of work she did. Hallelujah, she kept the dessert windows filled in the cafeteria!

She said if I just did a little tap on the window, she would spring the door open for me and give me a free dessert. It was great until that H&H moved. No more freebees.

The dance community was a very busy one. One thing I have learned is that you can't just wait for success to come to you. You have to work hard and get out there and show the world what you can do. I joined Theatre Dance Inc. and we created our own productions. I choreographed numbers with the different members and danced in the productions as well, all the while still taking class with all these valuable teachers. We put on our shows at the uptown YMHA on Sunday nights. We all volunteered our time and scraped together costumes with what we had. We put on some pretty good shows. People noticed.

The first dance piece I choreographed was "La Promenada" and the dancers with me were Jean Hulouse, Frank Westbrook and my partner was Phyllis Gehrig. Fortunately we got good reviews, which encouraged me to stay in the theater world.

Photo by Fritze Henle

Performing for the Sunday night concerts at the Young Men's Hebrew Association.

We often used the Charles Weidman Studio for rehearsals and one day Agnes de Mille was working there and her ballerina Nora Kaye was late. When Agnes saw me she said, "Oh Tony would you stand in for Nora until she gets here?" Well of course you'd do anything for the great Agnes especially when you're just a student (No, I didn't have to go on pointe to stand in for Nora). Fortunately Nora wasn't too late.

On one occasion, Will and I went to the Met to see the premiere of Agnes' new ballet *Harvest According*. My seat happened to be right next to Agnes. Her lead dancer Lydia Franklin was on stage and was supposed to start in silence but as Lydia started so did the orchestra. Frantically Agnes grabbed my arm and said, "That's wrong. She's supposed to start in silence." Mistakes like this happened several times during the performance and Agnes's punches and grabs kept getting tougher and tougher until at the end I was sore and Agnes was exhausted and slumped way down in her seat. She was a mess and I was hurt. I didn't care much for the ballet and turned to Agnes and said, "Agnes, you've done it again." Whatever that meant. And she smiled and said, "Thank you." Will didn't care much for it either.

Photo by Fritze Henle

Classes with Martha Graham opened up a new world. I had learned some modern dance technique with Gertrude Lippincott in Minneapolis but it was different to be taught by the master herself. Knowing I wanted to become a choreographer, I felt I should become well versed in all forms of dance. Pearl Lang was an expert in Martha Graham's technique as were other teachers like Ethel Winter and Helen McGehee. But, I especially enjoyed doing Martha's technique when she taught class. If Miss Graham wasn't teaching she sat on a bench on the side and observed. I did my best on those days, but didn't realize I was being observed for a reason.

One day, Pearl Lang, approached me and said, "Miss Graham would like to see you in her office after class." Class ended, I dried myself off and sprayed a couple whiffs of cologne, and knocked on her office door.

A voice said, "Come in."

I entered and saw Martha at her desk. "Mr. Charmoli, I have been observing you in class and have decided I would like to have you in my junior company, and for you to join my professional company when you're ready."

I know I should have been overwhelmed by this offer coming from the High Priestess herself.

But, my answer? "Thank you Miss Graham, but I want Broadway!"

The meeting was over in a flash. I later learned she detested Broadway. I continued to take her class but she never observed again when I was there.

Photo by Fritze Henle

With Phyllis erforming in the first piece I choreographed for the Sunday night concerts at the YMHA.

Years later, I was living in California and scheduled to direct a TV special on dance hosted by Julie Andrews and Rudi Nureyev. It was to cover all forms of dance including one of Graham's works. I and the whole crew went to New York to visit Miss Graham, as we had informed her we wanted to include one of her solo pieces "Ruth" in this special telecast.

We all arrived at her studio and our advance man went in to inform her we had arrived. After a few minutes he came to the door and announced, "Miss Graham will see Mr. Charmoli alone. The rest will have to wait." I walked in and had a wonderful reunion with Miss Graham. She and the dancer who was going to dance the number were waiting. In full costume she did the whole work for me, bit by bit, as I told her how I would shoot it. When I mentioned one particular high angle shot, Miss Graham became excited and suggested she would even make some changes in the choreography to accommodate my camera angles (We made no drastic changes). We had a grand old time and she thanked me for being one of her students and congratulated me on my success in the industry. Incidentally the number was well received on the telecast and the show won an Emmy. I had forgotten to enter my name as director or I could have won an Emmy as Director. C'est la vie!

My year to make it on Broadway was speeding by quickly, and though I was not yet on Broadway I was in the middle of everything dance - so I remained hopeful. I really didn't want to take that teaching position in Louisville that my brother Butch kept suggesting I should take.

We moved mid-year to a new apartment across from the Gardenia Club. One night I was sitting on our apartment stoop and watched Billie Holiday arrive to perform at the club. New York is a city like none other. Seems as if you rub shoulders with everyone after a while. Our apartment shared a bathroom with the neighboring apartment of Georgia Peach, who was a hat-check girl who worked at Club 21 upstairs. She made a little extra money on the side with customers who wanted a little extra entertainment. Inevitably Will or I would be in the shower and she'd suddenly pound on the door so she could do a quick cleanup before a gentleman caller arrived. She'd squeeze it all into her break from upstairs. She was an industrious girl. We got along great. She was beautiful with porcelain skin and blonde hair - she lit her apartment with blue light which made her look even more exotic. Good lighting is useful in many professions. One night, one of her drunken customers wandered into our apartment accidentally and scared the heck out of me when he climbed into my bed. I shoved him out and told him to go across the hall.

It was a non-stop routine of class and auditions. I kept in touch with all the announcements of auditions and went to everyone I could. It made no difference if I thought there was a chance of being called back or not. I bravely went out and did what they asked for whether I could do justice to it or not. While watching auditions I could easily see I could measure up to what the others were doing and many times knew I could surpass them. I was often put on the call back list and last until they called out the girls who were on call back. They would march out and line up in front of us and of course those amazons blocked me. But I stuck with the belief my time would come when a short dancer could fill the role.

But sometimes I could be distracted from the constant pursuit of performing on Broadway. Charles Weidman had a good looking assistant teacher named Peter Hamilton who often gave me special attention. I didn't mind it one bit. One time I told him I had to go to an audition right from class. He jumped on that and said, "You don't want to go all sweaty. I live near here, come and have a shower at my place." Heaven! I was in the shower just a few minutes when another gorgeous naked body joined me. I never made it to the audition and later found out they were only looking for acrobats, which I'm not.

One morning in Spring 1947, in Lucas Hoving's class, Lucas was on the phone so his assistant took over. Soon, Lucas came in and announced, "Tony that call was from somebody asking you to go downtown after class to the Dumont Studios in the lower floor of the Wanamaker Building and bring some dancers with you." I collected four other boys and told them to bring their dance bags with them. We took the subway to the designated place.

When we walked in we were graciously met by a gentleman. "Mr. Charmoli it's a pleasure to meet you. I've seen you dance in many of the YMHA concerts and I've enjoyed your work a lot. Now let me introduce you to this new thing we call Television. This camera can take an image of this lovely lady seated here and we can receive an identical image in the studio uptown. Now here's where you come in. Seeing you dance in concerts around town gave me an idea, we can transmit a stationary image but we've never tested a moving image like dance. We would like to see if dance will hold as well. Could you work out some dancing in this little set we have over here?"

TV test photos by Jack A. Partington Jr.

I said, "I think this is wonderful but first this bank of lights is so hot we'd melt in no time, they'll have to be moved back."

He countered, "They have to stay right where they are for technical reasons."

So I said, "Okay, boys. Eddie you put on your tap shoes, we'll wear ballet slippers and Bill you do some acrobatics. We'll work in eight-bar segments. I'll start with some jazz and clear then we rotate 8 bars at a time."

"Okay, we're ready and you sir, tell us when to stop. Good luck boys." A great hush fell over the room. Then "Here we go! Music!" The first boy went, then the next, then I went, and the studio was suspended in silence, next and the next and then great shouts of, "It's working. It's holding. It's holding! YEAH! YEAH! You can stop now!"

Out came the champagne and shouts of joy, it was absolutely thrilling to see such joy personified, the birth of dance on Television!!!

❦

I continued to dance in small productions all over town. In one of those concerts I danced in Talley Beatty's "The Southern Landscapes." It was an all-black cast except for me. My partner had the unfortunate name of Ora Leek but she could dance. In concert one afternoon at the YMHA, Talley's ballet was the last work in the first act. As an exit step ending the first act, my male partner and I were supposed to do a series of double tours across the stage. It's an exhausting step and we had never rehearsed this combination so we did our best. We did our first preparation jumped straight up and turned twice in the air before landing took one step to our left and repeated the combination. We executed another. We did it another time and I heard George take a deep intake and exhale. We did it one more time totally exhausted and we looked at each other and just walked off. Talley was up front doing his thing and saw us with a quizzical look on his face. Then we rushed back in to do the very last variation to end with the entire company. Talley was forgiving and agreed we needed more rehearsal time.

During intermission one of my dance teachers, Hanya Holm was in the audience and ran into my friend the dance critic Walter Terry and he asked Hanya, "Well what do you think?" And typical of a teacher her reply. "Well he certainly kept up with them." Naturally being one of my dance teachers she was watching me.

After these shows, we often went to someone's apartment to dine on the poor dancers' staple, "Fairy Pudding" - which translated into tuna casserole. But, when we went to Don Pippin's apartment in Greenwich Village, he would cover the coffee table with newspapers and dump out a whole pot of cooked shrimp and serve them with beer. Fingers and paper towels were the utensils.

Coincidentally years later, Don was the music conductor for the last Broadway show I worked on, Woman of the Year. It was a good way for us to reconnect as good friends.

Our summer home.

Summer of 1947, my year was technically up but I just knew I was going to make it on Broadway. I just had to stick it out a little longer.

We had to give up our hotel room for renovation so we moved to Franklin Coate's barn in Westport Connecticut for the summer. Franklin was the organist for a nearby church. He had an apartment in town but would go up to the barn when he wanted to get out of the city.

We lived there for the summer with our friend Bob Richley and his cat Cora Ann Louise Charles the Second. The barn was just an open space with blankets strung out on ropes as room dividers, a hot plate for cooking, a toilet, and the shower was a garden hose strung up to a shower head on a pipe - or you could go to the river nearby. The train took you from Grand Central Station and would drop you off in Westport within walking distance to the barn. The whole set up was pretty primitive but there was no other choice.

There was one saving grace, however. Not far from the station was the Westover Inn, which served late and Will would meet me there on my return from the city and we'd have dinner.

One memorable evening Tallulah Bankhead was there in the far corner waiting for her boyfriend who was acting in a play at the Westport playhouse. On this unforgettable evening the mayor was having a birthday party for his teenage niece and at one point she got up and went over to Tallulah and asked,

48

"Excuse me, are you Tallulah Bankhead?" And Tallulah, well into her beverage, growled out at her, "Of course I am, you dumb cunt. Who the fuck do you think I am?" And the young girl clapped her hands and gleefully said, "Oh you are Tallulah! You are Tallulah!" and ran back to her table. That incident became the story for the whole summer.

On another occasion Will and I went to a Tallulah Bankhead party in Manhattan as escorts for Esther Williams. Upon our arrival, the butler opened the door and there was Tallulah, drink in hand and immediately upon seeing Esther, Tallulah put her drink down on the floor, pointed to it and said to Esther, "Dive in!" It was a hoot and got a big laugh. Even Esther thought it was funny.

And since I am on the subject of Tallulah, I should share a great Tallulah story going around town at the time. Tallulah liked to be in the all-together when lounging around at home. One night after ordering dinner to be delivered to her door, she heard the doorbell ring and realized she wasn't wearing a single stitch of clothing. So she grabbed a mink stole that was lying across the back of the couch and draped it casually around her shoulders and opened the door. The delivery boy was speechless and just stammered till Tallulah said, "What's the matter? You've never seen a mink stole before?"

Well, my one year deadline to get on Broadway had passed and all I had to show for it was a lot of great adventures and wonderful classes and a short acting stint playing Buck Tillford, a jockey, in *The Love Wagon* which opened April 14, 1947 at the Papermill Playhouse. It was fun and it paid, but it wasn't Broadway.

Papermill Playhouse's Love Wagon

In late summer I finally got my break. It happened mercifully when Esther Junger the choreographer, hired me to play the role of St. Peter in a Robinson Jeffers' work, *Dear Judas*. It seemed funny. Here I am, recently graduated from a Catholic College and my first Broadway show was to play the role of St. Peter as a dancing mute. Well, at least it would be Broadway.

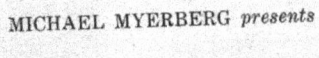

MICHAEL MYERBERG presents

"Dear Judas"

A Drama from the Original Work of ROBINSON JEFFERS
Adapted and Staged by MICHAEL MYERBERG
With the music of JOHANN SEBASTIAN BACH
Selected and Arranged by LEHMANN ENGEL

With

FERDI HOFFMAN • MARGARET WYCHERLY •

And a Company of Forty

Dances and Mimes by ESTHER JUNGER • Costumes and Masks by MARY
Scenery and Lighting by ALBERT JOHNSON

MANSFIELD THEATRE, 47th Street

OPENING SUNDAY EVENING, OCTOBER 5

Here, in terms of great plot and stirring language is an exciting mingling dramatic force with the proportions of spectacle. Mr. Mye premise of universal interest and mounted it against a tapestry of and dance, of unrivaled power and beauty. Here, is an evening fil wonder, great music and inspiration for all.

IN THE PLAY: "Listen to me now and remember. There is not one creature, neither yourself nor anyone, nor a fly nor flung stone, but does exactly and fatally the thing that it needs must." —Ferdi Hoffman (third from left) to the masked figures played by Tony Charmoli, Richard Astor and Betts Lee.

Make Mine Manhattan and Kyle MacDonnell, Tony on far left
Photographer: Alexander Bender

ON BROADWAY!

Dear Judas opened on Broadway on October 5, 1947 and ran for 17 performances at the Mansfield Theater. I played Peter as a dancing mute. It was a fairly experimental approach to the familiar Easter story which incorporated modern dance and poetic tableaux. One odd thing was that the director of the show, Michael Myerberg, was always wheeled in on a sort of hospital bed and directed the show from it propped up by a pillow. He was a rather odd fellow, but the choreographer Esther Junger liked me and was fun to work with. My friend, Walter Terry, reviewed it for the *Herald Tribune* and gave it a generally kind review, but all in all a somewhat forgettable show other than being my first credit on Broadway.

Fortunately for me I had auditioned for other shows and right after *Dear Judas* closed, I got a call back for *Make Mine Manhattan* starring a 26-year-old Sid Caesar making his Broadway debut. *Make Mine Manhattan* was a musical revue about New York City. It opened Jan 15, 1948, at the Broadhurst Theater and ran for 429 performances. I danced throughout the show and was featured in the second act as "Phil the Fiddler."

It was a great cast. I got along great with Sid Caesar, we made each other laugh. There was a talented blonde named Kyle MacDonnell cast in one of the principal roles who was always a lady on stage, but talked like a sailor off stage. It was always unexpected to see that type of language come out of such a beautiful girl. She was a lot of fun. Kyle and I kept in touch and I saw her years later in New Mexico where she had retired after she married.

We had a comic, David Burns, a short chubby man who always kept us in stitches. One afternoon, he was late for rehearsal and we were all getting annoyed when we noticed him sneaking in from backstage in his hat and overcoat, crawling across the floor pretending to be extremely inebriated. He got to his place and slurred out something about "a rough night last night." He couldn't just walk in discreetly and apologize for his tardiness - he had to make us laugh so hard we would forget that we were sore with him. And it worked.

The choreographer was Lee Sherman and my dance partner was Annabelle Gold. One outstanding thing about Annabelle was her bust. For a dancer hers was quite large. During one rehearsal Lee was quite brisk with her. He came over to her and was about to grab her by the shoulders when she reached into her blouse, grabbed one of her tits, pulled it up out of her blouse and threatened him with, "You touch me and I'll kill you!"

We all yelled "Bravo!" and applauded. It certainly did the trick because he never did that again.

Lee was generally not a couth gentleman. I learned one thing from him. When I become a director if you have to raise your arms a lot in front of your actors, never wear a shirt with short wide sleeves. Being on the short side, I was always in the front and it was pretty disgusting whenever Lee raised his arms to demonstrate something, I had to look right down his sweaty, hairy armpits. Not a pretty sight. I learned something else. Never manhandle a dancer. To demonstrate or correct something, ask if it's all right to touch them or just be gentle.

Photographer: Alexander Bender

Photographer: Alexander Bender

Tony as Phil the Fiddler in **Make Mine Manhattan**, *along with the cast. Left: Sid Caesar*

53

Lee and I got along pretty well and he gave me some extra dance roles in the second act. One as a prancing pony, which turned out to be a rather special thing. People told me I looked HOT in my white tights galloping around the stage. Well, I was. Dancing is hard work!

Lee could run hot and cold but was always nice to me. I got a dancing break in this show. I understudied the lead dancer, Ray Harrison, and during one show when it was time for Ray to do the number, he was not there. His partner, Nell Fisher, was right next to me and said, "You're his understudy aren't you?"

Eagerly I said, "Yes!"

She just grabbed me, "Let's go!"

I felt so wonderful dancing as a principal. I just gave it my all and sold like crazy and gave it a slam-bang ending. It paid off for we got a big hand from the audience and also the cast on stage. When I ran into the producer Joe Hyman backstage, flushed from performance, I asked, "Joe how did you like my dancing? With a sly sense of humor he said, "Oh, was that you out there?"

And Ray didn't miss his cue again.

LOVE LIFE

When *Make Mine Manhattan* closed in January, I decided to not go on the road with the show as I felt I needed to stay in New York. I trained a young dancer named Bob Fosse to take over my role, and I looked around for another Broadway show.

Love Life had opened at the 46th Street Theatre on October 7, 1948. It starred Ray Middleton and Nanette Fabray. It was directed by Elia Kazan, and choreographed by Michael Kidd.

The show was about a married couple, Sam and Susan Cooper, who never age as they progress from 1791 to 1948. The storyline of *Love Life* was interspersed with vaudeville numbers that reflected the themes.

I heard one of the dancers, Forrest Bonshire, was leaving *Love Life* and Michael Kidd needed a replacement. Forrest and I were the same size and I liked Michael's work so I filled in.

My partner, Arthur Partington, was very tall. He and I had a dance number that wasn't getting the audience response I thought it was capable of. I thought we could stop the show if he was willing to make some slight adjustments to the choreography. I said Michael Kidd didn't have to know. He agreed.

I suggested that when we danced side by side, we dance so close that when he put his arms out - I have to duck. We would be the mirrors of each other, but with him towering above me it brought a sense of difficulty. Every time I ducked under his arm we got applause and a roaring laugh. No matter what, we stayed perfectly together. The Big and the Little of it. By the end, the audience was really laughing and we always got big applause. Too bad Michael Kidd wasn't around to see us do his number.

Nanette Fabray was a fun leading lady. The first night I appeared in the show, as I danced around past her she mouthed, "You're new here" and after that she'd always applaud as I came dancing around.

To this day I still tease her about the horse.

For better or worse, *Love Life* used a live horse on stage during the show. For some reason, when Nanette made her entrance, the horse always got a hard on - talk about being upstaged! Time after time. Nanette maintains it was the blaring of the trumpets that accompanied her arrival that excited the horse. I of course think it was just Nanette. Eventually we put the horse behind the bottom half of a stable door, "Mr. Ed" style, so that his enthusiasm could be discreetly hidden from the audience.

Nanette at a party at my house all these many years later. She still can make me laugh.

Nanette is one of the funniest raconteurs I have met. She can get a room laughing like few others. I am privileged to call her a friend. One funny story is how she got her name. Her birth name was Ruby Bernadette Nanette Fabares, and in her early years she performed as Nanette Fabares. But Ed Sullivan emceed a benefit she performed at and reading a cue card - mispronounced her name as "Nanette Fa-bare-ass." So, she changed her last name to Fabray.

Love Life closed on May 14, 1949 after 252 performances and garnered Nanette a Tony award for "Best Performance of a Leading Actress". It gave me great pleasure to see her talent recognized as she did a great job in the role.

While I was performing with *Love Life*, I also discovered opportunities in this new medium called Television.

Stanley Simmons, Louise Ferrrand, Geneve Dorn, Bruce Cartwright, Marina Palmer, Martin Kraft perform "Fascinating Rhythm".
STM Publicity Photos/ Charmoli Photo Archive

Chapter 3
Early Television (1949-56)

STOP THE MUSIC

One morning Lee Sherman rang me. "Tony, somebody called. They are looking for a choreographer for television."

I knew what television was because of the dance demonstration we did.

I reported to Charles Henderson and his wife Mitzi Mayfair at Steinway Hall and introduced myself. They wanted a choreographer for a show called *Stop the Music* and needed someone who could do all kinds of dances.

Right off, Charles said, "Show us some choreography."

Right off, I knew I was talking to someone who knew nothing about dance. I said, "I need dancers to show you some choreography."

He then sat down to the piano and said "What would you do to something like this?"

I said that's a tarantella so I would do this." I danced a few bars and he immediately said, "You're hired." Through all this, his wife Mitzi just kept sipping her Martini and repeated "Yeah, you're hired."

Next we went to the Forrest Theater from where the show was going to be televised. I hired some dancers and went right into rehearsal during the day, while I performed in *Love Life* during the evenings. Between the two shows I was working very long days, but I loved it.

Stop the Music was one of the first game shows on television. Bert Parks emceed the show and the orchestra played tunes for the home audience to guess. Dancers danced to musical interpretations and singers would sing the lyrics to popular songs.

At the first orchestra rehearsal for *Stop the Music*, Mitzi appeared with a fresh Martini in hand and just kept getting increasingly inebriated until she had to be whisked away. We first went on the air on May 5, 1949, with no mishaps and everybody seemed pleased. I don't remember if Mitzi was at the theatre for the air show or just passed out at home. I didn't see the show myself because I was performing down the street in *Love Life*.

The Times gave it a good review but got my ire up when they wrote "The dance numbers were beautifully choreographed by Mitzi Mayfair." I hired a PR agent immediately and had this corrected in a flash. It was corrected in several newspapers and Mitzi Mayfair never showed her face in rehearsal again. In fact I lost total track of her.

I would choreograph three or more different songs weekly for audiences to guess the title, and on weeks when I didn't have time to work out so many dances I would ask Bert Parks to "*Stop the Music*" earlier. Fortunately he knew music so I could tell him the exact number of bars that had choreography. It all worked out perfectly.

The dancers gained a certain notoriety on the show especially Geneve Dorn who had quite an ample bust and was very proud of it and loved to display it. She could manage to break a strap and allow her bust to come flying out in a shot. She loved facing the live orchestra when going through this maneuver. We always knew this happened when the orchestra fell apart and went blowing notes all over the place. Geneve would fake embarrassment and go through quite a maneuver putting her bust back into her costume. The orchestra guys would always show appreciation with enthusiastic hoots and whistles.

One of my dancers, Bruce Cartwright came to me at rehearsal one day with Geneve in tow and said "Tony have you met Miss YoYo Tits our Japanese dancing girl?" She loved all the kidding and attention.

The other dancers were Louise Ferrand, Marina Palmer, Martin Kraft, Stanley Simmons and Bruce. The dancers became an important part of the show and developed fan clubs of their own. One of the singers, Betty Ann Grove sometimes joined in some of the dance numbers. Estelle Loring and a male singer

Yo-yo tits Geneve & Stanley in "Wedding of the Painted Doll"

Marina Palmer & Stanley Simmons in "Paree"

filled out the cast, while Bert managed to keep the whole thing together.

Stanley Simmons was always particular about how the costumes looked - and on his own time he would fit, recut, and embellish all the rental costumes we used on the show. I always wondered if the costume rental agents noticed that the costumes were always significantly improved when they were returned. I wasn't surprised at all when Stanley later became a successful fashion designer.

I had continued my ballet classes with Helene Platova during all this time. Even the top Broadway choreographer Jerome Robbins took her class. Of course he was doing so many Broadway shows as well as performing with the New York City Ballet he didn't have time to appear in class very often. With the introduction and the popularity of television and my career taking off, I had to give up a lot of classes too.

One day after being absent for quite a while I appeared again while class was in progress. Plotsy tapped her cane several times, stopped the music, got up from her stool and slowly walked over to me. Utter silence. She didn't ask questions about my long absence she just said, "Tony for you and Jerry I give special price. Two dollar a year. You come two times." Titters from the students and class resumed. She meant of course, where the hell have you been?

STM Publicity Photos/ Charmoli Photo Archive

Choreographing *Stop the Music* in the day at the Forrest Theater on 49th Street and then running right from rehearsal down Broadway to dance in *Love Life* on 46th Street, and then squeezing in the odd class when I could - absorbed all my time. After theater I'd go right home to Will who would have a simple supper waiting for me. Then I'd get on the phone and start calling people for rehearsal the next day. By the time I got to bed I was bushed!

Stanley Simmons & Geneve Dorn doing something Christmasy

*Martin Kraft, Bruce Cartwright, Geneve Dorn, Marina Palmer,
Tony Charmoli "In The Good Old Summertime"*

Meet Me In St. Louis?   *Visiting San Francisco*

Will observed this for a while, then said to me, "Tony, when you get home after the theater, why don't I take over making all those calls for you so you can have supper and get to bed at a more decent hour?"

This arrangement was a lifesaver. All of those years living and working in New York could never have been possible without Will looking out for me at every turn. Will dropped his Park Avenue job and took over as my manager.

When *Love Life* closed, I was able to perform an occasional role on *Stop the Music*, too. It was up to me to come up with all the ideas for the dance scenarios. I'd talk with the scenery folks and see what scenery was available for rent, and sometimes that would trigger a concept. But it all was very fast. There wasn't much time for doddling. It was always, "Here! This is what we are going to do!" And we'd just do it. It was all pretty quick.

On these pages are some rare production stills from *Stop the Music*. You can see we had a lot of fun on the show. I suspect that is one reason why it was so popular. I worked on the show till the spring of 1950, when I got an important call.

My work had captured the eyes of the powers behind the upcoming TV show, *Your Hit Parade*. They were impressed that I had to create concepts for and choreograph three or four dance numbers each show in a very short space of time and *Your Hit Parade* was going to require the same format. I couldn't refuse their offer. So I made the move to *Your Hit Parade*.

STM Publicity Photos/ Charmoli Photo Archive

The South Seas!

Appalachia

Something in the spirit of Swan Lake

Something exotic

60

Betty Grove & Tony in Hucklebuck

Winter Wonderland

I stayed in touch with many of the dancers. Geneve captured the eyes of someone on the West Coast and relocated and was never heard from since. Stanley became a well-known fashion designer and I can't account for the rest.

STM Publicity Photos/ Charmoli Photo Archive

Stanley Simmons & Geneve Dorn in Paris

Dancing toys!

Many people may not remember *Stop The Music* these days, but we put on a great show. It was an ambitious endeavor for early TV and the response from the audiences encouraged the development of Dance on television and paved the way for shows like *Your Hit Parade*, and dance shows that have followed. I very much enjoyed being a part of it.

61

HOBNOBBING

Fortunately, when we moved back from the barn in Westport that summer before I was cast in my first Broadway show, we moved into a large apartment uptown on Riverside Drive. It was a great space for entertaining friends and came in handy for production meetings later on with *Your Hit Parade*. We hired a live-in houseman named Moon who cooked and cleaned while Will and I worked.

Dancing with Jane Kean at a cast party

The dance world in New York was a large one, but in spite of that it seemed everybody knew each other and would check out each other's work in support of the art of the dance. We'd socialize before shows and after shows and kept track of what everyone was doing. Between Broadway and *Stop the Music* I was always busy - but I still managed to get out and have a bit of a social life. Above, I am dancing with Jane Kean at a cast party.

One evening Will and I were invited to the choreographer John Butler's apartment for dinner. His guest list was quite something. Besides his friend, and Will and I, there was John Gielgud and Greta Garbo herself. It certainly was an interesting dinner party. Garbo was a natural human being with no "Look at me, I'm a big Movie Star" attitude about her at all. She was more interested in John Butler and I being in the dance world, and she had lots of questions about my working on Broadway. In fact the whole evening was pleasant and unpretentious. Garbo lived nearby so John Gielgud escorted her to where she had to go, and came back where a cab was coming for him. As John started for the cab he asked Will to join him, but not me. John got in but left the door open and called out for Will to get in. Will again indicated I should be included. John just closed the door and drove off, alone.

Our next encounter with John Gielgud was in 1951, in London when we went to see him in A Winter's Tale. The play was good and so was John. We went backstage and of course he was glad to see Will, so we invited him to join us for dinner. He said he had to refuse because he was already engaged with a very important appointment. Will and I called a friend and asked him to join us and he said he would love to and let's meet at a certain club. We cabbed over and were happy to see our friend Tom who said this was one of the best men's clubs in London. We were having a good time when Will called me over to a window and pointed out and said, "Tony Look." We were on the second floor looking right down into an outdoor men's toilet with no ceiling - totally exposed and brightly lit up. There standing at a urinal with his manhood in hand... cruising... was the great actor, John Gielgud. An important engagement indeed. We never ever told him we had witnessed his so called "important date." And Will never engaged him either.

With Will in Paris

Each summer, Will and I made a point of getting to Europe and visiting and making new friends. A wonderfully wealthy friend named Joe Kennedy (from Minnesota) had moved to France and lived just outside of Paris with his friend Herb Bigelow. We had an open invitation to stay at his villa each summer. It had a beautiful courtyard where I spent many hours painting and I created quite a bit of work whenever I visited there.

While there, we made the acquaintance of Fern Bedeau, who owned The Chateau Conde in the Loire Valley. It was a true castle and Will and I stayed in the Duke and Duchess of Windsor's suite. Will had the Duchess' bedroom which was pink, I had the Duke's room which was blue. But, it was back to New York when vacation was over.

On one of our annual trips to Europe, another extremely wealthy friend Sally Bondy invited Herb, Will and me to drive down to Madrid with her. When Sally traveled south to Spain or the Riviera, a separate car would follow behind just to carry her luggage. She invited us to join her a few times and it was truly traveling like royalty (when we visited Portugal with Sally, we even stayed at the royal palace).

Fern's place.

When we arrived in Madrid, right on the side of the highway was a large billboard sign announcing that Josephine Baker was appearing at a famous outdoor restaurant showplace. We all agreed we had to see her. Sally happened to be lightly acquainted with Josephine. We checked into the Palace Hotel, where Sally knew the owners - from whom she got tickets. We quickly got dressed and made it to the restaurant just in time for the show.

We were surprised to see that there were just a few people up near the stage with the rest of the theater was totally empty. We felt embarrassed for Josephine and decided we should sit at a table way in the back under the trees where she wouldn't be able to see us. She did a great professional job and the few people there loved her.

The next evening, the owners of the hotel gave Sally and us a very nice cocktail party to which they invited Josephine. She arrived to great applause of recognition from the guests and she was very pleased. When she got around to us we were greeted with big smiles, as she and Sally knew each other. Sally lied and apologized for arriving too late to see her show, but asked, "How was it?"

Josephine responded with a great big smile, "It was great! There wasn't an empty seat in the house! I'm sorry you missed it."

The artist's life is about self-promotion, no matter how big a name you have.

> *Years later, Will and I did go to see her show when she appeared in New York and the show had improved a hundred fold.*

One evening in New York, Will and I were driving around the city in a rental car and came upon a movie theatre showing an old Mae West Film, *She Done Him Wrong*.

I got so excited I said, "Will, park the car! Let's go to see that movie." I explained. "My father took me to see it when I was a little kid and he just loved it, but I didn't understand what was so good about it. I was too young..."

Well, Will and I sat through the whole thing and the rating for my father went way up. I loved Mae West. I followed up with going to all her movies - but more on Mae later...

Dear Moon passed away while working for us, so Will and I arranged for his burial. We knew he went to church every Sunday because he often had the priest over for lunch in our rather spacious kitchen. The priest was very grateful to us for being so nice to Moon and thanked us for asking him to come visit. A ceremony was arranged at his Vietnamese church and after the ceremony we stood to receive a large line of handshakes from all the parishioners who thanked us for doing this for Moon. Will and I thought that perhaps in the future a relative might show up, and rather than say he was dumped in potter's field we could direct them to where we had given Moon a proper burial.

Our next move was to the wonderful duplex penthouse apartment at 16 West 71st overlooking Central Park. It was quite grand with a garden and studio on the upper floor overlooking Central Park, The Museum of Natural History on the uptown side and Central Park on the east, and The San Remo Towers on the west. The two stories could accommodate many parties of which there were many.

My mother and Claire visiting our apartment in New York. The woman on the right was our friend, Lou Nelson's mother who used to ride for the Pony Express!

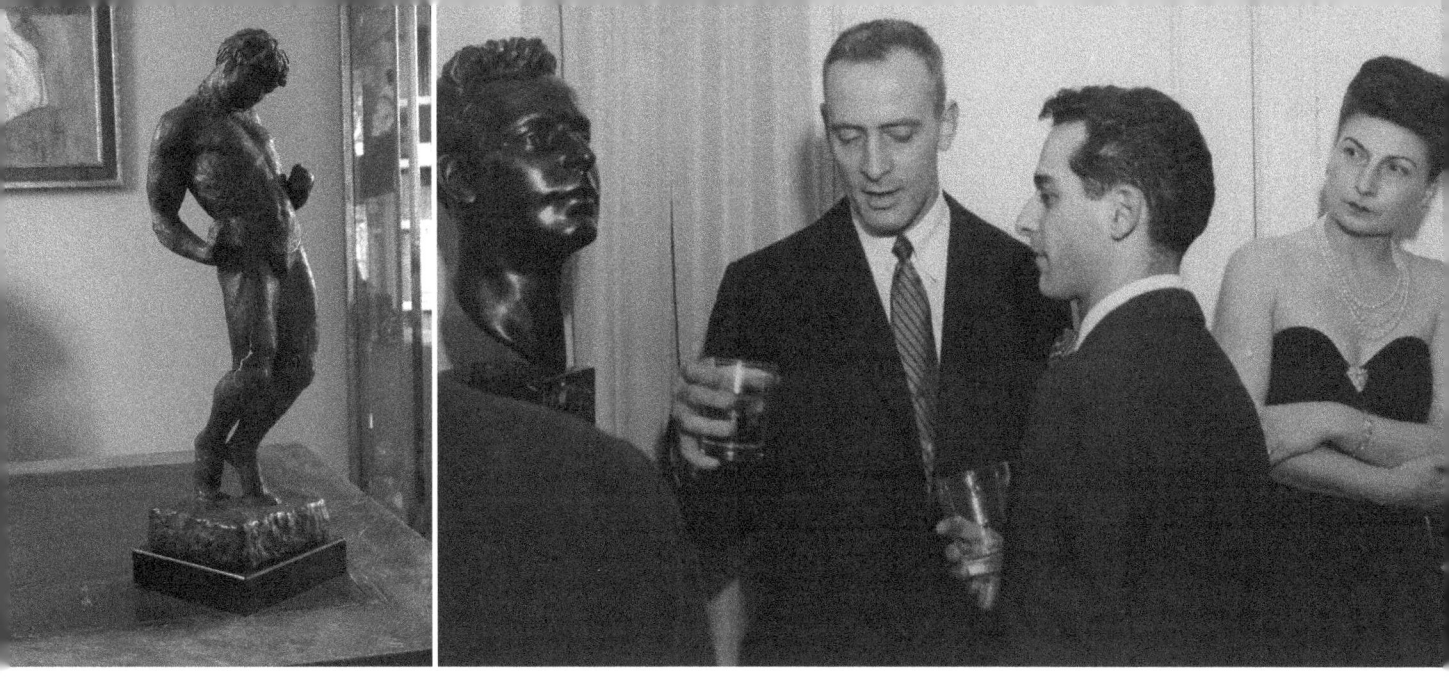

Left: one of the figure sculptures for which I modeled. Originally, the arms were up in the air above the head- but she couldn't fit the sculpture on the shelf where it was going to dry- so she pulled the arms down into this position- which both of us liked much better anyway. The sculpture has had its bumps over the decades, but it is still a wonderful reminder of the fun times I spent with Charlotte Dunwiddie. Right: Charlotte considering the bronze she did of me.

My mother and Claire visiting our apartment in New York. The woman on the right was our friend, Lou Nelson's mother who used to ride for the Pony Express!

Charlotte Dunwiddie was a dear friend in New York who was outstanding in many ways. First off, she spoke five different languages quite fluently. I witnessed that one evening at a party in her grand Park Avenue apartment. She would greet the guest in the language of their country and continue a rather long conversation with them and turn on a dime and speak to an American in English. I was fascinated the night I observed her speaking to a handsome black man in an outstanding wardrobe with a half cape thrown over his shoulder and gold cords with small tassels holding the whole thing together. I asked who it was and she quickly introduced me, in his language, to Prince Rene Douala Manga Bell the ruler of the French Cameroons in Africa. She later told me he was interested in marrying her and wished her to move to Africa and help him in his work.

Well that never happened. She loved New York too much to even consider the suggestion. She also was quite good at sculpting but said she hadn't been encouraged to do it for some reason while married to her previous husband who was a top executive with Goodyear. He had passed away a couple of years before, so I offered to model for her if she wanted to start sculpting again. She jumped at the offer and we started the next day.

I was working on *Your Hit Parade* at the time and she loved coming to watch, but we always found time for modeling until she finished the clay original which was prepped for casting. Later when she finished casting the bronze of my head, we had a *Hit Parade* party and invited the cast to the unveiling. Charlotte was so happy with the evening, she asked me to do more modeling and she completed several more pieces.

The prize came when she called one day to tell me she had an offer to do a bronze of a horse for the entrance to the prestigious Jockey Club. This was a tremendous joy for her because in Germany and South America she was quite a horsewoman and loved sculpting horses. Now the elite of horse lovers and owners in America would see her work. Charlotte always had a driver take her everywhere and the three of us went out to the Jockey Club to see the sculpture and it was marvelous. Many club members congratulated Charlotte on her elegant sculpture which pleased her - and we finished with a great celebratory dinner!

Will and I moved to California shortly after that. Once we moved, we lost track of Charlotte. We talked a few times by telephone, then once I called and there was no answer. There was no answer for a long time and we never saw nor heard from her again until we finally were able to reach the building manager who confirmed that Miss Dunwiddie was no longer. She helped glorify a wonderful chapter in our lives and still the detailed memories live within me.

Above is one of the figure sculptures for which I modeled. Originally, the arms were up in the air above the head - but she couldn't fit the sculpture on the shelf where it was going to dry - so she pulled the arms down into this position - which both of us liked much better anyway. The sculpture has had its bumps over the decades, but it is still a wonderful reminder of the fun times I spent with Charlotte Dunwiddie.

NBC publicity photos/ photog: Roy Schatt/ Charmoli Photo Archive

YOUR HIT PARADE

When *Your Hit Parade* hit the airwaves in the summer of 1950, it became an overnight hit. It was both fun and challenging to quickly come up with innovative stagings for each of the hits on the billboard charts.

Eileen Wilson, Snooky Lanson, and Dorothy Collins were the first stars, but were soon equaled by the *Hit Parade* dancers who quickly developed fan clubs of their own. Every time I attended a party or any social event I was pounced upon with questions about the *Hit Parade*.

It was a live show, as was *Stop the Music*, and as a consequence, there were a lot of funny moments. If you goofed up, it was in front of a national audience. There was no time to redo a number.

Eileen Wilson, had commitments on the West Coast so had to leave after the first season. Gisele McKenzie was her replacement and she was the easiest one to break up during a song.

One number was set in the courtyard of an Asian palace and Gisele was lounging as a queen on an ornate chaise and regally looking off into the distance. But there were supposed to be dancing girls whirling in very full skirts entertaining her. But she noticed that they were behind her, seen only from the waist up dancing behind the chaise. Gisele then turned to casually take a peek to see why and burst out laughing when she discovered the girls had no skirts on. They couldn't make the change in time. Then Gisele turned front and in runs Jerry Duane as a skinny half naked messenger bearing a proclamation. He threw himself down before her and held up the note. The sight of this funny skinny naked creature was too much for her and she burst out laughing, which started the girl dancers laughing, then Jerry on the ground started bouncing with laughter. So the song never did get sung. I guess the

Gisele McKenzie

television viewers also thought it was funny because the mail poured in about that number, or non-number.

Another memorable moment with Gisele McKenzie was when she attempted to sing, "Let Me Go Lover" in the Tower of London. She entered the scene as old Queen Elizabeth carrying a parchment with the title of the song on it and also a pardon. During the music intro, the Lover, played by Russell Arms, peered through the bars to read the pardon she's held up for him. He shook his head "No", and she crumbled up the paper into a tight wad and threw it at him. It bounced off the tip of his nose and hit Gisele in the face, which sent her into hysterical laughter, then he also lost it. They never did get through the whole song.

"This Old House" was another catastrophe. Snooky was sitting in a rocking chair on the porch of an old ramshackle house. Ginny and Lenny were groveling and making love in the dirt beneath a tree and a goat was tied to the tree right next to them. They are poor barefoot hillbillies.

Snooky started to sing, the goat is chewing and Ginny and Lenny are making young love. All is going well until the goat starts to relieve itself. Snooky sees it and starts to slur his words, Ginny and Lenny are trying to move away from the steady stream which keeps getting bigger and bigger and wider. Snooky is now singing only every other word and Lenny and Ginny are getting soaked with goat urine until they can't take anymore and are laughing hysterically and no more lyrics from Snooky either. Ginny and Lenny get up and leave and when Snooky rises to go, the house collapsed and came crashing down. Total hysterical disaster, never to be forgotten.

When Eddie Fisher came in to sing his hit single, "Oh My Papa", I was surprised to find out that he didn't know the words. Ray Charles, our choral director had to mouth the words just off camera. It worked out okay but I had never seen that done with the person who had the hit recording.

It was my turn to goof with the song "Ebb Tide". Before each song, we would show the chart number themed to match the set. The number title in this case, appeared in a flat of sand, which filled the frame to look like the beach. A wave of water was supposed to wash in and wipe away

Snooky Lanson

the title. I threw the bucket of water. But, I guess I was too energetic because my hands also were seen throwing the bucket of water into the shot. I felt awful but the mail that came in said they just loved it. They thought it was very funny.

One of the dancers, Dusty McCaffrey was very vain and had quite a large fan club. He liked to keep himself perfectly groomed all the time he was on camera.

He kept a mirror and a can of hair spray next to each camera. Once the TD cut to his shot too early and Dusty seeing the little red light go on just threw the spray and comb and mirror into the air and faked a step to cover the mistake. I thanked him for covering the error and he said. "Honey! When I'm crossing the street and the light turns red, I dance."

Dusty McCaffry

Once during warm up just before air, Dusty sprained his ankle and couldn't go on to do his solo. He said, "Tony I can't go on. You know the number you'll have to do it." I hurried and got dressed in his costume (way too large for me) and the other dancers were laughing hysterically at how funny it looked on me. My cue came, I slapped the too big hat on my head and went on. It was a trick dancing in that big costume but mercifully the end came and I did my somersault ending flat on my stomach but my hat fell off on the floor in front of me. I grabbed it, slapped it on my head right on the last beat of the music and ended in a triumphantly big smile. The dancers all yelled "Bravo!" I had saved the day. Dusty never sprained another ankle.

Rehearsal sequence- Notice Dusty is worrying about his hair.

When the tour of *Make Mine Manhattan* closed, I hired Bob Fosse to be one of the *Hit Parade* dancers. At the time he had a tap act with Mary Ann Niles - they partnered each other well, so I hired her for the show too.

We were a top show so we had to stay new and inventive. I thought of something that was rather daring at the time. I wanted to shoot dance sequences outside of the studio setting. I asked if I could have a camera in the lobby of the theatre so I could choreograph a number for Bob Fosse on the grand staircase in the lobby of the theater. It was a big request as it would mean the director would only have three cameras for the body of the show. Our director liked the idea and was willing to risk it. The show didn't suffer the use of one less camera. The number was a hit with the viewers.

At the time Bob was mostly considered a tap dancer, which is what he did with Mary Ann. Bob liked doing jazz numbers and wanted to go beyond what he'd been doing with Mary Ann, and perhaps be a choreographer someday. I gave him more jazz choreography after that. Years later he met Gwen Verdon and she introduced him to the styles of choreographer Jack Cole. And eventually he combined all he had learned into what became his signature style as a choreographer.

I hired Bob Fosse and dance partner Mary Ann Niles to dance on the Hit Parade.

> We were both standing in the wings years later - we each had been nominated for an Emmy - me for Shirley MacLaine - Live at the Palace, and he for Liza with a Z, Bob was very gracious when he won. He came back into the wings and smiled very sweetly, "This really belongs to you - but I think I'll keep it!"

The dance in the lobby was a big hit and this started a trend. I did a number on the rooftop of the RCA building, and another on 50th St. with the *Hit Parade* Dancers, and another to "Steam Heat" which I danced a solo down in the boiler room of the RCA building. This was a complicated affair as cable had to be laid from the studio out to wherever we were shooting - sometimes it involved a lot of cable. These numbers done on location were considered revolutionary. It's amazing to see how far TV has come.

At Christmas time we always did Christmasy things. One year we filmed holiday show in front of Rockefeller Center. The closing number was "O Holy Night" sung by Snooky. But just as Snooky opened his mouth to sing, he completely blanked out on the lyrics. There were no cue cards and the first verse was jibberish until Dorothy Collins, who was standing next to him, whispered the second verse's lyrics to him. He was incredibly embarrassed to forget his lyrics on live national TV. He was in tears afterwards

Snooky attempting to sing "O Holy Night"

and we just tried to console him the best we could.

On another Christmas show, Mary Ann and Bob followed the opening number with one of their own so they had to under-dress. Being a holiday show and the first number called for them to be reindeer. That meant Mary Ann had to stuff her ball gown into her reindeer costume giving her a giant belly. They rushed to the set in time to make the opening number but when the dancers saw this overly pregnant reindeer join them the whole company broke up including all the guys in the control room. Mary Ann was the damndest looking reindeer you have ever seen. Bob tried to ignore it but the big stomach would get in the way. It was very funny.

NBC publicity photos/ photog: Roy Schatt/ Charmoli Photo Archive

When a New Orleans type of number came up, I thought it would be just the thing for Bob Fosse to do a solo. We worked out a kind of sexy strut that spoke of New Orleans. I said, "I think this needs a hat like a derby." It proved to be just the thing. I called a guy I had seen do hat tricks in a vaudeville act. He came to rehearsal and taught us some hat tricks. Bob caught on very quickly. That hat became a standard in Bob's dance numbers because he liked a hat to cover his thinning hair.

On another show the boys were to wear white tights. On my rounds of checking, I found Bob dressed early and standing in the doorway of the dressing room with his big "schlong" hanging half way down to his knees under his white tights. I said, "Bob, get right back in that dressing room and put that thing into a dance belt. What do you want, everybody to faint?"

He laughed but did jam it into a dance belt where it was still conspicuous.

The singers did well but most of the fan mail came for our singer Dorothy Collins. Her fan club kept growing with each show, but her husband Raymond Scott our orchestra leader was a Royal Pain in the A. Dorothy was interested in growing into Broadway musicals where she could act and move around while singing. Over and over, I would stage her numbers to include movement and in rehearsal Raymond would get rid of my choreography and tell her to stay still. This routine went back and forth until she would be in tears. She wanted to prove that she was more than just a singer. I spoke to the producers and we finally worked it out with her begrudging husband so she could move while she sang. She was vindicated when she finally was cast in a Broadway show. We were all so happy for Dorothy. She showed that she could really act in the original cast of Stephen Sondheim's *Follies* for which she was nominated for a Tony Award for Best Actress in a Musical.

On Monday mornings we'd go to BBDO to find out what the hits were for the week, and in the afternoon, just the creative staff, the director, the writer, and I would meet at my apartment uptown on Riverside Drive. We would be in telephone contact with the Music Director and the Scenic Designer. My houseman, Moon, would fix dinner and we were allowed one cocktail at the dinner break. Come to think of it, the *Hit Parade* owes me money because I paid for all of this. I guess it's too late now.

I have to honor David who was the operator of Camera no. 2. I gave him assignments out of the

Having fun with Dorothy Collins

ordinary and he often would skip lunch to rehearse shots so he could do them on the live telecast. On occasions like that I always brought lunch in to David and his dolly operator.

I liked to experiment with different camera things and talked to my Technical Director about putting a camera below in the pit to give a more dramatic low angle shot of the dancers. He agreed and so we gave it a try with the dancers wearing in multicolored petticoats.

The girls lined up one behind the other and picked up their skirts and danced sexily right into the camera. When they got near the lens I had them twist their hip so it wouldn't be too crotchy as they leave the shot. The girls danced down one by one and the last one was Eleanor Boleyn but she danced right down to the lens with her skirt high in the air straddling the lens. I called a cut. I scolded, "Eleanor." She said, "What's the matter? Too much zuk!" "Yes. Too much zuk. Though, the crew loved it and wanted more.

Talking with David about a shot.

I mention Eleanor and I'm reminded of another occasion when we were in a photo session. The photographer was a middle-aged dandy and a little on the plump side, or was his suit too tight? He also had a well-clipped tiny mustache that wiggled when he talked and would always purse his lips. He was setting up the cast in various groups and finally came to Eleanor and me and put us where he thought best. On the way to our positions Eleanor said to me, "Doesn't he look like a well-kept asshole?" When I told the group privately what Eleanor had said, the photographer

Ruth Lawrence & Lenny Claret

blissfully ignorant found he had no difficulty getting us to smile.

On another occasion with choreographer Jerry Robbins, Eleanor wore a full dirndl skirt to rehearsal, which annoyed him tremendously so he angrily said to her, "What's the big skirt for, trying to cover up your big fat thighs?" The next day she came to rehearsal completely redone. She wore a tight form fitting leotard, long sheer hose, high heel shoes and a tiny silk scarf tied tightly around her neck and she looked fabulous. She was purposely late and when he saw her in the wings he stopped the rehearsal. Eleanor strutted across stage in silence to her place. The whole stage was in complete silence waiting for what Jerry would say. When she stopped and turned front, he spoke, "Lovely scarf you're wearing." Eleanor said, "To cover my goiter!" She was never bothered again.

NBC publicity photos/ photog: Roy Schatt/ Charmoli Photo Archive

For relief from always doing the current hit tunes on *Your Hit Parade*, we would do one or two numbers called "Lucky Strike Extras". These could be done by our singers or dancers. On one occasion I thought of doing a dance number for our blonde Bobbie Trelease. I came up with something I thought her fan club would like. I chose the exotic rhythms of Ravel's "Bolero". I had our set designer Paul Barnes build a four sided pyramid of six inch high steps, wide at the bottom and tapering to a four sided platform at the top.

NBC publicity photos/ photog: Roy Schatt/ Charmoli Photo Archive

Bombshell Bobbie is posed on the top platform in a long black very form fitting gown. The four male dancers are on each side at the bottom in tight black Spanish bolero costumes topped with wide brimmed black hats. The rhythms of the Bolero start rather quietly at first as the men start to move exotically then start to mount the steps increasing their sexy moves as they slowly advance to Bobbie who is moving provocatively. The music increases in volume and intensity until the dancers reach Bobbie, surround her, lift her high into a spectacular lift and then let her drop into their midst as the lights go out.

Bobbie Trelease

The applause was tremendous and fan mail and phone calls praising the number poured in. The dancers were thrilled at this great reaction and thanked me over and over. We were surprised when the client's wives complained. They said the number was too sexy for Television. Even the mail and phone calls praising the number saying it was the best thing on television didn't appease them. My reaction to all this, "TOUGH!! They can go to their church, I'll go to mine!" is what we used to say back in Minnesota.

Politics with clients and producers

Also on *Your Hit Parade* I wanted to do a number in a large elegant ballroom dressed with two very large candelabras. Paul, our set designer, searched every prop house in New York but couldn't find any that suited my requirements. Finally I came up with the idea of putting two tall singers in long white underwear as the base with each holding a large candelabra on their heads. This seemed to work out pretty well until they started to giggle. Then we had wiggly candles but once the dancers filled the set nobody noticed our brave candle holders.

Considering how quickly these shows came together, there were some wonderful production values. Both the set designer and costume designer knew the stock available to pull from and they did a great job within those short time frames.

NBC publicity photos/ photog: Roy Schatt/ Charmoli Photo Archive

Television was changing! Color TV was on the horizon. But the government had to be sold on its feasibility before they invested in the infrastructure. Having done the very first test for movement on camera, I was asked to do a test for color and movement on camera with a little show consisting of a comic, a singer and dancers to be done in the Colonial Theater in Columbus Circle. We used Dolores Grey and alternated with Nanette Fabray and the *Hit Parade* dancers. I asked Sal Balosni our costumer to create a special gown for the dancers to test color with. I knew that blue was the most stable of the colors on video, so I designed the scene around the

My Candelabras

Below left, Tony explaining some blocking to Eileen Wilson. (She was never terribly good with props.)

NBC publicity photos/ photog: Roy Schatt/ Charmoli Photo Archive

74

color blue. The blue bodice was tight with a very full blue skirt. I had the girls dance up to the camera and flash their petticoats which showed off all the other colors to be tested - red, yellow, green, and lavender.

One crane camera would shoot the entire number so of course I used my favorite crane guy from the *Hit Parade*, David. The dance started with Nanon Millis on the floor with her legs tucked under her so all you could see was her upper body surrounded by a full blue skirt. The camera was high shooting down on her so you saw only blue. As Nanon slowly rose, the camera craned down and to one side. The boys came in with their partners and one picks up Nanon. They waltz in a circle and away from the camera as the camera booms down to the floor. The boys leave their partners and the girls one after the other waltz into the camera flipping their petticoats revealing all the other colors being tested. One after the other so now the powers that be can see the colors in movement. The boys recover their partners and wind up doing a wild waltz in a big circle with the girls flipping their petticoats as they pass the camera. Now the inspectors see the colors in rapid motion. The waltz comes to an end in a very rapid spinning motion. Thank goodness the inspectors applauded.

In the number above, the man is making a date with all four women.

Then, the inspectors moved to a studio uptown and we repeated the show so they could check it from an out of studio location. Next they moved to another location across the river into New Jersey and we repeated the whole show over again. After that demonstration they returned to the theatre of origination but asked to only see the dance numbers. Will, now my manager, came in time to see this last performance and asked "How many times have the dancers had to do this number?" When I told him, he immediately asked, "Where is the producer?" I told him and he was gone in a flash. He returned in a few minutes and wanted to see the dancers. He told them they would be paid twenty-five dollars for each time they had to do the dance. They screamed with joy and smothered him with kisses. In those days that amount for dancers was very acceptable.

NBC publicity photos/ photog: Roy Schatt/ Charmoli Photo Archive

They also took pride in being so important in helping in the birth of color television.

In the summer breaks, I often visited my friend, Fern Bedeau in her home in France - The Chateau Conde' in the Loire Valley - a magnificent place. On one of her visits to New York, I invited her to the *Your Hit Parade* telecast, which she loved. I had primed the dancers that they would have a visitor after the show - so don't get dressed until after she leaves. I

I had the dancers perform this number in with the orchestra.

Hit Parade Dancers dancing in the streets!

asked Fern if she'd like to meet the cast. She said, "I'd be delighted." I knocked on the dressing room door and Lenny very invitingly said, "Come in." I opened the door and two dancers were completely naked and one was wearing a skimpy dance belt. Fern made a little gasp and said, "Oh Tony, this is lovely." I said, "Welcome to America." You can get dressed boys, and thank you!" Unfortunately Bob Fosse was not in that group or she might never have left.

I was now very busy doing the *Your Hit Parade*, when one morning Charles Weidman, a very well-known dancer, choreographer and teacher, came to my rehearsal in Steinway Hall. I was very busy with my *Hit Parade* dancers when an attendant came to tell me to answer the door. Before I got there the door opened and in walked a very drunken Charles. I was very angry for this falling down drunk to walk in and disrupt my rehearsal with my dancers. But, all he could say was, "Tony I need some money, you got any money?" All I had in my wallet were two twenty dollar bills so I gave him one and said, "Charles don't ever come and disrupt my rehearsal again. You're a disgrace to the dance world." I never did see him again, he must have been put away somewhere to dry out. Poor guy, it's such a shame for a talent to be wasted like that. Of course, the dancers wanted to know who the drunk was and I was ashamed to

NBC publicity photos/ photog: Roy Schatt/ Charmoli Photo Archive

Script meeting with Eileen

tell the truth. I had a lot to do with the dancers before lunch and another number after lunch so there was no time to fool around. Looking back, we always accomplished a lot more in the morning.

In 1954, *Dance Magazine* honored me with their first TV Dance award and presented it on *The Steve Allen Show*. The representatives from the magazine were seated in the audience and I was escorted backstage. There I ran into Bambi Lynn and Rod Alexander, the most famous dance team at the time. We greeted each other and they continued with their warm up. They were expecting to go on in the next five minutes when the stage manager came back and told them they would be going on later.

Quite some time went by before they thought to start warming up again for surely they would go on this time, but no they were delayed again. I got a little miffed because it takes a lot for a dancer to warm up. Well this happened about twice more and by now I was really angry with Steve for being so inconsiderate.

Suddenly he announced me and as I walked out I was still rather angry when he introduced me to the audience and said, "Tony congratulations on this award! I watch the *Hit Parade* and see your wonderful work every week. How do you come up with these wonderful dances show after show? What's your secret?"

Above: Dorothy Collins and Tony; Below: Bob, Nanon, Ginny, & Lenny

By now I really disliked him and I replied, "I don't think I'll tell you." I took the trophy and walked off. He went into gales of laughter and couldn't stop, it struck him so funny. His laugh was contagious and even the audience started laughing. Then the next night he mentioned it on his show again and several times after that.

The *Dance Magazine* people were furious that I didn't mention the magazine but we made it up by doing a radio show from the famous Sardi's Restaurant and that went

*Bob Herget, Lenny Claret, Tom Hansen,
Ruth Lawrence, Ginny Conwell, Nanon Miller*

NBC publicity photos/ photog: Roy Schatt/ Charmoli Photo Archive

very well with several mentions of *Dance Magazine*, and everybody was satisfied. Even *Dance Magazine* got this extended publicity and thanked me for the publicity.

In 1955 I was nominated for my first Emmy (for a *Hit Parade* episode in the '54 season). I didn't win, but it did bring me some publicity. But the style of music had been changing to rock 'n roll and that changed the whole method of presenting songs on the *Hit Parade*. I chose to leave the show to discover more interesting possibilities. After I left the show, I won my first Emmy award for Best Choreographer for *Your Hit Parade* (for the '55 episode "Showbiz"). But, I was already on to many other projects. I was busier than ever.

ANKLES AWEIGH!

I had been getting quite a bit of notice in the five years that I had been with *Your Hit Parade*, and I was hoping to be chosen to choreograph Gwen Verdon's new Broadway show *The Belle of the Klondike*. But it went to Jack Cole. I was disappointed, but I knew better opportunities would come around. Later one day while I was busy with *Your Hit Parade*, two men came from *The Belle of the Klondike*. I had them wait till I was done with my rehearsal, then met with them.

"Could you come and choreograph the chorus numbers? Jack has too much to do with the principals."

I thought for a moment, then I turned it down. I knew whatever I did would be attributed to Jack Cole. I didn't want to be listed as anyone's assistant. And I was glad I did, as *The Belle of the Klondike* flopped.

Soon after, I finally got an offer to choreograph my first Broadway show, *Ankles Aweigh!* starring Betty and Jane Kean. *Ankles Aweigh!* opened April 18, 1955. It didn't get terribly good reviews, but it did have a solid run of 176 performances. I was working mostly in TV at this point, so it was nice to still keep my toes in Broadway.

It's often said you do your best work under pressure. I guess that's true. In *Ankles Aweigh!* it became obvious they couldn't make a set change in the time allowed so I was called in to a meeting and asked if I could create a dance number in one, which means I had only the space in front of the closed curtain to work with. Plus, I had only piano and drums for music because there was no time to make an additional orchestral arrangement overnight.

Jane Kean and the sailors

I called the dancers back for a late night rehearsal and warned them that we had a whole new dance to do, and one day to do it in, so we'd be doing "high kicks at midnight". I came up with an idea of dancing to a code just using drum and a few accents on the piano. Well that's all I had to work with anyway. No time to get new costumes so I suggested trench coats and Fedora hats. The traditional look of a detective. There would be a piece of paper that would be secretly passed from dancer to dancer. It would appear and disappear as the secret item had to be kept from getting into the enemy's hands. The stage is dramatically lit. An occasional police whistle cracks the silence. The drums pierce the semi dark stage sporadically - sometimes shattering the silence like a machine gun. You really had to see it to understand the suspense it created. It always got a big applause and it gave the stage hands plenty of time to make the set change.

Anchors Aweigh photos by Will Rapport

After the first performance of this new number the whole cast came out and gave me a big hand. It was very touching. The dancers always said they enjoyed doing it because it gave them an opportunity to act as well as dance. Jerry Robbins also liked this number and congratulated me. I was always pleased when he very openly expressed his pleasure in liking my work. I had a very good relationship with Jerry. I know he could feel I had tremendous admiration of his talent as well.

Another popular dance number that consistently stopped the show was a strip number, but a different twist on the idea. The scene opened on the craps table at a gambling casino. A beautiful woman in fur coat and jewels is sitting downstage of the table and her high rolling boyfriend is playing with his back to her. When he loses all his money, he reaches out his hand without even looking at her and she divests herself of the fur coat which he throws on the table. With each successive loss, she blithely strips till finally she drops her last items and is covered by the other dancers while she is carried off stage. It was always a hit and combined sex, and comic timing, and talented dancers.

Cast of **Ankles Aweigh**

Not long after opening, I was summoned to a meeting with the producers one night at the theatre - and for some strange reason the meeting was held very privately. My dance numbers were stopping the show with great audience reaction and the producers taking note of that, secretly called this meeting to ask me to take over the direction of the whole

*Cast of **Ankles Aweigh** (photo by Will Rapport / Charmoli Photo Archive)*

show and fix it. I felt it was too late to try to do anything with it and declined. The book was so bad it needed a complete rewrite.

They should have brought in new writers. They called Jerry Robbins in to do it but there was not much Jerry could do. The best part was I got to meet Jerry the king of Broadway choreographers and we worked well together. He complimented me with, "Tony your dance numbers are the best dancing on Broadway." Coming from Jerry it was mind blowing. I guess he meant it because during the show I often stood in the back of the theatre to check on the dancers and Jerry would arrive at the theater and stand there with me just before the number closing the first act. I guess he really liked that particular number. It proved to me he meant what he said.

I also discovered Jerry could be very funny, One day he asked if I would come in and help him fix the book, I arrived but no Jerry. Suddenly I heard, "I'm down here." I went down to the dressing rooms and Jerry stepped out in full drag in one of the show girl's costumes. Drag is not for Jerry, but I laughed. He was pretty ugly funny. Then he said, "Don't you dare tell anyone!" Come to think of it I didn't, except my friend Will who also laughed and agreed, "He wouldn't be a beauty in drag!"

I had a great time with the show. Betty and Jane were always wonderful to work with. In fact, I was at Jane's last Christmas party.

BUSIER & BUSIER

All in all, 1955 and 1956 were very busy years. I could not now list all the shows I was doing during the period. I only can say that it seemed I was always working. Somewhere in here I signed a five year contract with NBC and they kept me busy with a lot of specials and movies that they were doing. But, there are a few shows that do stand out in my memory.

I choreographed *The King and Mrs. Candle* for Producer's Showcase with Cyril Ritchard, Joan Greenwood, Theodore Bikel, Richard Haydn, and Irene Manning. It aired April 22, 1955, four days after *Ankles Aweigh!* opened on Broadway. It was a busy time.

I was doing more and more work for NBC and flying from coast to coast for the various projects. In the summer of 1955, Alan Handley called on me to stage the musical numbers for a TV musical special *Svengali and the Blonde* based on the book, *Trilby*, starring Carol Channing. The talented Basil Rathbone was cast as the villainous Svengali. Russell Arms (from *Your Hit Parade*) was the romantic lead, and Ethel Barrymore was the narrator. Basil was good in his role, and Carol was the funniest Trilby I've ever seen. You couldn't take your eyes away from her. She was a big camp! But the prize goes to Ethel Barrymore as our narrator. She despised the interruptions for the commercials by announcer, Tom LeMonde. At each commercial break, she would speak with a low growly tone of disdain in her voice, "And now…let's have a word from Tom LeMonde." Then she'd snarl as we went to commercial.

It was worth just waiting for her announcement. It would set the entire cast to giggling. *Svengali and the Blonde* aired on August 22.

That Christmas Carol sent me the book, *Trilby*, and included a sweet inscription from her and Basil.

Basil wrote:

> "In appreciation and with respect for some beautiful work. Yours, Basil"

And Carol wrote:

> "For dear, dear Tony who captured this - and me completely with deep appreciation and love, Carol Channing"

I treasure this token and we remain good friends.

Carol as Trilby

I filmed *Svengali and the Blonde* in Los Angeles and stayed at the Chateau Marmont while we shot it. Living at the Chateau when Carol Channing was there was a circus.

She was in one of the new Bungalows living alone until she met Charles Lowe who was living with Wally Seawell in a suite kitty-corner to the one Will and I were in. Both suites were furnished with the same heavy maroon drapes. One morning Will and I awakened to see Wally and Charles' drapes were still closed but soon they were whipped open revealing Wally standing on the back of the couch stark naked and seemingly jacking off. Soon a big white ejaculation shot out spraying all over the window then the drapes were snapped shut. What a way to start the day! It was so funny. Charles had used a spray can of shaving cream to simulate the huge ejaculation.

*NBC Publicity Photos for **Svengali & The Blonde**/ Charmoli Photo Archive*

At cocktail time, we would go to Carol's and she would fix cocktails for Will and me. They were the damndest you have ever tasted. She'd have three

Rehearsing Svengali & The Blonde

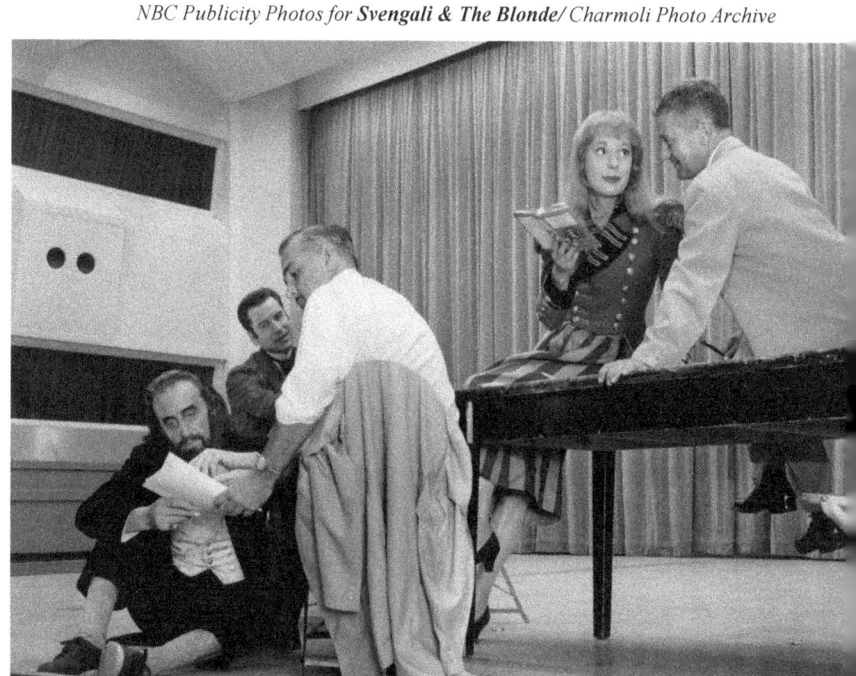

Svengali & The Blonde production number *Basil and Ethel*

to five different bottles out and start with, "A little of this, and a little of this, and now a little of this and a drop of this, then stir it up or shake it." They were pretty potent drinks. And Carol didn't drink. But it was fun.

Years later, when Carol was in Las Vegas sitting out her divorce from Charles, Will and I went up a couple of times to visit and keep her company. One time we were all set to go to dinner and she couldn't find her house keys so she brought her big handbag over to the bed and started to go through it. She pulled out a lipstick and said, "Oh there's that lipstick I've been looking for." Then something else she had been looking for. Then something else. And something else. This kept getting funnier and funnier. Then she dumped everything out and had a story about each item.

We finally got to dinner just before closing. We offered to pay but she insisted. We were walking to

NBC Publicity Photos for **Svengali & The Blonde**/ *Charmoli Photo Archive*

Basil, Russell, & Carol

our car, when the waiter came running after us waving his arms yelling "Miss Channing! Your change! Your change!" Carol had left well over a hundred dollars lying there and she had already left a tip. In those days that was a lot of money and still is, and how honest of the waiter!

Carol loved Will's laugh. If she was doing a show in town or somewhere nearby, she always made sure Will had tickets. Plus those tickets were always second or third row center. She said she wanted to hear his laugh because Will's laugh always tickled Carol and made her feel good.

While at the Chateau, Carol was slated to do a film with Ginger Rogers. She called and asked me to come over as she had something to discuss. She told me about the film and she had a song to do but the director didn't give her any help with how to stage the song. Would I help her? I was there in a minute.

The song was to be done in a living room so we arranged her furniture to resemble the set and started from the top. Carol sang and I would walk her through maneuvers around the furniture because it wasn't a song you'd just stand there and belt out a la Ethel Merman. The next day she did the number in the film as we had worked it out. Sorry the picture didn't measure up. *The Traveling Saleslady* was more like The Death of the Saleslady.

Eva Le Gallienne was a Broadway producer and actress who was noted for being tough, hired me to stage the TV Production of her *Alice In Wonderland*, a TV movie that aired October 23, 1955. We shot it in New York.

The cast included many Broadway notables including Maurice Evans as the narrator, Bobby Clark as the Ugly Duchess, Burr Tillstrum as the Mock Turtle, Elsa Lanchester as the Red Queen, Eva Le Gallienne was the White Queen and a little English girl Gillian Barber was Alice. Many more rounded out the cast, including Marc Breaux who played The Walrus. I later used Marc in a successful stage show in Italy.

When Miss Le Gallienne was not in a scene she sat across the room strictly observing the proceedings. One day I was staging a large cast scene, which took place in the kitchen. I had lots of crazy moments and wild goings on. Characters throwing things at each other, characters bumping into one another, the Cook throwing flour into the air as he was cooking. Sheer mayhem and crazy action. When it ended and everybody was hysterically laughing at each other and their shenanigans I looked across the room at Miss Le Gallienne who had the reputation of being tough, and had been observing all this, giving me the finger to come over to her. On the way I thought to myself, "Oh my God she hates it." I arrived and said, Miss Le Gallienne, you wanted to see me? She said, "Mr. Charmoli, I want you to know I have been observing you working and I think you have caught the spirit of *Alice* perfectly." I almost crapped in my pants I was so happy. That coming from the high priestess herself. I never forgot it.

There was a delicatessen downstairs, and at lunchtime Elsa Lanchester said in her English accent, "Tony, let's go to lunch."

On our way down Elsa sighed, "Tony, have you noticed whenever there is a child actor on the set, one DAIN say Fuck?"

It made my day. She was rare!

Sometimes Burr would do a very amusing announcement on his arrival at a party. He'd remain in the foyer or somewhere out of sight and have a discussion between his characters Kukla and Ollie - loud enough so all the guests could hear. They would be complaining about not being invited to the party. Sometimes Beulah the Witch would join in and spark it up a bit. It always was very funny and certainly got everybody's attention then innocently Burr would enter as himself and act as nothing had happened and join the party. What an entrance!!!

The oddly named *Dateline II* aired Nov. 14, 1955 and it was one of those cavalcade of stars events with singing and dancing. There were a lot of shows for NBC during this period that came and went.

The NBC Comedy Hour ran from January 8 through June 10, 1956, and they listed the Tony Charmoli Dancers as one of their regular guests. It wasn't my idea to call the dancers that, as I didn't train them and the cast of dancers varied depending on the number I was doing. It must have come from NBC marketing making use of the name that I was making for myself.

Above: Burr as the Mock Turtle ;
Below: Visiting Burr on the set with Kukla & Ollie

Scenes from a ballet I did for a newspaper convention with the comic strip, Steve Canyon, a popular strip at the time. Steve Canyon was played by my assistant, Dick Beard, and I used Barton Mumaw (from Jacob's Pillow) to play one of the dancers (Left photo, right side and in crowd above)

JAYNE MANSFIELD

I was offered a special I felt I couldn't turn down, an NBC Sunday Spectacular. *Atlantic City Holiday* was a 90 minute special starring Jayne Mansfield. Also booked were Jack Carter, Polly Bergen, Pat Boone, Bill Haley and his Comets, Jonathan Winters, Rocky Graziano, and Carole Morris who was Miss Universe at the time. It aired August 12, 1956.

Locations were shot in Atlantic City but I wasn't needed there, I did my work on a stage in New York. Jayne and Rocky played aliens from the planet Venus who have come to Earth as tourists. There is an intentional running theme of Jayne playfully spoofing Marilyn Monroe. In Jayne's opening scene, she is sitting in a bathtub on Venus reading *The Brothers Karamazov,* as Marilyn had recently made news by announcing that she wanted to make a movie of Dostoevsky's book.

I immediately got to work hiring dancers and developing the musical numbers with my pianist Roger Adams so I'd be ready for her hugeness Miss Mansfield when she got in. Knowing what I had to work with I thought the song, "Heat Wave", would suit her to perfection. I was right. Her arrival didn't disappoint. Her famous bust entered first and her bouncing hips immediately followed. I knew we'd get along just fine when I saw and heard her squeal and shimmy of approval to what I had planned for her.

I introduced her to Roger our pianist and all the dancers and everyone loved her right off. I just knew this was going to be an unforgettable experience. We first went to the piano to work on the vocal with Roger and she purred out the lyrics. Roger didn't mind at all that she was bent over him with her tits caressing his ear while she whispered out the lyrics. I think he got an erection each time he had to turn to correct her because his nose would brush her bust. I wondered what would happen when I gave Jayne the dance moves.

Then, the studio door opened and in came her boyfriend, Mickey Hargitay, the 1955 Mr. Universe, carrying her little daughter Jayne Marie on his shoulders. When he put her down, Jayne ran across the room to him and he picked her up into a straight arm Angel Lift over his head. Little Jayne Marie turned to all of us and squeaked out "That's my daddy, Mr. UNIVARSE!"* Well one of my dancers Mary Ann Niles just blurted out a big half spitting laugh which got all the dancers laughing. A circus couldn't top this.

Next I started teaching the choreography to Jayne, simple at first then I noticed she loved to get close to the mirror and at times touching it in self adoration and I said, "No, Jayne not like that."

"I'm doing it like you said," she replied. "I'm just using a little more expression."

"Well, you'll never get away with that," I explained. I knew the censors.

Another section had a few subtle hip moves which she turned into out and out bumps. When I stopped her she said, "But Tony, it's a modern movement called a contortion."

I countered with "No, it's called a contraction and you're not going to get away with that either."

Well it was a trial but we managed to get through a routine that I thought would be approved by the censor who was coming the next day. The censor arrived on time but Jayne was late and wearing a dress of that heavy crochet silk clinging to her body like a second skin, revealing everything and leaving nothing to the imagination. I met Jayne at the door and quietly scolded her, "Jayne, of all days to wear a sexy dress like that, I'm not sure the censor's going to pass on the number."

Jayne gave the female censor the once over and said, "Don't worry, Tony, I'll take care of this."

Jayne giggled and ambled over to the censor and purred, "Good morning, I'm Jayne Mansfield and I understand you're here to look at the number I'm doing on the TV special. I must tell you that this is not my costume. You see this dress is very..." then she purred very Marilyn Monroe like, "ANATOMICAL." I think the inspector's eyes giggled as well, and she later okay-ed the number.

When Jayne was around you would be guaranteed a laugh somewhere along the line, she was a wonderful sport. On rehearsal day for the other talent, everybody got together and worked on the material they'd be doing. Jack knew his material, Pat certainly knew his song and Jayne would be fine by show time so we were ready for the run-through. The producer, lighting technicians and all the behind the scenes people it takes to put on a show came in to observe. Jayne wowed them with her number much to the producer's enjoyment. Pat Boone did a great job with "I Almost Lost My Mind" and "Tutti Frutti".

Only Jack Carter seemed testy and unpleasant and annoyed about something much to the dismay of the company. We didn't know what was bothering him, so I didn't invite him to the telecast party I was giving afterwards. The studio theater was packed and everyone performed very well, the producers loved Jayne's gyrations and thanked everybody.

Curious as her father was actually Paul Mansfield, who initiated custody proceedings that same month because of Jayne posing for Playboy earlier that year.

Right after the taping I rushed home to our penthouse overlooking Central Park to see if the caterers had everything under control and there sitting on the couch was Jack with a drink in his hand and said, "Thanks for not inviting me." I just let it go by and asked if he'd like another. (An aside, I've seen him in California, a changed man and quite pleasant, I guess the NY bit was one of his off days.) The caterers did have everything under control and ready for everybody to have dinner and enjoy the show. Cocktails flowed and the cast and crew were had a good time. The show went by with everybody enjoying what they saw and they applauded themselves on the screen.

Everyone was whooping and singing and having a grand old time when the doorbell rang. I went to answer it and there in the foyer was Mickey sitting on a little fragile ball chair, and Jayne on his lap with her arms wrapped around him. I opened the door and standing there were two police officers.

Jane Mansfield publicity photo (Wikimedia Commons)

Upon seeing them Jayne raised her arms in the air and threw herself over backwards into a full back bend until her head touched the floor and her strapless dress allowed both tits to fall out practically to her chin and she purred, "Oh, officer do come in."

They just stood there mouths open in shock.

I said, "Yes?"

One spoke, "We've had several complaints, perhaps you could close the windows to cut the noise."

The other one muttered to the other, "Can't wait to tell my wife what I just seen!"

Jayne didn't attempt to cover herself and purred, "I can give you a drink."

I think they're still standing there open mouthed.

Variety gave her a generally good review - *"Jayne Mansfield ... held up her end as well as the others, even taking a go at a song with breathless intonation which must have conjured up to many a certain other charmer."*

By the way, Mickey Hargitay was in Mae West's muscle-man review at the Latin Quarter at the time. So, through him I finally ended up meeting Mae West backstage after her show. I loved Mae West. She measured up to everything I expected. After we had moved to Hollywood, she invited us to a party that she gave at her apartment at Ravenswood. She was smart and gracious.

Will and I buy a house in California!

Chapter 4
Dinah Shore

MOVING TO CALIFORNIA!

Summer of 1956, I got a call from Bob Banner, "Can you fly out to California and meet about *The Dinah Shore Show*?"

I flew out. The meeting was brief. Bob was the producer and said that Dinah was going on the air with an hour long show, and would continue with her fifteen-minute one as well. He then asked if I would be interested in doing the fifteen-minute show as a sort of audition for the longer one. I was a little shocked. I was coming from the successful *Your Hit Parade*, with an Emmy under my belt, and working non-stop with high profile celebrities. I stood up and drew myself to my full five feet plus, took a deep breath and said, "Mr. Banner, I audition for no one." I turned to the exit, taxied to the airport and flew back to New York.

A short time passed and a call came. "Mr. Charmoli would you consider coming to California to do the fifteen-minute as well as the hour show with Dinah?" I was at the airport flying to California in a dash. *The Dinah Shore Show* aired October 5, 1956 and became a big hit. Dinah and I hit it off immediately.

For a while I had been flying out to do *The Colgate Comedy Hour* and as soon as the show signed off the air, I'd go straight to the airport and fly back to New York. I couldn't do that with Dinah's show.

With Dinah, I was working more in California than in New York and we were aware, much as we hated it, the only thing to do would be to move to California. It would be tough giving up our two-story apartment with penthouse and garden overlooking Central Park and also near the theater district. It seemed almost impossible to leave it all behind. We decided to keep the place for a while and see how it went. During that period, Judy Garland was making her second appearance at The Palace and wanted to rent our penthouse while she stayed in New York, but Judy did not run with the best crowds and we knew we would not get the penthouse back in the same condition, so we turned her down. It was safer to let our friend Marc Breaux and his new wife keep an eye on things.

It was near Christmas of 1956, and Will and I were in New York for the holidays. I heard Dinah Shore was in town, and also Dixie Fasnacht, or Miss Dixie as we called her. She owned Dixie's Bar of Music in New Orleans. Will and I decided to give possibly our last big party at the penthouse.

It turned out to be quite an affair. We also invited Gisele McKenzie and Dorothy Collins and a few others from the Hit Parade and my pianist Roger Adams, plus a whole bunch of theatre people. There were guests upstairs in the garden terrace bar overlooking Central Park and downstairs in the spacious living room area.

The party was in full swing when I approached Miss Dixie to give us a couple of songs. I introduced her to Roger and told him what a great barrelhouse singer she was. That was the first time I saw Miss Dixie become shy about performing.

A peek of our NY penthouse.

She said, "Tony, I can't sing with all these celebrity singers here, I'm just an old barrelhouse broad croaking out the songs."

"Well croak some out at this party, they'll love it." I told Roger to get with her and work out some stuff together and tell me when they're ready.

Soon I announced to everybody upstairs and down to gather in the living room for a great treat. The place was packed and I announced, "A Christmas gift for everyone, direct from New Orleans... in person... Miss Dixie!"

She growled out "Just give me a pig foot and a bottle of beer!" And the whole room shook with thunderous shouts of approval and applause. Miss Dixie just bowled them over and they wouldn't let her stop. It was a hell of a good way to get the

Holiday Season started. No others wanted to follow that and didn't have to. Everybody seemed happy with just Miss Dixie's performance.

While we were downstairs enjoying Miss Dixie nobody knew that outside we were having a huge snowstorm. We turned on the news to hear taxis weren't running but buses were. This didn't seem to upset too many and Gisele said she would accompany Dinah because their destinations were near each other. Everybody seemed to work things out quite well.

The next day Dinah called to tell me what happened. She said, "That darn Gisele! We covered our heads with scarves, put up our collars and did everything to disguise ourselves because the bus was loaded and the only seats available were way in the back and we got to Gisele's stop without anybody noticing us. But, when the bus stopped and Gisele stepped off, she stuck her head back in the bus and yelled, "Goodnight, Dinah Shore"! Right then I could have killed her. All the riders rushed me for autographs and stories about how they 'loved *The Dinah Shore Show*.'" The short ride to my hotel seemed like an eternity."

Photo by Jay Thornton

Soon afterwards, we finally chose to let go of the dear New York two-story Penthouse overlooking Central Park. I missed New York but didn't have much time to brood over it, I was working non-stop. Besides, the Chateau Marmont proved to be a rather marvelous place to be.

I must say life there was very enjoyable. Celebrities everywhere you looked. Sometimes in unexpected places but always interesting. Paul Newman would generally be at the pool on Sunday afternoons. Beautiful eyes, but suffered from chicken legs. There's a reason you don't see his legs too much in the movies.

In not too great a time, Will started shopping for a house, and soon found a house he thought could work as our California home. It was not very far from the Chateau. My only request was that it should have a foyer. I don't like the front door to open right into the living room and the backside of a couch. I went to see his selection and meet the owners.

When we stepped into a high ceiling two-story foyer I said, "Yes! we'll take it!"

They said, "Don't you want to see the rest?"

We did the tour and I asked why they were selling, what was wrong with the place? They said Mr. Gold had to move to a more arid location for health reasons.

They asked why we were moving to California when New York was such an exciting place.

I told them I was coming out to do *The Dinah Shore Show*. They exclaimed, "Oh! We love Dinah Shore! The house is yours."

We took it. After we settled in, we put in a new pool and gave an inauguration party. Our friend Richard said he would do the christening. Before guests arrived Richard went out to the back garden and pulled up a bunch of ivy and disappeared. When it was clear all the guests had arrived Richard appeared naked except for a crown of ivy and a banner of ivy across his chest and wrapped around his hips and covering his private parts. He appeared at the top of the steps to the pool walked around to the deep end too much applause. He then made one grand gesture and dove in. Of course all the ivy came off in the water as he swam the whole length of the pool under water. He came out the shallow end totally naked and turned front to the guests then stretched both arms out to the sides and swung his torso from side to side causing his big dick to sexually slap his thighs from side to side causing a loud sexy slapping noise. The guests went wild with screams as he announced in tempo with the slapping of his dick, "The pool is now officially open!" A couple jumped in with their clothes on and the rest however they were inclined. It was an unforgettable initiation. Richard moved back to Pennsylvania but the pool is still happily entertaining swimmers.

Missy and Jo liked to nude sun bathe at our pool -just like many other folks.

One day when I returned home from the studio I noticed a painter painting the house next door. When he turned around, I was surprised to see Russell Arms from years earlier on *Hit Parade* and *Svengali and the Blonde*. Evidently work for singers was slow and he was painting houses in Los Angeles. It can be tough finding jobs as a singer.

Through the years our house has undergone extensive remodeling. Bud Holden, a dear friend and an excellent designer, immediately drew up renovation plans. The house was enlarged and glamorized and made much more enjoyable with bigger rooms, and a studio for me to do my painting. We also added a terrace, cocktail bar and treillage for outdoor dining. He did a wonderful renovation. He not only designed and supervised the building but also physically pulled the house together. His vision was super and the end result was magnificent. These days, we miss him as he spends much of his time in Ireland working for a chemical company. Fortunately, he has been able to enjoy many of the celebrations we've had in the house and we look forward with hope to his return to this country.

The house has been a great place to entertain the many people I work with. Dinah Shore, Danny Kaye and others have come over for home cooked meals and good times. Frequently they even helped with the cooking! But, back to *The Dinah Shore Show*...

DINAH

My first meeting with Dinah proved it was a match meant to be. One meeting was all it took and we were into rehearsal and it took off from there. We also happily stayed together until the contract ran out.

Each show had several dancers and a group of singers as regulars and a quite varied list of guest stars.

Dinah and Frank Sinatra worked together on a radio show years before TV. So she asked him to be one of her first guests on the first episode of her hour-long TV Show. Frank accepted and we were all thrilled until we started rehearsals. Fortunately he could dance a bit and moved quite well.

Dancing with Dinah (photo taken by dancer friend)

I worked out a little soft shoe for the two of them and I had to keep it quite simple because he didn't want to work very much. All through rehearsal he seemed edgy but we got through it by holding our breath.

Dress rehearsal was always with full cast in costume, and a full live audience. Dress rehearsal time came, the audience was in and eager for a show, but Frank was nowhere to be found. Panic time. Ticker, Dinah's pianist pulled out some music Dinah could do to fill in the time that usually was with Frank. This had to do as we couldn't delay any longer or we would jeopardize the broadcast show. The dress rehearsal proceeded without Frank and seemed to be ok. Now we had only a short break before the live telecast.

Of course everybody was on edge. Poor Dinah. Airtime comes and still no Frank. The show starts without him

Frank Sinatra, Peter Lawford, Dinah and some boys play poker for chocolate bars.
(NBC Publicity Photos/ Charmoli Archives)

and just as the announcer says: "Ladies and gentlemen, Dinah Shore!" Dinah is making her entrance and Frank comes walking into the studio. Dinah sees him out of the corner of her eye and kicks it up a notch she's so happy. But what an injustice to put the whole company through this. The show turned out great and Frank did come back again the next year. I guess he behaved better that time as I don't remember otherwise.

Betty Grable made a few guest appearances on *The Dinah Shore Show*. One time, I thought she'd have fun doing a number with about six muscle men. When I proposed it to her she was delighted and anxious to get started. She agreed it would play off her image nicely.

Betty Grable's entrance
(NBC Publicity Photos/ Charmoli Archives)

She enters on a beautiful white horse looking like the film star she is and is greeted by several big quite handsome men. The men fully dressed in white suits approach her and help her off the horse and most of her costume is left behind on the horse - revealing a rather naked Goddess. Betty now scantily clad goes into the number while the men exit. She looks great singing and strutting about the stage. The men return in no time at all as six handsome very naked hunks and join her. Betty singing and dancing with six hunks was quite a picture. Rehearsal went well. But...

But when we went live on the air, all went well until the handsome naked hunks wearing little loin cloths form a tight backs-to-the-center-circle with Betty singing her heart out until she is almost hidden in the center. They slowly bend forward lifting Betty with their butts till she is sitting on their backs looking like the center of a giant exotic flower. Betty is still singing through all this. The effect was beautiful and earlier drew applause from the rehearsal audience.

But, during the break, the men had lavishly greased themselves from head to toe so their muscles would glisten more sexily. The men looked great and drew applause for about five seconds then laughter as Betty, still singing, slowly slid down the center of their well-greased slippery backs and disappeared behind a big wall of muscular legs. Their greased backs were just too slippery to hold her. Dinah and the whole studio audience were bursting with laughter including Betty trapped behind those huge legs. It was funnier than funny to see this barrier of flesh with a beautiful blonde

Dinah, Betty and Tony Randall
(NBC Publicity Photos/ Charmoli Archives)

in the center, still singing, trying to get out. The fan mail simply flew in asking for a repeat but we never did do it again.

She did finally get out to dance and sing the last eight bars and got a huge audience applause, whistles and standing ovation. It was a memorable guest appearance. Accidents like that seldom bear repetition so we never did try it again.

Sometime later, Betty was appearing in Las Vegas as the starring act at one of the Casinos and I made a visit to her after her show. I got to her backstage dressing room and the door was open with a heavy cloth draped across part of it. She was seated at her dressing table with her legs up on the board, and doing her nails when I arrived. I threw back the drape and said "Hi Betty!" She quickly responded with a flip, "Oh hiya Tony! How about that - they got me out there singing and dancing, and I even got lines!" She was a character.

Betty was never one to tout herself as being a Big Movie Star. When she was with good friends she preferred being "just one of the girls" and always was great company.

Betty also told me of the great sexual encounters that took place on the valley side of Laurel Canyon Blvd. Because there were no streetlights there it was a safe very dark place to carry on in parked cars, out of parked cars, often on blankets on the ground, anyplace they could find. It seems on Saturday nights it was the favorite place for young lovers to engage in the sports to their hearts content. She said anything and everything went on until the cops discovered this and lights were installed along the route. She was sure young lovers found someplace else to carry on but she didn't know where. She too was one of a kind and always a lot of fun.

When I first joined Dinah's company, she was doing a 15-minute show with a vocal group called the Skylarks made up of two girls and three boys. I joined them on a tour of some Southern States and we were housed in hotels. The two girls shared a room, two boys shared and I shared with Joe Hamilton, who was the handsomest of the whole group. Dinah had her own room. We all rehearsed together, dined together, but went to our separate rooms at night. Joe, the handsome one, was in my room long enough to clean up then disappeared only to return in the early morning. Where he had spent the night is anybody's guess but we did all notice every morning at breakfast, Dinah had an extra big smile on her face. Incidentally, the tour was a success. Joe eventually married Carol Burnett.

Shirley MacLaine came into my life right after she made a big hit on Broadway by stepping in to do

"Steam Heat" for the ailing Carol Haney. Fortunately for her a big Hollywood film producer was in the audience and snapped her up. We got her as a guest on The Dinah Shore Show. She arrived for rehearsal carrying her rehearsal bag and she started to change into terribly beat up dance shoes. I said, "Shirley you're a star now you can afford some new shoes." She replied, "Are you kidding, all my steps are in these shoes." (A reply Gwen Verdon was going to repeat several years later when she came in to her first rehearsal with me.)

Rehearsals with Dinah were a pleasure. She was always so positive and willing to try things she had never done before. I came up with a dance I thought Dinah could do with her.

Dinah said, "But Tony, Shirley's a dancer and I don't dance - but I'd like to."

I said, "Well you're going to dance with Shirley."

I put together some dance movements to "Ballin' the Jack." It was singing and dancing - and Dinah was good at it and loved doing it. I had their costumes designed with stripes to accent their movements. That night they did it on the show and they were perfectly together and the audience gave them a rousing standing ovation.

Dinah came away breathlessly and said, "Tony I don't believe it, we got a standing ovation with a dance number - and I was dancing!"

From then on Dinah was game to try anything.

This number pretty much bonded Shirley and me for all we were going to experience in the years to come. Shirley guested on the show regularly.

Dinah and Bea Lillie were rehearsing with me one day when the costume designer's assistant came in and asked, "Could I interrupt to take Miss Lillie's measurements for her costumes?"

Before Dinah could answer, Bea unsnapped her dress letting it fall to the floor, leaving her in underwear looking like a plucked chicken.

Above: Shirley MaClaine and Dinah;
Below: Shirley, Dinah & Maureen O'Hara

95

Dinah, in pretended shock, exclaimed, "BEA!"

Bea chirped "What, too sexy?"

It broke up the room. She was the funniest... and fun to work with.

Dinah was rumored to be the luckiest gal in Beverly Hills when she married George Montgomery in 1943. It was rumored he had the biggest "schlong" in Beverly Hills and all the movie queens were after him. Lucky Dinah! One day George paid a visit to the NBC studios to attend a Dinah rehearsal. Not long after he arrived I called a five-minute break. George went to the men's room and stood at one of the urinals. Tom Hansen, one of my dancers, followed at a short distance. George was already relieving himself when Tom stepped up to the urinal next to George and proceeded to relieve himself and peek over to check out George. George made no attempt to withdraw or conceal himself in any way so Tom had a good view of the envied piece of manhood. When Tom returned to the rehearsal we were all eager for the news. Tom's first hand report, "It's true, and it's BIG!"

Dinah might have been the luckiest gal in Beverly Hills to have married George Montgomery in one respect but we suspected he might be impossible to live with. Dinah always invited the cast over to watch the TV show on the air and she'd serve dinner as well. We all agreed it was a good show and everybody was having a good time, when George comes in. I guess we were disturbing his bedtime. Now mind you, he was far away in the back bedroom on the split-level in a large home where it must be quite silent. He appeared suddenly carrying all the ladies coats and threw them over the railing to the floor below, and wish us all an angry "Good night!" We were all shocked as the ladies gathered their coats. Bob Finkel's wife had just received hers as a birthday gift from Bob, she let George have it straight and direct, then turned on her heels and left. We calmly thanked Dinah and left feeling very sorry for her. In this respect Dinah didn't get a bargain. I got on fine with George, but then I didn't see him every day.

After rehearsal in the Valley each day, I would follow Dinah in my car to make sure she got home safely as we lived relatively close to each other. She'd give me a honk and a wave as I turned off onto my street. But sometimes she'd pop by and have dinner with Will and me at my house, just so she'd get home after George went to bed. She also

Tony, Andy Griffith, Dinah, Ethel Merman & Cyril Ritchard; Bea Lillie above

had a kitchen installed at the studio so she could fix dinner for folks there and again delay coming home to her irritable husband. They eventually called it quits in 1962.

Dinah and George had a sweet daughter, Missy, and an adopted boy named Jody. Typical of young boys Jody often got into trouble. One evening when we were on tour with Dinah in Denmark, Dinah and I were on our way down to dinner in the Hotel restaurant. As we approached the swinging doors to the dining room Jody came flying out, literally tossed out by the maître d'. We didn't ask questions we just stood there and laughed. He wasn't hurt so we knew it was just Jody being Jody.

Betty Hutton was on the show about four times. In 1958, Dinah had heard she was having

Betty Hutton & Dinah
(NBC Publicity Photos/ Charmoli Archives)

a tough period. Her film *Spring Reunion* had just opened and didn't do very well at the box office and her career was still a bit on the outs since Paramount hadn't renewed her contract a couple years earlier. Dinah took pity and wanted to help get her back on her feet by bringing her back for another guest spot on her March 23rd show.

Betty accepted and arrived at the scheduled hour, bright-eyed and bushy-tailed. We did our greeting and welcoming bits, but Dinah (who was always on time) hadn't arrived yet because her son Jody got into some trouble at school and had to go over to the school to sort things out.

Betty asked, "Where's Dinah?" I explained what had happened and that she would be right here.

Betty, on hearing this, stood up to her full height, put her hands on her hips, announced, "I wait for no one!" and left.

I couldn't believe what she had just done. Dinah out of the kindness of her heart is doing Betty a big favor and she behaves like this? Soon, Dinah arrived only to find Betty had been there and gone.

Dinah instead of saying let's do the show without her said, "Poor girl! We have to get her back." Betty disappeared for a full day.

The following day, Betty arrived and the two went into a mad welcoming embrace like nothing had happened. Go figure. Rehearsal resumed. Fortunately Betty was a quick study and she learned the big and elaborate production number in a record time and we went on the air as scheduled. We couldn't believe it. The mail and phone calls of loving praise for the production poured in. They wanted us to repeat the number. In those days we couldn't just run the tape so horrors we had to have Betty back for a repeat performance a month later on the April 27th show. She behaved better but was never asked back.

Louis Jourdan was a guest for a show that aired January 18, 1959 and scheduled to do a song and dance with Dinah. My assistant Dick Beard and I were in the rehearsal room working out the dance they were going to be doing on the show. Dick played Louis and I was Dinah. We were in each other's arms in a deep back bend, one on top of the other, when Louis opened the door and blurted out, "Oh! Excuse me." and slammed the door shut.

I immediately rushed into the hall calling, "Louis, come back!" An explanation cleared the situation.

When Dinah arrived and was let in on what had just happened she got a big kick out of it and said, "Maybe you should do my part in the show." Needless to say they looked wonderful together and did a great job on the telecast.

When Lana Turner guested on *The Dinah Shore Show*, she got right into the rehearsals and had a good time. All three of those broads, Dinah, Kay Starr and Lana, got along just great.

One late night after rehearsal, we were all standing outside talking in the driveway just before getting our cars. Lana was first to go to her car leaving Dinah, Kay, and me. Dinah went to her Chevrolet, and Kay was standing next to her Lincoln when we all turned to see Lana going by in her chauffeur driven limousine. She waved demurely and said, "Good night girls!" Then slide down into her seat and disappeared. Dinah and Kay just looked at each other and you could see "Bitch" written all over their faces, but never spoken. Very Hollywood. I got a good laugh out of it all the way home.

Later, Lana showed her appreciation for the fun we had on the show by giving me a very glamorous autographed photo of her. It's hanging on the wall in my trophy room with the other treasures. Her daughter came to party at my house a while later and saw the photo. She gasped when she saw it on the wall in my office, "My mother gave you that photo? I love that photo, but she still hasn't given one to me!" I teased her with, "Well, I guess I'm special."

To start off a new season, Dinah always threw a big party at her house for the clients from Chevrolet and their wives. I was always included and at one of these parties the clients got into some intense discussions and they all disappeared into the surrounding bushes of a fairly large backyard.

Lana Turner, Kay Starr, & Dinah
(NBC Publicity Photos/ Charmoli Archives)

Dinah came to me and said, "Tony, I don't know what's going on but dinner is ready. What am I going to do?"

I said, "I'll do something." I proceeded to take all my clothes off, handed them to Dinah.

She said, "Tony stop, you're crazy, what are you doing?"

I said, "I'm getting your guests to come to dinner." I ran, stark naked, to the upper diving board, beat my chest and did a loud Tarzan yell. "AAAOOOOAAAAOOO!" I could see the guests start to come out of the bushes. I did another Tarzan yell and dove into the pool.

I swam to the side where Dinah met me and said, "Tony, you're crazy!" as she wrapped me in a large bath towel.

I said, "You can serve dinner now."

Mahalia Jackson & Dinah

On another show Dinah, Tab Hunter, and Dean Jones were singing and dancing in a number when suddenly Dinah's multi, multi-layered tulle petticoat unsnapped and fell to the floor tripping up Tab, Dean and Dinah into a pile of hysterically laughing trio. They never did finish the number. They just lay there laughing while the orchestra played out to the end. The rehearsal audience laughed right along with them.

Tab was a good-looking guy and had a pretty good hit with the song "Young Love." He was rather shy at orchestra rehearsals and I loved to tease him. He'd be standing next to Harry Zimmerman, the conductor and when he caught my eye I would mouth, "You're beautiful" and he'd turn beet red.

Dean Jones, Nanette Fabray, Danny Thomas, Dinah Shore & Tab Hunter
(NBC Publicity Photos/ Charmoli Archives)

Carol Channing & Dinah having fun
(NBC Publicity Photos/ Charmoli Archives)

If I was out at the entrance to the NBC Studio when he would drive in, in his convertible with the top down I'd wave to him and call out "Kim Novak!" You could see him blush or was that a suntan? He was a sweet man and besides he was just as pretty as Kim.

When I was still living in the Chateau Marmont, I returned late from rehearsal one night and the elevator wasn't working so I started up the stairs and ran into Tab Hunter coming down the stairs in nothing but a white bathrobe. I just looked up at him smiled knowingly and said, "I won't ask questions." He just smiled and went on, he knew I knew that Tony Perkins was living up there, and everyone knew Tony Perkins was extremely well-endowed. I was surprised to see Tab walking so well.

Once when we were in Las Vegas with Dinah performing her latest act at one of the hotels, I saw Eartha Kitt was also doing her show at another hotel. I had worked with Eartha on *The Colgate Comedy Hour* so I called and invited her out to dinner with myself and Dinah. She accepted and we met at one of the popular restaurants in Vegas at the time. She was wearing a full-length fur coat and when she let it fall back onto the back of her chair, she was wearing a beautiful China silk dress that I complimented her on. We got to visiting while we waited for Dinah to arrive.

When Dinah and her singers came in, Dinah was also wearing a fur coat, and when she took it off, I saw she was wearing the exact same dress. Eartha did a slight gasp and casually reached

Ginger Rogers

back and slipped her coat back on and wrapped it enough to cover her dress so Dinah wouldn't notice. What a noble gesture. The evening went on without a further hitch and the ladies got on just great.

One of the strangest requests from one of the guests for *The Dinah Shore Show* came from Ginger Rogers. She would do the show if she didn't have to dance.

Dinah asked if I could come up with something? I thought how strange for a movie star who didn't want to do what she was famous for. In answer to Dinah, I said how about "New Fashioned Tango?" The lyric says, "Don't move, why move?"

Dinah said, "Perfect!" Ginger was hired. I called two dancers Mark Wilder and Jimmy Brooks and both were available so we were on. I asked Ginger if she had a long tight evening gown - and she did, so I told her the idea. She liked it!

Before rehearsals with her, I worked out the movements with the guys while I did Ginger's part. Since she didn't have to do any real dancing, she learned her part very quickly. I called Dinah into the rehearsal room and we did it for her. I guess we were a hit because Dinah said, "You just have to do it in the show!" Kiddingly I asked, "Me or Ginger?"

We did it and quickly the audience caught the humor and loved it. So did Ginger. I guess it was ok to have a great dancer like Ginger on as a guest and not have her dance. Perhaps she couldn't dance without Fred Astaire.

I didn't meet Fred Astaire until I went to a birthday party for his daughter, Ava. She saw me there and asked, "Tony, did you see Daddy?" I said, "I saw him, but Ava, I've never met your dad." She immediately took me to where he was sitting and said, "Daddy, This is Tony Charmoli."

Fred immediately stood up took my hand and said, "I'm honored!" I was absolutely amazed and shocked that this icon of the dance world would greet me with a standing handshake.

I said, "I'm more than honored!" It was an unforgettable moment.

He double flipped me when he told me how much he liked my work on *Your Hit Parade*. I used all the superlatives I could think of in telling him how much I loved his stuff. I haven't seen him since.

We had a tall handsome French actor Yves Montand on the show a few times and one could quickly see he really rang Dinah's bell. Hell, he

Dinah, Julie & Chita

NBC Publicity Photos/ Charmoli Archives

rang my bell too, but Dinah comes first. He did ask for some private tap dance lessons from me and I went to the Beverly Hills Hotel for those and up to his room. That's what he wanted, tap dance lessons - and that's what he got. Damn! However the sparks continued to fly between Dinah and Yves. There is no proof that anything went beyond just sparks, but he was great on the show.

Dinah got us all stirred up one day when she announced she got Joan Crawford to guest on the show. She was coming to NBC to watch a dress rehearsal. When she arrived, she was dressed like the big movie star she was. Big fox coat, black floppy hat, gloves and sunglasses. It was a little dark in the studio so thankfully she took the glasses off. With a pound of makeup on she looked the same. Every inch a star.

Everything went well in Dinah's office, and we walked over to the stage where the door was opened to the studio and there the audience was already seated and the place was packed like it always was for Dinah's show.

Yves Montand with Dinah

Joan made a huge gasp and put her gloved hand to cover her mouth.

Dinah asked, "Joan what's the matter?"

Joan took a deep breath and said, "You have an audience! I could never work with a live audience. I'm afraid I can't do this. Sorry Dinah."

That was that. We were all so disappointed. I didn't even get her autograph. I had the lipstick already out and ready.

We shot an episode in New York where we got Chita Rivera sort of the last minute, so I had to work out a routine for the song, "It's All Right With Me" in a hurry. Fortunately I had done a lot of work in New York so I knew quite a few dancers. I contacted four guys all excellent dancers, Hank Brunges, Grover Dale, Pepe DeChiazza, and Kelly Brown. I warned them we had very little time to rehearse. It's called throwing it together. It went together rather nicely and Chita was very happy.

She said, "I'd like Tony to see this!" She meant Tony Mordente who was a dancer/choreographer and her husband at the time.

We did it full out for him and when it ended he exclaimed, "Tony write it down, write it down!" I think that meant he liked it - I hadn't heard that expression before.

Above: Dinah and Art Carney duet on "Back in the Old Routine"
(NBC Publicity Photos/ Charmoli Archives)

Pearl Bailey guested on Dinah's show several times and we always loved to see her. She would always bring some very good fried chicken and all the tasty things that go with it. After each visit we could almost feel the pounds creeping on, but it was delicious and irresistible. She said that she cooked it herself, it was fried to perfection.

Pearl did *Hello Dolly!* on Broadway covering for Carol Channing while Carol was on vacation. I told her I was going to be doing some work in New York while she was in the show and she arranged for me to get a box seat right near the stage.

During the big "Hello Dolly!" number, she came to the side of the stage where I was sitting and looked up to my box and called out, "Hey! Tony, look. They got me singing and dancing! How about that?"

The theatre was full of servicemen and they gave her a big hand and a standing ovation. We had a good visit in her dressing room after the show. No signs of fried chicken though, not even a bone. Maybe she was on a diet to fit the part better, but she made the part her own in her unmistakable Pearl Bailey way.

Tony and Dinah in their chimney sweep routine

Shirley Temple and John Raitt join Dinah and Tony for a toy number

One Christmas, I suggested we do a chimney sweep number. She loved my story of the number and thought it perfect for the holiday. We were the two Santa's elves who cleaned the chimneys before Santa arrived. Someone has to help keep his red suit clean! Again the audience reaction was tremendous and we had to repeat it the following year. After we did it the second time Dinah said, "Tony, I don't care if we get tons of requests, I'm not doing it again. I'm getting too old to be a chimney sweep." She meant it, we never did it again.

Dinah had another good time doing a number. This time with the Broadway favorite Gwen Verdon. I had them interpret colors in dance movements. This number required a lot of improvisation. We got yards of fabric to play with and they had a great time with billowing chiffon and they got more daring as the number went on and suddenly they got all caught up in the fabric and wound up on the floor laughing hysterically. It turned out to be better than anyone could choreograph.

When Kay Thompson & Her Boys hit New York with her gunfire of a song and sparkling energy she was an immediate big hit. Like wildfire word got around that this was an act you just had to see. When Dinah heard about it, she immediately wanted Kay and her boys on her show and she got them.

Shirley Temple, all grown up, was already booked and her music and number selected. It seemed natural to do a childlike number so we planned and rehearsed a piece around toys in a child's playroom. Naturally Shirley was the Doll, John Raitt was the Toy Soldier, Dinah was the Rag Doll, and Kay was going to be the Jack-in-the-Box. Upon arrival Kay was informed of the numbers she was in and she said she'd do everything except the Jack-in-the-Box. Kay had a thing about being glamorous and the Jack-in-the-Box didn't measure up.

When Dinah heard this it became the usual, "Tony what are we going to do?"

I tried the costume on and it fit perfectly. Having choreographed the number, I knew the part so I played the role.

In dress rehearsal, when Shirley as the toy doll climbed out from her shelf she stopped and said, "Tony, I don't feel any light on me here."

What a pro! Of course she was 30 years old at this point and had been performing her entire life. She knew you had to be lit to be seen. I immediately got on the stage manager's headset and talked to the lighting booth. She was lit and we continued.

This number was the last thing in the show so Kay joined us for the cast bow at the end. Incidentally her part of the show was terrific. In fact the whole show was good and I had a great time with Kay. Kay and her guys were rightfully the smash new big act in the USA.

Will and I happened to be in London that summer and I gave Kay a call. She invited Will and me to her flat. We accepted and had a great time visiting and went to the roof to have a grand look of the whole city. On departure we invited Kay to go to dinner with us but she refused saying she had a previous arrangement.

That night Will and I went out to dinner at a famous supper club, and there sitting alone way in the back was Kay. We didn't question her. We just left her alone thinking her date was late. Will and I were seated at a table out of her sight. We were there until almost closing time but her date never showed up. She was alone all that time. We talked with her the next day, but didn't ask what happened. We felt there probably never was going to be a date. C'est la vie.

To help up-and-coming talent, Dinah would introduce them to a large audience by having them appear on her show. One performer of note was Barbra Streisand.

Barbra came to rehearsal in her thrift shop clothes (which were just starting to come into vogue) and pretty much stayed to herself in a corner of the rehearsal hall. When it came time for her to run through her number with the pianist she walked up to the piano looking very dowdy in her thrift shop garb, and started her song. Well, a tornado struck! She simply blew everybody away with "Happy Days are Here Again!"

When asked what she would be wearing on the telecast, she said, "What I have on."

Well, Dinah immediately said she couldn't endorse such a talent looking like a street person. She had her housekeeper bring out a few of her gowns. Barbra selected a chic orange crepe evening gown with a long sheer flowing chiffon scarf. It was too big for Barbra and there was no time for alterations, so wardrobe pinned it up the back with safety pins.

Barbra was to walk up a spiral staircase between her two songs so I told her, "When you get to the fourth step, twist your hips away from camera so we don't see the pins up your back."

Barbra Streisand

Come show time, Dinah introduced her. The intro starts and Barbra steps up the stairs and remembers my direction and also does a big flip of the long chiffon scarf as an added distraction. I'm in the control room and remarked "Bright girl!" She certainly knew what she was doing, and that appearance became an important introduction to millions of Americans.

It was a special treat to have Violette Verdy and Jacques D'Amboise come from the New York City Ballet to guest on *The Dinah Shore Show*. I had asked Dinah to book these two dancers because I had an idea, which would be something novel on her show. It aired February 22, 1959.

The story was set in a small New England town and immediately it is obvious through the dance of a young man and young woman that they are falling in love. The dance develops from a grey and rainy day into full blown love. The scene changes into a sunny romantic setting and their costumes change into sweet and romantic colors as they dance a romantic pas de deux as they express their love for one another.

When the love pas de deux ends, the scene dissolves back into the opening setting only this time Jacques is standing on a platform next to a hanging noose on a grey about-to-rain day. Violette is in the foreground in front of a crowd in raincoats and open umbrellas who have come to see the hanging.

She is looking up to heaven as the camera moves in to a close up of her, blocking Jacques out so we don't see what's about to happen. It starts to rain as we see a close up teary-eyed face of Violette in front of the raincoat-covered crowd. Suddenly a loud crash and thump from the gallows. She faints and falls to the ground. We fade out on the passed out young girl on the ground in the pouring rain.

Not a pleasant ending but very moving and provocative for a dance number on television in those early days. A prop man on a ladder with a sprinkling can created my rain.

So the audience is not too disturbed, Violette and Jacques come back as themselves after the number and talk to Dinah. The mail came in commending the wonderful dance and wanting more work like that which pleased me. I thanked Dinah over and again for allowing me to create such a moving dance piece on her show. So totally different from what is usually seen on TV. She praised me for my work and thanked me for working on her show.

Jacques D'Amboise liked to come by and swim naked in my pool when he was in Los Angeles. I'd be in my studio painting and I'd hear him let himself in at the side gate. He was straight but I always teased him and asked when he was going to have sex with me, and he'd just laugh and say, "I'm thinking about it..." It was all in good fun. He is a handsome man, a talented dancer, and it was always pleasant to have him swimming naked in my backyard.

Laurence Harvey... the mad kisser

NBC Publicity Photos/ Charmoli Archives

Violette Verdy and Jacques D'Amboise from the New York City Ballet

My first Producer credit was shared with George Schlatter on *The Dinah Shore Show* in 1961. Laurence Harvey was a guest and an amusing remembrance of Mr. Harvey is every time he arrived for rehearsal he would grab me and throw me into a big back bend and plant a big full kiss smack on my mouth then jokingly say. "That's to make Dinah jealous." Of course Dinah couldn't have cared less. He loved to joke around.

My first shot at directing a TV spot happened when we were on location in the Bois de Bologne in Paris. The French crew always insists on wine for lunch and our director joined them. Then they always take a nap after lunch and our director apparently not used to wine for lunch fell asleep.

Donald O'Conner, Dinah, Roy Rogers and Dale Evans

Dinah was ready and gung ho to get on with the show and said, "Tony you know how to shoot the show don't you?"

Of course I did, so I got our camera operator and said, "Dinah's ready let's go."

I cued the tape, cued the music track and rolled the tape. In one take we wrapped the number, packed up, and were moving on when we punched the director.

He awakened with, "Are you ready to record?"

Dinah said, "I've already recorded this song. Tony did it. We're moving on."

That director never dared have wine for lunch again. I loved doing it and eventually wound up in the director's chair with a different woman star - the fabulous Cyd Charisse.

Burt Reynolds' star seemed to rise quite rapidly when he hit California. It wasn't long before word got around that he was courting Dinah Shore. Eventually, after I was finished with *The Dinah Shore Show* and launched into directing with Cyd Charisse, Burt got a show of his own and I was hired to direct and Anita Mann did the choreography. There was a young band, The Keane Brothers, that appeared regularly, and Anita had dancers when we needed them.

Bing Crosby was very quiet and an easy guest to work with.

The very proud folks involved with the show and our Emmys

The producers would arrive to see a run-through of the show. Just prior to their arrival Anita would always slip into a very tight form fitting top which would make her bust stand out.

Acting naïve I asked, "What's that for?"

Her answer, "The producers always like the dances better when I'm dressed like this."

I said, "Sure. You can get away with anything with THEM, but I'm still here."

If Dinah was seeing Burt on the sly, as it was rumored, she certainly kept it a secret around his show. We never saw any sign of it, nor walked in on any phone calls he might be having with her. That still didn't change our minds about the affair. Whatever blows her dress up, I guess.

Years later we were invited to Bob Banner's house at Dinah's request. The Skylarks, myself, and of course Bob and his wife Alice. We all had a sneaking suspicion that this might be our last time for seeing Dinah. She arrived wearing tennis shoes and sport clothes ready to enjoy a casual affair. We drank a toast to her, had a wonderful dinner then sat down to screening many excerpts of Dinah shows we all had done together. What fond memories, we laughed and reminisced and poked fun at the videos. It was a memorable evening and what we had suspected earlier, proved we were right. On departing, our good byes were chock full with held back tears. We all felt this was our last good bye. Dinah passed away shortly after that.

In memory of Dinah I have life size photos of the two of us in our Chimney Sweep costumes framed on the wall of my bar, and another very large one on the wall of my garage dressed as ourselves and obviously enjoying dancing together. She'll be in my memory forever.

Cyd on The Dinah Shore Show *Photo by Marcia Roltner*

Chapter 5
Some TV Specials 1960-1966

CYD CHARISSE

Cyd is one of my favorite dancers on film, and in rehearsal she is something else. She puts on a pair of little flat shoes while learning the choreography, then changes into shoes with rather high heels to try out the number.

One day I asked, "Cyd how do you ever dance in such high heels and not hurt yourself?"

She said, "Practice Tony, lots and lots of practice."

The first time I worked with Cyd was when she was a guest on *The Dinah Shore Show*. I had seen her in films many times and immediately went to see any and all of her other films. I first did an elaborate production number, which served to reflect her career as a film star. I hired Bob Lone, a dancer I had worked with in New York who was movie star handsome and would make a good partner for Cyd. They both looked very handsome together and partnered beautifully. I later learned Bob had a big crush on Cyd and was nervous as hell to finally be working with her - but grateful at the same time.

The second number was a simple pas de deux partnered with my assistant Dick Beard to the then big hit "Days of Wine and Roses." They did justice to the number on the dress rehearsal, but on air the ending didn't work out so well. They were to do a lift where Cyd would wrap her body around Dick as he lowered her to the floor. I guess it was performance nerves or something, because this time Cyd hung onto Dick so tightly she pulled him down with her and wound up sitting on his face on the floor. They both started laughing and never did stand up to acknowledge their applause. They just remained in a heap on the floor and giggled. Dinah also came out laughing and thanked them for their stellar performance, which started the audience laughing even more. It was a hoot. Nothing like live TV.

Cyd was asked to do *The Ed Sullivan Show* so she called to ask me to choreograph a number for her. Of course I accepted and went to her house with an idea. I suggested she should do a number to a big hit of the day, "MacArthur Park."

She hadn't heard of it. Thankfully, her son Tony was right there said, "Yes, mother do it! It's a great song!"

How could she refuse? As we worked out the dance she grew to like the music more, and felt the choreography was marrying itself to the music, in other words, she could feel it. I called the set designer of Ed's show and told him what I needed and when we arrived in New York we were pleased to see they had everything ready for us.

My next request was, we would have to pre-tape the number. When that was refused, their point being it's a live show, I returned with there would not be enough time to set the stage and take it down during a live show. Well, they finally acquiesced, so we taped the number and ran the tape for the live telecast.

Photo by Marcia Roltner

Cyd on The Dinah Shore Show

It was a knockout. The audience went wild with applause and even Ed smiled and applauded. When Cyd walked out on stage looking like a million bucks she got a standing ovation. Something a TV audience seldom does.

We were informed the public reaction to the number was so terrific they repeated the TV show the next night.

⁂

Some years later, my first job as a TV director came on a phone call from Cyd who said, "Tony, I have an offer to do a television special and I'll do it if you'll choreograph and direct it."

I called my agent Jules Sharr and he said, "Do it. You've been doing both jobs anyway, you might as well get paid for the work."

So I called Cyd and accepted. I had choreographed the dance numbers for her appearances on *The Dinah Shore Show*. They went well and she was very happy with them so we were well acquainted.

Now the challenge. I knew from the beginning I didn't want to start the special with the usual walk down entrance of the Host that was overused. I went back to my old methods of calling a technician. I asked if the crane on a camera is strong enough to hold a person and the camera? When he answered, Yes, I had my opening. I had a support built so I could put Cyd in a chair at the required distance from the lens of the camera and during the opening song, ride her around the set and out over the audience to relieve her from having to dance an opening number and wearing her out at the top of the show. I immediately called and told her what I had planned.

She was delighted and repeated, "Then I don't have to dance an opening number do I? Bravo!"

Rehearsals were called for the dancers whom I knew from previous shows and who were of the right height to work with Cyd. I started with them first so Cyd wouldn't have to get up too early to start working. She liked that because it was easier on her for the guys to know who would be lifting and partnering her. I often used Sonya Haney to work out lifts and steps so they would be ready for Cyd.

When she arrived we went through the usual introductions and put her into the chair and gave her a little trial run for the opening number. Surprise! She liked it! One great hurdle crossed.

Now we moved on to the dance she does with the boys. First she learned it in flat shoes then she did it in heels. Cyd seemed comfortable with the number so we went on.

The next number that Cyd had to do was with The Electric Prunes, an English boy band. The Prunes were used as the interludes between Cyd's changes of wardrobe in the fashion-modeling segment. They were a great touch.

In that number alone she had three costume changes, so we took our time to carefully sort it out and make sure the costumes would work and do what we wanted them to do. This took some time but it worked out wonderfully. Everybody seemed happy with it.

Next she had an Adam and Eve song and dance followed by a talk dance with the Sid Krofft puppets. This was a little tricky because she couldn't see the puppets but had to imagine they were there. They were in Chroma key and in a completely different location. Then finally the long tricky "Bolero." It was an exhausting show to do in one day. Getting in and out of costumes, touching up make up, reviewing dance steps and lifts all start to take its toll by the end of the day. When we came to do the last big dance number she said, "Tony, I just can't dance another step, I'm exhausted."

What to do? We had only one big dance number left. It would be a major expense to ask for another studio day!

One of the girls in the group said she knew the number and could dance it. She could also fit into the costume. I told Cyd this plan and she sighed with relief and agreed it was fine. Saved by Jackie Gregory who had worked with me on *The Danny Kaye Show*. Cyd got dressed and into the headdress and did the movements that I was shooting in close-up. She looked fabulous and did it in one take then got out of the costume, rested a bit and into her "Goodnight" and closing speech dress while I shot Jackie Gregory in Cyd's costume dancing the wide shots.

No one ever wrote in or called to ask whom the girl was who did the long shots so I presume nobody even noticed it wasn't Cyd. As a souvenir I have the headdress Cyd wore in that dance.

After Cyd had an opportunity to rest, she came to the set looking every inch the movie star and ready to do her good night speech. I had her back lit so you could see the silhouette of that great body through her sheer gown then slowly brought up the front light as she walked down to camera into close-up for her goodnight speech.

She said about three words then slurred and stumbled she was still so tired. After we did that several times I went to the client and asked if we could shorten what she had to say and just bring up their logo. They were satisfied with what they had seen so far and granted permission.

I ran to Cyd and told her to say, "I hope you enjoyed the show and thank you for watching. Good night."

She did it in one take. I thanked everybody and it was my turn to wish the cast and crew a "Goodnight!" My first show as Director and Choreographer was in the can and under budget. I thought I'll have a beer or maybe a glass of wine and a long lie-down. From then on I always did both jobs.

Over the years we would see each other at various dance events and it was always a pleasure to catch up with her.

I visited Cyd at her place to interview her for this book. It was rather sad to see her in her late years. She was frail and her memory was not the best. But, she knew me and as I told her about the things we had done together, she would remember them too. And it was like her younger self coming to the forefront and waking up there for a bit. We had a grand time reminiscing and going over old times. She brought out stacks of photos and reviews and when we said our goodbye's I knew it was the last goodbye. At the door, Tony thanked me for giving her a very special afternoon. She died just a few days later.

Cyd was a talented dancer and a good soul. And she will always hold a special place in my heart as she believed in me, and gave me my first boost into the director's chair.

Director Barry Shear, Cornel Wilde, Janet Blair, Tony Charmoli

JANET BLAIR & NELLIE BLY

My first job of producing a show was *Nellie Bly* starring Janet Blair for *The Chevy Show*. It aired Jan. 30 1960, and I did it while still working on *The Dinah Shore Show*.

It was a low budget production so everything had to be done on the fly. Janet was always prepared and ready for the shoot, but Cornel Wilde, my leading man, had to have lots of retakes. On occasions like this I'd stay up with the editor putting together what we had shot, so I would know how to proceed with the actors in the morning. The edit took all night and morning, so without sleep I went right into the next day's shoot. Fortunately the second day went much faster and I believe we were able to finish with just a half-day shoot.

I must say Janet was a gem to work with, and Mr. Wilde was very handsome. The fact that there were no costume changes sped things up a lot. The small detail that Nellie wore the same outfit around the world was never a point to be considered. I guess one could say that in those days one could get away with anything. Margaret Dumont, Patsy Kelly, Iris Adrian and Lyle Talbot were also excellent and never presented any problems. They always knew their lines and came prepared for the day's shoot. Under so much pressure I can't tell you how grateful one is to have actors like that.

KIDS ARE PEOPLE

George Schlatter called one day with an idea to do a show with only kids to air April 17, 1960. It would be a special for *The Chevy Show* called *Kids Are People*. Immediately I loved the idea and started thinking. My first thought was to do an opening number with kids in a playground. George agreed with another of his "Fuckin' great Charmoli!" exclamations of approval.

I started auditions for the kid to open the show. I thought rather than open with a wide shot of a playground loaded with kids, I would like to start on a close-up of a young boy yelling, "Olly olly oxen free!" Something we used to call out while playing hide and seek. I think it meant everyone is finally free to come out of hiding.

I auditioned lots of kids until one little red head caught my attention and I hired him to open the show. This kid eventually grew up to be one of Hollywood's successful film directors - Ron Howard. This

*Jay North, Angela Cartwright,
& Teddy Rooney with Tony*

was about the same time that he was cast as Opie on *The Andy Griffith Show*. Little Ron was perfect for the opening as he did his call and slid down as the camera zoomed back to reveal a playground full of children, many of whom were in the show.

The host was Angela Cartwright, assisted by Jerry Mathers and Jay North. I had seen a book of poetry by Joan Walsh Anglund titled *A Friend is Someone Who Likes You*. I thought it would be perfect for the show. I had Angela read it to me just to see how she would do. I immediately reacted and said, "Angela, that's just how I want you to do it in the show." Then I gave her the poem so she could learn it.

Rehearsals were a pleasure. When the time came for Angela to tape it, she looked adorable in her overstuffed chair. We rolled tape, cued her and in one take she had worked magic and left a lump in my throat. The whole crew was in awe and had nothing but praise. I had cue cards for her just in case, but she had memorized it and sailed right on through.

There was a cute number where Angela sings "I Enjoy Being A Girl," where I thought it would be fun if she was playing dress up. At one point while posing in front of a mirror with her fancy dress clothes, she kept getting too far away from the mirror. I stopped the camera and went up and quietly told her, "When you are too far back, the camera can't see your reflection in the mirror." She got what I was saying right off and for a very young girl I have to say she was very professional.

Thanks to Angela and Joan Walsh Anglund. If I remember correctly I did write to Miss Anglund to thank her for writing such a heartfelt poem.

I seem to remember the boys did a song too. The show was such a success that Chevy wanted us to do another special the following fall for Halloween called *Ghosts, Goblins and Kids*. Teddy Rooney joined us for that show and performed a musical number. Another kid even played an animal trainer. All the kids did a great job.

FEATHERTOP & JANE POWELL

John Marsh, the writer, came to me with a script he had written for a musical version of Nathaniel Hawthorne's *Feathertop* which aired on October 19, 1961.

The locale was changed from Massachusetts to colorful New Orleans. I had worked with Jane Powell on her own TV Special and she was unanimously cast as the lead on this one. Hugh O'Brian was *Feathertop*. I was hoping to secure Louis Jourdan as the Gentleman of Breeding but due to previous conflicting commitments, Mr. Jordan was not available. But Hugh did a great job.

When I read the story *Feathertop* I kept seeing Cathleen Nesbitt as the witch. When I suggested this to John Marsh, he said, "She'd be great, but she's a big star, you'll never get her."

My response was "Try me!"

Fortunately it was my luck to be at a dinner party when in walked Cathleen Nesbitt. I jumped with joy for I immediately saw she would make the perfect witch. I didn't hesitate in approaching her and as I described the character, I assured her she would not be the typical snaggletooth, black pointed hat cartoon witch, but beautifully gowned, sophisticated and charming. She loved the idea so I contacted her agent who gave the go ahead and Miss Nesbitt was cast. I was ecstatic.

Mary Rodgers wrote some of her best music and Martin Charnin's lyrics won me over completely. Together they made a wonderful team. I'd work with them anytime.

One example I remember, is the morning after Jane's character Julie Balfour, has met and fallen in love with her handsome gentleman of breeding. Upon rising from a night's sleep, she throws open the shutters of her bedroom and sings "I think I'll Have the World for Breakfast." I applauded I loved it so. In fact Jane made a perfect choice playing a southern belle. She was radiant in the role.

Dean Whitmore was a director and a close friend of mine in New York. I felt I had so much work on the floor handling the choreography and moving actors and dancers around, I couldn't also be in the director's booth. I laid out all the shots for the musical numbers and the choreographed pieces so I could be on the floor helping the dancers and actors. I could make corrections and any changes immediately. This combination helped us get through the shoot in record time. It also helped the actors from having to do and redo shots over and over again.

Hugh O'Brien and Jane Powell

Hugh O'Brien, Tony Charmoli rehearsing with Mary Rodgers

Cathleen Nesbitt with Mary Rodgers

One thing stands out in my mind as funny to me but was embarrassing for Bob the costume designer. In the evening of the great ball, the uninvited witch Cathleen Nesbitt appears at the top of the grand staircase beautifully gowned, and everybody freezes in horror. The ballroom goes silent in anticipation of what might happen next. In complete silence, she starts down the steps when suddenly Bob runs onto the ballroom floor and yells, "Stop! Stop! She's wearing the wrong shoes."

Miss Nesbitt stops, gently picks up a slight corner of her gown looks down at her comfortable shoes then slowly back up and says to Bob still standing at the bottom of the staircase. "My dear man, if at my age I can't command the audience to look at my face instead of my feet, I should not be standing on this staircase. Continue!"

And we continued. The taping finished with resounding applause from the entire cast and it also was well reviewed by the press which made all of us happy.

> "A bright original musical comedy bursting forth from that tired blinking little screen. A gem of purest ray serene." Harriett Van Horn, N. Y. World Telegram

> "We would like to see this musical Feathertop done every season." Larry Walters, Chicago Tribune

---

Before *Feathertop*, I had choreographed *The Jane Powell Show* which was aired by NBC on April 28, 1961. This is what gave me the idea for casting Jane. The cast for this special was outstanding with Art Carney, Steve Lawrence and Gwen Verdon. It was a pleasure for me to choreograph dance numbers for Jane and one for Gwen.

I called Roy Fitzell to partner Jane. In the story of the dance, Jane is at a Party Dance sitting alone and forlorn at the end of a row of empty chairs. All the girls have dancing partners, and Jane is made up as a plain ugly duckling looking girl - just as dowdy as can be. All the other girls are out on the dance floor with their dance partners having a good time. Jane sits sadly with her hands folded when soon handsome Roy arrives and invites her to dance. As he touches her she immediately transforms into a beautiful princess and the dance floor immediately becomes a very grand ballroom. All the guests stop to watch this prince and princess do a sweeping magical dance. It was a moving and very heartfelt moment. The fairy tale ends as everyone joins in for a big dance finale and all leave with their partners including smiling happy Jane as herself with Roy as himself. Once again Love triumphs.

Gwen's dance was set in a western horse corral. She was in the center of the corral, dressed in a tight fitting leotard. Around the corral, cowboys leaned and sat in various attitudes on a split rail fence. These cowboys were sizing up this hot number as they would one of their prize colts. Gwen's pony movements were prancing, stomping the ground, galloping, flipping her tail very provocatively and other moves of a sexual nature. Finally, the guys join her in the corral and the

One of my favorite photos of Gwen is from this show.

galloping and gaiety takes off until it reaches a height where the whole set transforms into a big barn dance hall on a Saturday night. Gwen transforms from pony to dance hall girl and really goes to town with a fast cancan. Soon the frenzy and gaiety reaches such a soaring dancing height celebrating this beautiful pony transformed into a vivacious dance hall girl, it seemed the energy would blow up the set. You had to see the number to know how entertaining it was. Gwen was absolutely at her peak and charming in this role.

Of course Jane was a delight as always to work with. She is one of those people you are instantly fond of. Both a star and a big heart.

ALICE THROUGH THE LOOKING GLASS

In 1966, I was asked to choreograph *Alice Through the Looking Glass* which was produced by Alan Handley. Bette Davis was cast as the Red Queen, Nanette Fabray was the White Queen, Jimmy Durante was a very funny Humpty Dumpty, Jack Palance the Jabberwocky, and the Smothers Brothers were Tweedledum and Tweedledee.

I had done Eva Le Gallienne's *Alice in Wonderland* before in New York, and it was a treat to do another version of it here on the West Coast. Bette Davis as the Red Queen was perfect casting. I never had seen anybody so perfectly cast. We did a rehearsal run through and all was going well until the Tea Party.

Nanette Fabray as the White Queen was a good roller skater so I put her on skates and gave her crazy things to do on her entrance to the Tea Party. The doors open and in rolls the White Queen, banging into things, hanging on to the drapes and pulling them down, knocking over chairs, banging into plants while making high cackling noises as she bumbles and rolls to her place at the table. The cast and crew were howling with laughter at Nanette and so was I. That was my mistake. Putting Nanette on roller skates was outrageously funny. Too funny. I blame that mistake for the loss of Bette Davis.

The next day Bette called in sick with a terrible back pain and couldn't continue with the show. It seems she thought she would be upstaged by Nanette. It is hard to believe that the great Bette Davis didn't think she could hold her own, but that is my gut feeling. So instead, Agnes Moorhead made an excellent replacement - and I must confess she was much easier to work with.

When done, the whole thing turned out to be an imaginative production of *Alice Through the Looking Glass.* It is available on DVD if you look for it.

NBC Publicity Photos/ Charmoli Archives

Chapter 6
The Danny Kaye Show

I always liked the films of Danny Kaye so when I got a call to come to join his staff for the *The Danny Kaye Show* I accepted without hesitation. The timing couldn't have been better. In 1963, Dinah was moving on to do a talk show so I was free to accept Danny's offer. The minute I walked into Danny's office I could feel this was going to be a good match.

I was right from the first meeting. Danny and the producer discussed musical numbers for the show and made it quite clear I could create dances which stand on their own, he would not have to be in them. As the weeks went by I found that to be true. Danny loved the dance and would often come into the rehearsal room just to see us working and loved it when I put him in a dance number.

Danny would generally be in the opening and then we'd would work in one of the special guests. One of his favorites was Gwen Verdon. He would have her on the show every week if he could. He really had a hot nut for her.

Once when she was on the show, he invited her to dinner after rehearsal. Gwen was afraid it was just going to be the two of them, so she asked me to go with her. We kept it a secret from Danny until we got to his house. Gwen rang the doorbell and I ducked behind her. Danny answered the door with a big greeting to Gwen until I stepped out from behind her. I think he said something like "Oh I meant to ask you to." Yeah, sure. But it helped Gwen to feel more comfortable.

Showing how it's done with Jackie Gregory, Jeri Jamerson, Sally Mason, & Nancy Martin

Elaine Joyce is dancing on the far left.

Danny loved dancers and some of the more regular girls were: Elaine Joyce, Jackie Gregory, Nancy Martin, Sally Mason and Bonnie Evans. The boys were: Lee Roy Reams, Roy Fitzell, Johnny Harmon, Jerry Jackson, Gary Menteer, and Nicholas Navarro. Others were added as needed. Over the many shows they did some beautiful work - from comic to serious - Danny really allowed us to explore true dance on prime time TV.

I have never seen Danny in a rage like he was when we had Tammy Grimes on as a guest. She had made quite a splash with *The Unsinkable Molly Brown* on Broadway and we were looking forward to working with her. She was fine at rehearsing the things she'd be doing on the show and all was going well until the break came.

Everybody went to his or her dressing rooms, or to make up or to whatever they had to do to get ready for dress rehearsal. Dress rehearsal was called and everybody was ready except Tammy. She was nowhere to be found. Danny was furious. The audience was in and anxious to see the show. Danny told his pianist, Ticker, to get the music for his Las Vegas stage show. Danny did his entire one-man show to the delight of the crowd, then stormed off the set to get ready for the TV Air show. By now Danny was pretty tired. Finally Tammy was found passed out in the ladies room from doing pot or something stronger that her mystery boyfriend brought to her. The TV show went on, Tammy pulled herself together for a reasonably good performance. By then Danny had done two full shows and was the last to take his bow and he walked off the set shouting "Get that woman out of my sight, I don't want to see her ever, never, never again!"

Danny and Gwen
{NBC Publicity Photos/ Charmoli Archives)

121

NBC Publicity Photos/ Charmoli Archives

We had a visitor who often came to our rehearsals - Judy Garland. As a young boy, I tap danced in her relatives' night club in Grand Rapids, Minnesota, when the Gumm Sisters were also making an appearance there, but we didn't meet until many years later. I don't know exactly when we first met, but by the time I was working with Danny and she was doing her show down the hall, we had already built a history between us. In the rehearsal room she was just Judy. She popped into our rehearsals a lot, much to the annoyance of her producers who wouldn't be able to find her. Judy's rehearsal room was right next to ours. I'd often remind her that they needed her on her set but she always preferred to watch what was going on with me. None of us minded. In fact we loved having Judy as an audience. There's only one Judy and no one has imitated her to perfection. Liza fortunately made it on her own.

Bob Mackie the talented designer gave a Halloween party at his house around that time and Will and I thought of wearing black tie. As luck would have it just as we arrived a big black limousine pulled up and out stepped Judy Garland wearing a long black evening gown, probably one Bob had made. After we did our hugs and kisses we all immediately thought the same thing. We would be her escorts. She took Will by one arm and I got the other and we walked to the front door and rang the doorbell. Bob opened the door. The minute he saw this trio he exclaimed "Tony only you could come up with something like this only you!" Needless to say, we were the hit costume of the party.

Lucille Ball was a favorite guest. They got along famously. I guess they respected each other's talents. Lucy and I got on just fine.

On one occasion I told Lucy I had something I thought was funny that she might consider for the sketch she and Danny were doing. I had worked it out with the prop men and I would show it to her right after lunch if she came a little early so Danny wouldn't see it. She agreed and I demonstrated.

The scene was a Japanese restaurant. There were two low tables and of course no chairs. It was difficult to sit way down on the floor pillow gracefully so I pretended to move my hips from side to side and just finally plopped down and quickly straightened my legs out under the table, laid back flat and the prop man way down beyond the other table pulled me through on the pillow until I wound up at the second table, sat up quickly and broke into conversation with guests at that table. Lucy finding it hysterically funny burst out laughing and did it on the first try.

When Danny got back from lunch, we ran the sketch. The prop men were ready to do the trick with Lucy. Danny and Lucy entered the restaurant and were escorted to their table. Danny still has no idea of what we had planned. Lucy started her maneuver to sit and she finally just plopped down, the prop man pulled her through and she wound up at the next table with other guests so she engaged them in Japanese. It all happened in a flash and the trick worked perfectly.

Danny almost burst a gut he laughed so hard. He loved it and so did the writers. Lucy was great in telling it was all my idea. I worked with the writers quite a bit. They even encouraged me to come up with more.

Danny began inviting me to the writer's meetings, which is unusual for a choreographer. But I've always thought choreography is storytelling which isn't too different from telling a good joke.

Another sketch took place on a ship. The entire set was put on a rocking platform and the scene was

Danny and Lucy

the dining room. The joke was to maneuver Danny's chair away from the table every time he was about to take a bite of food. Sometimes the chair with Danny in it would go rolling out the door and disappear and suddenly come rolling back in. Sometimes with Danny in it and sometimes empty.

It was first rehearsed with a stand in and it worked every time and was indeed funny. I told the stand in I thought it was funny and he said, "Yeah but wait till the porcelain princess tries it."

He was right - Danny wound up with banged up elbows and adjustments had to be made but it all came together for the air show and all the laughs perked Danny up and made it all worthwhile.

I loved Danny, but not when he had those seemingly unprovoked fits of temper. Fortunately they didn't happen too often but often enough to be discouraging. However he also had good taste, he bought one of my paintings.

Danny and Lucy were a good team. She came back multiple times. On another show with Lucy guesting, we were doing a big spiritual number of "Song of the Swamp," popularly known as "Chloe" (Louis Armstrong recorded it in 1952), and I had an idea. The lyrics by Gus Kahn go like this:

> *Chloe! Chloe!*
> *Someone's calling, no reply Nightshade's falling, hear him sigh Chloe! Chloe!*

Danny is singing the plaintive number up front. I put Lucy in amongst the dancers and singers and gave her some of the steps they were doing to make her one of them. At one point the dancers and singers are reaching a climax in the music singing, "If you live, I'll find you." They abruptly stop dancing and singing as Lucy is rapidly lifted high in the air and wails, "CHLOE' then drops down into the group and they resume dancing.

Danny fell apart laughing. It really was funnier than any of us thought possible. Even Lucy broke up. Unfortunately Sylvia had just stepped into the rehearsal and saw it. She called Danny over and quietly discussed matters with him.

Lucy talked to me and said, "You watch Tony, it will be out. It's too funny and she didn't think of it." Well, it stayed in for the rest of this rehearsal period but the next day it was out. Sylvia was a tough cookie. I think what really bothered Sylvia was that Lucy had the joke line and not Danny.

Sometimes it was a chore to go to the house as both Danny and his wife Sylvia Fine Kaye were very strong personalities with differing opinions about staging and material. *The Danny Kaye Show* was technically led by Danny, but Sylvia was a distinct voice behind the scenes. She later produced a TV series that I directed and choreographed on the history of the American Musical Theatre in the 70's and 80's called Musical Comedy Tonight. The decision making process was frequently a battle of diplomacy and sometimes I had to draw on all my resources to be attentive to both of them in a room. But they both liked me and I had a good relationship with both of them.

Danny was sometimes challenging to work with. Once while taping for Sylvia's musical comedy archives in a theatre, Danny was performing and I had a camera guy go right up front to get a low angle on Danny. The camera guy crunched way down to make himself as small as possible and invisible to the audience. This taping was not being broadcast it was for the archives.

A camera in the front of the stage is a common practice. Danny blew his top. He stormed off the stage with "How do you expect me to be funny with a camera blocking me from the audience?" The camera was below the audience level and never blocked their view. They understood what was going on. They were historians. Danny's performance would not even be in the part Sylvia was doing. Danny was being a real Pain ITA. It took a while for the good little wife to calm things down, and Danny picked up where he left off. These fits of temper did more to upset the audience than any good to the production. Sylvia got what she needed for her theater history in spite of Danny's tantrums.

While working on *The Danny Kaye Show*, I noticed that right across the hall at CBS was Kathryn Kuhlman, the very popular evangelist. She was in rehearsal for her TV Show, *I Believe in Miracles* and I was curious to see her in operation. So one day I sneaked in the back door of her studio.

It opened up behind the cyclorama of the stage of the studio she was in. I stopped in my tracks when I overheard her voice giving directions to one of the parishioners who was about to appear on her TV Show. I had always been curious about what made these religious mongers tick and was absolutely floored when there behind the cyc hidden from the audience was Ms. Kuhlman coaching a young black girl on how she should deliver her testimony.

Mary Tyler Moore in a Twenties number
(NBC Publicity Photos/ Charmoli Archives)

She told the girl that she would call on her to come forward during the show to give testimony on her commitment to the LORD. I heard her scold the girl with "No, no no! You should show more passion. Raise your arms to the Lord. Ask for forgiveness and burst into tears if you can, then drop to your knees as the Lord forgives you."

Those aren't exactly her words but the content is the same. Ever since that little encounter I loved watching those Holy Roller types. Kathryn Kuhlman was very good at putting on a show.

❧

Danny was a good cook. He often took trips to San Francisco to visit his many chefs in Chinatown. He had two kitchens in his lovely home in Beverly Hills, one Chinese and the other Italian. Danny liked to cook and give dinner parties.

I had a pleasant surprise one evening. The invitation seemed like all the rest and of course I was pleased to have it. I was a little late so when I walked into the living room and saw Yul Brynner, then my eyes fixed on one of my very favorite movie stars, Cary Grant. It didn't stop there. When we were summoned into the dining room, It was just the four of us. Danny seated Cary right next to me. It was a tremendous moment. I felt like the young boy from Mt. Iron who fell in love with Janet Gaynor years before. I said how happy I was to meet him.

With a smile he asked, "Disappointed?"

I was not at all. I found Cary every bit as delightful off screen as he is on. I'm sorry to say that was the one and only time I had the experience of spending time with him. This evening ran for quite a long time with just four of us. This happened several times at Danny's house; opportunities to meet and visit with famous celebrities.

On another occasion I hosted a dinner at my house and Danny said he would do the pasta. I insisted there was plenty of help in the kitchen to do the work, but when Danny says he's going to do the pasta, that's the way it's going to be. Soon word came from the kitchen, "The pasta is done. The water is ready to be strained." Danny jumped up to do it. He took two hot pads and lifted the big pot of boiling pasta, carried it over to the sink, and as he started to pour out the boiling water, hot steam came gushing out and burned his hands. He screamed in pain, the pot slipped and the boiling water poured into his boot. We tried to get the boot off to no avail. We brought a lot of ice and piled it onto the leg. He must have been in shock because he had no pain. He managed to sit down to eat his pasta, then decided to call his driver and go home. We were informed by the driver that half way home Danny hit the ceiling in pain and they raced off to Emergency. They had to cut the boot off of his foot as it was badly burned.

We had a show the very next day and in it he had a dance number with Shari Lewis. With his leg was all bandaged up he was able to do his TV Show sitting down. When the scene with Shari Lewis came up, she used her puppet with Danny, and then I stepped in to do the dancing with her. It seemed to work out pretty well. Fortunately Danny was up on his feet again in no time.

Danny loved to be in the dance numbers along with the dancers. In one number, Danny was singing while the dancers were kicking up a routine behind him. Just as he joined in the dance Lee Roy Reams kicked a little too high and split his pants right in two but kept on dancing until the pants dropped around his ankles and he just kept on going. Danny started laughing so hard he couldn't move. Lee Roy just improvised some hopping steps out to the end of the number. He fortunately was saved from total embarrassment by wearing a dance belt. Or maybe the audience would have liked it better if he had displayed the whole enchilada as the mail just poured in wanting more.

NBC Publicity Photos/ Charmoli Archives

I told Danny about Juliet Prowse (for whom I later choreographed the "Bolero" in '71 to much success) and he immediately said we should have her on the show. I chose "Love Makes the World Go 'Round." My story was to have a young girl sporting four romances then choosing one for marriage. Her romances would be with Nick Navarro, John Frayer, Brad Craig and Lance Avant. A maypole was the set and each of the boys would dance around the pole with Juliet in the center. The music stops and Juliet takes the boy nearest her away to dance a variation defining his character. Upon her rejection he returns to rejoin the other guys and the dance around the maypole resumes. This routine repeats until the boy of her choice. In this case it was John Frayer. The maypole goes away and the romantic couple goes into a grand pas de deux winding up with him slipping a diamond ring on her finger and he chases after her into the wings. I guess audiences loved it. The mail was all very positive, some even loving it. We didn't have e-mail in those days.

When Betty White guested on *The Danny Kaye Thanksgiving Show*, I staged a corny song for her called "Its Turkey Lurkey Time." At dress rehearsal she did it as a cheap strip joint hooker and just destroyed Danny and everybody in the cast. She was hysterically funny.

There were unseen hazards in some of these numbers. In one Sally Mason and Gary Menteer were submerged lying flat on their backs under a cloud of dry ice and on a certain count they would sit up out of the cloud. One can't breathe in dry ice and can't see either. The problem in this number was Sally and Gary couldn't find each other's hand to make their rise out of the dry ice cloud until just barely on the last second of music almost passing out from not being able to breath. The pay-off was it worked beautifully.

NBC Publicity Photos/ Charmoli Archives

Another dance using fog climaxed with two dancers tossing a girl in the air and letting her drop down below the level of the fog where they caught her out of sight. It was a tough maneuver, but paid off with a great gasp throughout the audience when it appeared that no one was going to catch her.

In another number the tempo was so fast and the dancing so energetic with many entrances and exits that the dancers had to have tanks of oxygen standing by in the wings so they could take a quick whiff on each exit. It was a long and difficult number. And remember the dancer must smile through this whole ordeal. Judging by the audience applause, it was worth it.

In another number three girl dancers are standing on three tall boxes wearing overly long black lace mantillas concealing the boxes by trailing down and to the floor. Their arms are raised over their heads holding the ends of the lace and they are swaying slowly left and right just enough not to reveal the boys standing up there with them. On a certain count the boys do a surprising leap high off the boxes down to the floor. Tragedy almost happened when one boy got stuck in the girls big lace mantilla and almost took her off the box with him. You could hear the gasp from all who saw the near tragedy. The good part was this happened in dress rehearsal and not on the air.

Fortune was on my side when the fan mail came in. It was a hit. It was sad to see this show run its course and not come back. I guess one has to live with fond memories.

One evening at a party at my house Imogene Coca and Danny Kaye were having a grand time when I interrupted them with the arrival of a guest. I said, "Imogene Coca and Danny Kaye this is Herbert Hirschmuller, courier to the Queen of Holland!"

I thought he would be thrilled to meet these television stars.

Herbert curtly said, "Oh, I never watch Television."

Imogene burst out into uncontrollable laughter and the next day at rehearsal said, "Tony, if you look on the curtains in your back room, I think you'll find my lashes stuck there."

When I was doing *The Danny Kaye Show* my dance teacher from Mt Iron, Ida Canossa, came out to California to visit me and I took her backstage to meet Danny.

It was thrilling because Danny was one of Ida's favorite movie stars and they connected admirably. He complimented her for taking me in to teach me to dance and complimented her on her looks. I guess it might have been her big hair which caught his eye. She never forgot this visit and thanked me over and over saying it was a major high point in her life.

When I got back from New York after doing the Shirley MacLaine special *Gypsy in My Soul* I was invited to a party at Danny's house. There was a big dance floor outdoors and a good band was playing dance music but nobody was dancing. Just then Danny crossed the floor on his way somewhere and I shouted "Danny! Let's dance!" He immediately dropped what he was carrying and partnered me. We were having a grand time and gathered quite an audience. Sylvie went by and said, "Thank you Tony." We got the party started.

After a while I went inside and the house was pretty packed but I found a comfortable corner where the view was very good, when someone caught my eye. One didn't need a second look to see he was handsome. No he wasn't just handsome, he was young and very handsome. Well, he's coming right to me. Wow!

He said one of the nicest things ever said to me. He said, "Thanks for taking such good care of my sister."

It was a young Warren Beatty. I called Shirley immediately to tell her.

She said, "He said that?" She was overcome, you could hear it.

Just then Eddie Fisher interrupted and I dissolved into the rest of the party.

Montefalcone, Italy

Chapter 7
European Adventures

ITALY

My first trip to Italy was to visit Montefalcone, the birthplace of my parents. My sister Mudge, Will and I spent the night in Naples and called the maid with some laundry we had to have in the morning. We were going to Montefalcone. She was curious about why we picked Montefalcone. This dialogue was being done in the best I could do with my limited Italian.

She said "But you're Americans aren't you?"

When I answered, "Yes, but our parents come from Montefalcone."

She jumped with delight and in Italian she said, "I come from there too." She was so delighted she ordered the limo and brought a packed lunch for us to have on the way up to the top of the mountain. What a great send off!

The trip up in the limo was quite beautiful. Montefalcone is a picturesque mountain village with cobblestone streets which looked much better when viewed from a distance. When we arrived, there were quite a few people out on the street to greet us. A little boy and girl put our luggage on their heads then led us to our destination. When we arrived we were met by a rather large group of people who immediately smothered us with big hugs and kisses and tears of joy. They were so happy to see their American relatives. We finally got into a decent conversation doing the best I could with my Italian-American accent when suddenly the hugging and kissing stopped. We were at the wrong house. We were informed we wanted the

Left: Welcoming committee with grandma on the right -with a surprise for me. Right: The priest/stamp collector.

Minelli's on the other side of town. The kids collected our bags loaded them into the car and they waved us off. We gained by this error because the other side of town was a much nicer side of the mountain.

On arrival we went through the same tears of joy and hugging but since we knew we were in the right place the second time had a better edge. Even the local priest was there to welcome us. There were tears of joy and loud greetings from relatives and other townspeople. It seems Italian women can command tears in an instant. We were thanked over and again while we gave gifts of American clothes that we had brought and that they just loved. Even the local priest was there. Knowing he was a stamp collector from my mother, I brought my stamp collection, which was quite large (l also collected stamps). I gave it to him and he was so grateful, I think he thought he had died and gone to heaven.

My uncle, my mother's brother was also there and informed me if I had to go to the toilet he had the only porcelain one in town. All you had to do was throw a bucket of water in when you had finished and it flushed. I thanked him for the information and passed it on to my sister Mudge and to Will. They were amused and graciously thanked the uncle.

Next stop was my Father's side of the family, and we went through the same tears of joy upon greeting. My grandmother pulled me aside and told me she had saved something special for me. I couldn't wait. She reached way down to her ankles and gathered up the hems of her many layers of skirts and petticoats, raised them up to her crotch and reached into

Family time.

a pocket right next to the pee hole in her bloomers and pulled out a handful of a dark strange looking object. I couldn't figure out what it was. Then she said in Italian, "I knew you were coming so I saved this 'specially for you." She then handed me the dark object and I smelled it and deduced it was a piece of dried ham. I thanked her and put it in my pocket. Later one of the dogs in the neighborhood loved it.

Will and my Uncle- who had the nicest toilet in town

When we got back to my uncle's house I immediately tested out his toilet. He was right - it worked. Supper that night was home grown salad and pasta with tomato sauce. Very familiar and really very good with that right out of the garden taste.

We went to church the next day and were invited to have lunch with the priest. After mass we were escorted to the parish house and into the living room.

It was a terribly hot day and all the shutters were closed three quarters of the way so it was quite dark. We could see there were things out for a tea and cake affair. In this rather dark room the cake looked like a luscious dark chocolate cake covered in dark raisins. Then the servant arrived followed by the priest who apologized for being late. He announced he was happy we could come and would we like some tea and cake? We couldn't say no, there was no choice. He told the girl to serve and as she reached out to cut the cake, all the raisins flew away!! We were polite and managed a small bite.

That night we were escorted to the empty barn where our beds were made of straw covered with blankets. The barn reeked of stale air. Fortunately there were large windows and we opened all the shutters and made the best of it. We were nowhere near a hotel and our driver was not due back until morning. We slept in our clothes and soon it got rather stuffy and we saw the shutters had been closed. Will and I got up and opened them again. After the third time this happened we just let it go. We were informed the next morning the shutters are closed because the night mountain air is very bad for you.

In the morning we were informed that the driver couldn't make it so we had to take the bus back. Right then and there we agreed this was our first and last trip to Montefalcone. Even the beautiful mountain scenery couldn't lure us back.

On the way down the mountain in a bus loaded with people, Will had an urgent need for a toilet and I asked the driver to stop at the next bathroom. He said there was no toilet until we get to Napoli. He pulled the bus over to the side of the road and handed me some toilet paper.

He said in Italian, "He can go here."

Left: Our Bus and Bus Driver. Right: The view from the bathroom.

We were on a country road with no town around. There were not even any bushes. The bus was packed with people and their kids and cackling chickens and products loaded in baskets for market, everybody talking up a storm.

Will in a panic asks, "Where shall I go?"

I said, "Go behind the bus, or out in the field."

He rushed into the road behind the bus, took care of his business and blushed as he climbed back onto the bus feeling much better. Not one person paid any attention or asked why we had stopped. They obviously had been through this many times before.

We've never been back. We chalked it up to an interesting experience. My sister and I were happy that we were not born in Montefalcone.

❦

My next trip to Italy was to do the choreography for the Musical *Il Terrone Corre Sul Filo* in Milano for Remigio Paone. It starred their lead comic Nino Taranto and actress Tina De Mola. The dancing stars were Gilda Mareno and I brought an excellent American dancer with me Marc Breaux whom I had known for years. I didn't trust what I would get with an Italian male dancer. I knew Marc from our meeting years before at the Charles Weidman studios and was very familiar with his abilities as a dancer.

The producer Remigio Paone gave us a very grateful welcome and introduced us to the rest of the staff and our translator Mariella de Sarzana, who was a great help throughout this Italian adventure. That same day we met the cast and supporting players and had a very good time meeting and greeting. The cast and stars were very open and gracious and I had fun practicing my Italian. One by one we went through the whole company. First we met the leading lady Tina De Mola. She was charming and apologized for not speaking better English. Her great smile made up for everything she thought she lacked. The rest of the company went by with a greeting and a handshake while the lead comic Nino Taranto very full of himself arrogantly announced he was the star. He said he didn't think he had to come to rehearsal every day.

As rehearsals progressed I tried to get him to do some of the more contemporary things we were doing, but his arrogance got in the way so I just stopped offering help. Tina on the other hand was ever grateful for my work in staging her numbers. She was a dear.

One day in rehearsal Tina sneezed, and I said, "Cresha sante."

She excitedly gushed, "Grazzi, grazzi. Mille grazzi!" Embracing me like mad and repeating "GRAZZI!"

I said, "To what do I owe this?"

She said, "You just turned me into a young girl, thank you, thank you!"

I then remembered that when one sneezes, "Cresha sante." is what you say to a child, but to a grown up you should say, "Salute." I scored points that day.

Another faux pas I made was on an afternoon with a group of boy dancers were playing policemen. I said, "Y carbonaras vene qui."

They didn't move. I thought I had said, "Would the Policeman come here." I was informed, "Policemen is carabinieri. "Carbonaras is a pasta with cream sauce."

So I laughed and said it the correct way.

But, they still didn't move. So then I asked what's going on?

They responded, "Noi saremmo piuttosto carbonaras" or they'd rather be pasta with cream sauce. We did have fun with the language and rehearsals were full of laughter. They were tickled that I was trying.

Gilda and Marc, our star dancers, and I were picked up by boat at the dock of our hotel, owned by Paone, and transported to Paone's beautiful mansion with an impressive Italian garden where we were supplied with piano and drummer on a rehearsal stage. The choreography just seemed to pour out in such beautiful surroundings. A maid and butler always served lunch. Who could ask for more? After rehearsal we were boated back to the hotel to clean up for whatever Mr. Paone had planned for the evening. Usually it was a grand Italian dinner and we were always entertained by Italian musicians and singers. This pattern continued until we rehearsed in the theater.

With props for Mark and Gilda the dance numbers really came alive and they looked great together. Finally the last run through on stage went very well and we were ready for show time. I checked out the theater and it had been decorated with hundreds of gladiolas stapled to the balconies and boxes. This being the grand opening night of the new season, the theater was packed with beautifully dressed women and men in formal attire. The theater was buzzing in anticipation of seeing a new show.

Gilda had arranged to arrive with Marc before the show in a horse drawn carriage. it was pretty magnificent and the press just ate it up.

In rehearsal with Marc and Gilda. These photos were taken by Giancolombo, a successful Italian photographer who later had a prestigious career shooting everyone from Winston Churchill to capturing life in small Italian villages. But of course, Paone would only hire the best.

Just as the show was about to begin, Marc's valet rushed in panic to tell me Marc was not getting dressed and was refusing to do the show. I raced to his dressing room and it was true, he was not dressed and violent with me for getting him into this mess. He even barked at the producer, I detected a bad feeling of stage fright. As he was bitching, his dresser and I were getting him into costume. Slowly and piece by piece we finally got him dressed despite his constant complaining. The dresser and I stayed with him until he had to go into the wings. Once there, I rushed to my seat. My heart was pounding until I thought it would burst. The orchestra started and Gilda with Marc danced onto the stage. I breathed a huge sigh of relief.

They were stunning and the audience was captivated. Marc showed no signs of stage fright and his power made Gilda even more captivating. They charmed the audience and were the stars of the show. As they came to the section I thought would get a good response, I was proven right by a tremendous burst of applause. Then, they came to the end brilliantly and WOW! A standing ovation and stomping of feet and bravo's. I thought, "Wait 'til they see what's coming up in the second act!"

I mingled amongst the crowd in the lobby during intermission and the buzz was all about their ballerina Gilda and the American dancer Marc. No one was talking about the star Nino Taranto. I've had my fingers crossed that Marc and Gilda's performance in the second act would knock their socks off.

The second act begins with the Bluebell Girls, then Nino, and finally Gilda and Marc. The stage is dimly lit except for the two beds on opposite sides of the stage. Marc starts slowly thrashing restlessly in his sleep. On the other side of the stage, Gilda slides her hands out from between her legs and fondles her breasts. Marc rolls over and hugs the pillow then puts it between his legs. Gilda pulls her hands out from between her legs and comes out to almost center stage. Marc throws the pillow on the bed and comes out to center stage. They are looking out over the audience and dance rather lyrically and suggestively away from center almost to the wings then suddenly they simultaneously stop, hesitate turn and look to center, then make a mad dash to each other and Gilda does a flying jump into his arms wrapping her legs around his waist. They go into a sexy, lovemaking dance, which comes to a hot passionate climax. Spent they separate, and slowly return to their beds as the lights dim.

The audience went wild and started ripping the flowers stapled to their boxes and throwing them down to Mark and Gilda. Then they started yelling "Choreographer! Choreographer!" and the stagehands reached down from the stage and pulled me up onto the stage and the place went wild. They started ripping more gladiolas off the boxes and throwing them down at us. Do you know those flowers hurt when you get stabbed by one of the hard stems?

We all attended the cast dinner, which was in a lovely outdoor restaurant, and the weather was perfect. Everybody was congratulating each other and Paone gave the customary thank you speech. Of course we were all anxiously awaiting the reviews. It was well into morning when Mariella said, "Tony, the papers should be out by now, I'll go get them. Of course we all were on pins and needles waiting. Soon Mariella arrived with a stack and she eyed me at the end of the table and gave a big wink. My heart started to race. The papers were passed around and we soon read a huge rave for the stars of the show Gilda and Marc and also a rave for the choreography. The supposed star of the show, Nino Taranto was barely mentioned.

Nino Taranto, the self-supposed star, came over to congratulate me then asked if I would work with him the next day. Of course I did. It was a little too late but I did my best. After all he's the star of the show in his own mind. To show his gratitude, Paone gave me a large sterling silver tea set. I brought it to Mariella's attention. I told her I loved it but he knows one can't take silver out of Italy. Is this an Indian giver gift? Mariella said "Don't worry, I'll ship it to you." She did and I still have it and use it.

Marc stayed and toured with the show for a year then decided he'd had enough. He returned to the USA, married and temporarily came to live in the studio of our New York penthouse apartment while we were in California. While there he discovered something and called our attention to it. There in the apartment across the street and slightly below us, one had a good view of a bed pushed right up against the window with a man lying in it covered only by a sheet. Every morning at precisely 8:30, a women walks in, kisses him then turns and leaves. The naked guy proceeds to give all those with field glasses a good show. I didn't know about this until Marc discovered it. I have since moved to California. I wonder if he's still in the window. If so I certainly hope he's changed the sheets.

Next came an offer to do a show in Rome starring Alice and Ellen Kessler and Enrico Maria Salerno. The "Kessler Twins" had appeared on *The Danny Kaye Show* with some success when I choreographed "The Boy from Ipanema" for them. So they asked me to do their show in Rome. The success of the Gilda Mareno show was also a big help. Fortunately I could do the show in English and if I did need help, the Kesslers could translate for me. Enrico had a mild Italian arrogance but was a very capable actor and dancer. Alice and Ellen were a joy to work with, so rehearsals were not work at all but something to looked forward to.

The same cannot be said for the lunch break. It was between two and three hours. One day I suggested if we cut one hour off we could stop at 6 o'clock and have a longer evening. Some agreed and others didn't but offered to try. The experiment lasted just one day. They had shorter days when I worked on Alice and Ellen's numbers. Enrico rehearsed in there as well. The next problem I had was the pianist had terrible body odor. I thought I had the solution when one day I brought a bottle of cologne to rehearsal, sprayed myself with some and offered it to him but he said, "No thanks, I don't' use it." I set the bottle on the piano and at intervals I would repeat the offer but he never used it. I did the whole show with a smelly pianist. Fortunately the principals were professional and accommodating and we had fun.

Carlo Ponti was also involved in backing this show so one day he brought his wife Sophia Loren to the rehearsal to see a run through thinking she might be right for the film version. Since the character is one and the other is her alter ego, Sophia would play both parts. She turned it down so the film never got made. It was goose-bump time just to meet her in such a private atmosphere.

Opening night was a show in itself. This was the first show of the new season so the upper crust of Roman society would be arriving dressed in their most outstanding finery of Italian couture. I was not disappointed. The foyer was packed with the beautiful men and women of Rome swigging cocktails and complimenting one another. I did another quick check back stage and indeed everything was ready.

It was time for the show to start but nothing was happening. I ran into Franco Zeffirelli and asked, "Franco, what are we waiting for?"

He said, "She's not here yet."

Just as I was wondering who "she" was, everyone parted

Alice and Ellen Kessler and Enrico Maria Salerno

and Anna Magnani dashed in. She was rather disheveled looking and trying to get her open raincoat on even though it wasn't raining, followed by an attractive young boy fussing with his necktie, giving the distinct impression they had just climbed out of bed. I'm sure it was an act so she didn't have to talk to everybody. She rushed right into the theater and sat down. I'm not sure what was better, the show out front or the show on the stage. Whatever it was, it was a happening I'll never forget. Incidentally, the show got good reviews and had a long run - although I thought the book was weak.

(Postcard) "Hi, Best rom Positano, above you can see the view from Franco Zeffirelli's Terrace -Ellen & Alice

All my warmest memories. Hope to see you soon. Franco Zefferelli

   It was great to reconnect with Franco. That evening, Franco invited the Kesslers and me to his estate just outside of Rome. I thought it would be a little get together but it was an evening one can never forget. The place was full of entertainers, mountains of food, glamorous people and something going on at every turn. True Italian hospitality. That man not only can put a show on stage but he does it at home as well. What a fabulous ending to my working in Italy.

FRANCE

  The Cabots consisted of Dick Beard who acted as my assistant on many shows, his friend Frank Sabella and Marion Sanders. I staged this group with a roster of crowd pleasing numbers and they began to get great notices performing around New York.

  Soon, The Cabots came to the attention of Don Arden who put together the Lido shows in Paris. At a meeting at my place in Manhattan, Don proposed the Cabot's appear at the famous Lido.

  I asked, "At what point in the show would they appear?"

  He then went into a lengthy description of each of the "FABULOUS" acts he had choreographed for the new show, and when finished he boasted, "Then The Cabots will follow that - if they can!"

  I said, "That's okay I just wanted to know where they fit in." I knew Don's work and was not a bit intimidated.

Frank Sabella, Marion Sanders, & Dick Beard lit up the Lido.
Photo by Maurice Seyklow

In The Cabots killer number, "Satin Wears a Satin Gown," Marion is in a skimpy form fitting bodice wearing a big black velvet cape with a high wing collar. The boys are naked except for a little loin-covering dance belt. Marion enters running in a full circle completely covered in her black velvet cape then suddenly stops. Next shooting out and over the top of the collar is a big shock of her blonde hair. On a loud cymbal crash she turns front and whips open her cape revealing a fabulous body dressed in a simple tight bodice hugging a great figure. Already this reveal gets applause.

There is a smattering of applause throughout the number. Approaching the climax the music gets more exciting until Marion circles the stage in a fast run right up to Dick who snatches her into a straight arm lift and carries her high in the air on a run to the front of the stage. She falls face forward to screams from the audience but to be caught just before hitting the audience by Frank who was hidden under a table.

The audience jumped to its feet yelling, "Bravo! Bravo!"

I missed the opening night because of other responsibilities, but Will and I flew in the next morning. Frank and Dick and Marion met Will and me at the Orleans Airport the next morning arms loaded with copies of the great reviews. The French papers carried huge raves with full page pictures. They were a SMASH!!

Don Arden never spoke to me again. That seemed childish and didn't bother me in the least. The Cabots were a big hit and that was what I had worked toward. It was an extremely satisfying project. The Cabots played the Lido for an extended period after that.

SYLVIE VARTAN

Sylvie Vartan, the famous French star called on me to direct a TV special she wanted to offer the French as a New Year's gift to the French people. It was to be done at the Palais des Sports in Paris, and that was an added inducement for me. When I lived in Manhattan I used to spend my summer hiatus from *Your Hit Parade* in Paris and loved it. She didn't have to twist my arm for me to say yes. I was assured I would have everything I needed to shoot this special specifically English-speaking cameramen, stage managers and lighting director.

Well, only one cameraman in the whole crew spoke English. I relied on that one cameraman to do all the exterior work. Everywhere we shot with Sylvie we collected huge crowds. Fortunately I had taken French in school - it helped - but of course I didn't learn technical terms.

I learned all the French terms during camera blocking through this one dual language cameraman. It was a test.

I asked for a tall ladder to get a reverse shot to see the entire arena. "Oh! Oui, oui, oui, Yes, Yes, Yes." No ladder appeared.

Show night on my way to the booth to shoot the show, I entered from backstage and there under the stage was exactly what I had asked for. I reached in and hauled out the tall ladder I needed, and put it up myself. Maddening.

Fortunately Sylvie was in top form that night and turned in a great performance. She did a terrific show. Sylvie very graciously stayed to do some pick up shots for the edit and thanked me and we all went out to a sumptuous celebration for some great French food. The French adore her and can't seem to get enough of her. I must hand it to her, she doesn't shirk from hard work and does everything she can to please her audience.

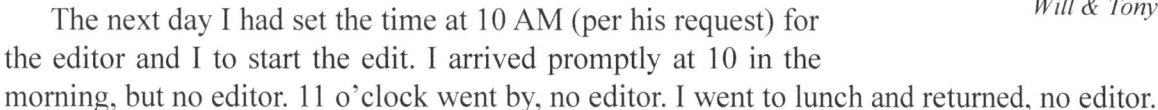

The next day I had set the time at 10 AM (per his request) for the editor and I to start the edit. I arrived promptly at 10 in the morning, but no editor. 11 o'clock went by, no editor. I went to lunch and returned, no editor.

Will & Tony in Paris

I did what I could to remain cool and finally at 4 o'clock, the editor, who had also recorded the show, arrived with no apology or explanation. Time being of the essence, we just proceeded to edit the show. On the next day of editing, so as not to get stuck with the long lunch break, I ordered lunch for everyone from my hotel to be sent in to the edit facility. The hotel outdid itself. At the specified time, in came four waiters carrying trays of food. They set up a table, dressed it and proceeded to serve the crew in a grand manner. Did I score points with this display? The trick worked. I had all the crew right there. I suddenly became a hero.

My contract had specified that I would be home in California for Christmas day. Because of time lost due to the French worker's lax attitude towards promptness, the production company had to fly me home for Christmas and then back again to finish the edit. We had only completed the first ten minutes of the edit before I left for Christmas.

Unbeknownst to me, those ten minutes were aired on French television as a Christmas preview of what was coming from Sylvie. I found the surprise more than a little frustrating. On my return to Paris, we went right to editing the rest of the show to everybody's satisfaction.

Lisa Kirk and her boys in "I Travel Light"

Chapter 8

Some Nightclub Acts 1958-1970

LISA KIRK

Lisa was a performer through and through. She was happiest when she was out there with the footlights and an audience. She found her niche with "Always True to You in My Fashion" in *Kiss Me Kate*. Her stage presence was remarkable and she used it well.

This talent also served her in the nightclubs. The Persian Room was like a second home to her. Her husband, Bob Wells wrote her some show stoppers. For the last club engagement we did in New York he wrote a song called "I Travel Light." I felt this opening number needed boys to fluff it up and it gave her a show-stopping opening.

Her boys Jim Brooks and Scooter Teague enter carrying a telephone in a hat box. Jerry Rush and Gary Crabbe carry a bag which when opened we see is really a bar. Lisa is sitting on a large traveling trunk carried by the four guys. In the song Lisa sings about why these items are necessary for a girl who travels. On her last note, the boys lift her straight into the air with the applause of the audience.

When we first performed this in the rehearsal hall for her husband Bob, he was overwhelmed and commented, "You stop the show with the first number? Amazing."

Then with Lisa still sitting on the big trunk up in the air, the boys start to sway gently left then right, and quietly Lisa segues into "I'm sitting on top of the world..." The audience breaks into applause again. It was remarkable. The whole evening became an unforgettable event. Each number seemed to resonate with the audience, which energized Lisa and her dancers to fill the room with overflowing energy.

> ***Lisa Kirk Captivates Plaza's Persian Room***
> ***Tips on Tables - By Robert W. Dana - September 18, 1958***
>
> *In her eighth return engagement last night in the Plaza's Persian Room, Lisa Kirk captivated everybody with the dramatic scope of her personality, illuminated by song, costumes, lighting, writing, musical direction and staging. Lisa was magnificent, opening with the froth of Robert Well's special number, "I Travel Light" and concluding with a colorfully contrived musically apt journey to "Far Away Places."*
>
> ...
>
> *In trying to come up with something new these days, cafe entertainers are inclined to stretch their act to the point of burlesque. When I heard that Miss Kirk would have four singing and dancing boys with her this time, I had grave fears. These proved groundless, as Jim Brooks, Jimmy Harris, Jerry Rush and Scooter Teague demonstrated.*
>
> ...
>
> *Staged by Tony Charmoli, with original music by David Saxon, Miss Kirk's performance, fascinating as it is throughout, probably will be remembered best for its finale/ "Far Away Places," in which she visits the Riviera in a brilliant yellow satin evening wrap with matching fox, goes Spanish with serio-comic overtones in a Spanish flamenco gown and concludes with an exciting interpretation of "Limehouse Blues."*
>
> *The boys join her in this finale, always embellishing the act, never cluttering it up. They say Miss Kirk loves her work so much she never takes a vacation. If this be so' let nobody gainsay her this privilege, for her performance in the Plaza's Persian Room is one that must be recorded among the greats of our time.*

The audiences in London gave Lisa the same reception. She

was a happy chicken and called to tell me. The show was recorded over there and they wanted her to extend her run. However, prior commitments brought her back home.

One thing about Lisa, she would never see a doctor. She had a thing about not going to them. Probably she was harboring maladies we didn't know about. Bob said the last time she really had to go, she looked smashing. She had her hair done. She wore a new blouse, a yellow suit and a matching coat and hat. He said she looked stunning. For years she had harbored a fear of hospitals and was afraid if she ever went in she would never come out. She was right. She got dressed for her very first visit to a hospital and never came out.

I have fond memories of her coming to parties at my house and knocking everybody out with her smashing wardrobe. She was lean and tall and could wear clothes well, plus she loved doing it. You could always tell Lisa was there by her laugh. She and Juliet Prowse were the two loud ones who could make chandeliers quiver with their glass shattering laughter. They can never be replaced.

THE FOLIES BERGÈRE

Around 1959, Michel Gyamarthy, the producer of *The Folies Bergère* in Paris, called me to choreograph an American production of the *Folies* for the new room in the Tropicana in Las Vegas.

I soon learned we had very different styles of working with showgirls and dancers. He'd yell out his directions with no consideration of how annoying they were, whereas I always simply directed and choreographed my requirements. Needless to say the cast preferred my way of getting things done and pleased me with good results. It soon resulted in my taking over and doing the whole show with better results.

One soon sees how difficult it is to be a showgirl carrying those big feather headdresses and walking up and down stairs in high heel shoes never looking down at where the next step is. I tried it and I can tell you it's a bitch. But, after long hours of working and dress rehearsals somehow the show gets pulled together. Only once did one girl come down the steep steps wearing a huge crown which kept slipping a touch with each step down and by the time she hit the stage her neck and crown had reached a steep angle trying to hold it on and she was supposed to say, "I am Messelina Empress of Rome," which always came out "Empwess of Wome." That didn't help. She looked like a drunken sailor and had the whole cast quivering trying to hold in their laughter. On her exit, the poor girl had to grab her crown before it fell off.

When things like that happened, Michel would get furious. On another note one could always tell when one or two of the showgirls acquired a Sugar Daddy by wearing a new fur coat and suddenly going out to dinner a lot. Why not?

In one sequence, the magician's trick was walking down the little runway right down to the footlights as he pulled a rabbit out of his top hat and holding it up for the audience to see. The trick was ok, but the problem was every night the little bunny would let loose with a big stream of piss right on the pianist below. One night he slammed the lid of the piano shut and climbed out of the pit yelling " I quit. I'm not taking any more of that rabbit pissing on me every night!" He got a big hand and a big laugh. The next night the magician and rabbit came farther forward to do his bit and spared the pianist who had been convinced to come back.

When I was next in Paris, Michel invited me to go to see *The Folies Bergère*, to see the French version of the same show we had done in Las Vegas. Before curtain time we were in the lobby and Michel ordered a glass of wine for me, then another, which I refused. We'd already had wine at his place before coming to the theater.

I looked at him, "It feels like you are trying to get me liquored up..."

He sheepishly shrugged and said that they had tried to duplicate what I had done in Las Vegas, but it wasn't nearly as good, so he thought a few glasses of wine would help. In a way he was right. The one glass of wine did help me get through it. The sets and costumes were great but the performances and staging in many cases were very French. Charming but no punch.

MARLENE DIETRICH

While I was in Las Vegas directing *The Folies Bergère* for the main stage of the Tropicana Hotel, Dietrich was appearing in the little theatre especially set up for her next door at the Desert Inn. Her show was carefully designed to make the aging star look as glamorous as she had been in earlier years. Her dress and invisible undergarments were so structured that they would practically stand up by themselves. Without them, she was a little old lady - but once she stepped into her costume (almost literally) and stepped on to a stage that was quite carefully lit, she became the Marlene Dietrich audiences expected to see.

I had to take the opportunity to see her on stage. After the show, I met her backstage. She asked me to join her for dinner at the Desert Inn. She said she'd like to talk to me.

I asked, "Where in the Desert Inn? It's a big place."

Marlene Dietrich

She said rather mysteriously, "Just come into the casino, you'll see."

I arrived, and there smack in the middle of the casino and surrounded by gambling tables and croupiers all roped off from the adoring public, there was her table - all set for dinner. She arrived and indicated for me to take the seat right next to her. Naturally we discussed her act and she asked me if I had any suggestions? So, I gave her a list of the changes I would make.

The changes I suggested were simple, but necessary and we put them in the very next show. She followed my suggestions to a tee and said it not only felt better but the audience response was better. She was very grateful. One more act saved. After that she went back to Europe and slowly faded to a glorious memory.

ELEANOR POWELL

My home town in Minnesota, Mt. Iron, was a typical small town excepting we didn't even have a movie house. The nearest one was in the next town of Virginia, five miles away. Rather than afford a bus trip, we'd hitchhike and sometimes risked hanging on to the back grid on the Greyhound bus and duck down so the driver wouldn't see us in his rear view mirror. This way was okay in the summertime, but in the winter, the rear tires would kick up a lot of snow and we'd be freezing by the time we got to Virginia. But what the heck, Eleanor Powell was worth it. It never entered my wildest dreams that one day I would meet her.

The day came when Richard Priborsky, a friend and pianist called one day with, "Tony, come down to the Goldwyn Studios, Eleanor Powell wants to see you."

I nearly passed out. I said, "I'll call you right back." I was in shock, I couldn't believe I was going to actually meet the star I used to hitchhike to see on the silver screen. I was in for a much bigger shock.

I arrived and there she was, I couldn't believe my eyes and when she approached and shook my hand I has in heaven. I was in for much more.

"Tony, may I call you Tony?"

"Why of course."

"I am putting an act together for Las Vegas and would like you to choreograph it for me."

Now I was sure I had died and gone to heaven. I was emotionally overwhelmed but was able to manage, "I would be honored to work with you."

Well we started right then, no pussyfooting here, we were in rehearsal.

In her old act, pre-Tony, she used to give the audience her recipe for making pancakes. I told her I wouldn't do her show if she continued giving recipes to the audience. I said that was so un-Eleanor Powell. I want the movie star Eleanor Powell.

We started discussing ideas and I told her of my admiration of her and what I would like to do for her. The idea was: Take the houselights down and in the darkened theatre you hear taps, the spotlight hits the curtain and slowly moves to the right down to the edge of the curtain, and tap shoes come into the spotlight, and they travel and keep tapping in the spotlight as the light slowly grows larger and larger as they get to the center and now the spotlight widens to full head to toe as Ellie turns, taps her cane, taps her top hat, strikes a pose and the announcer says, "Ladies and Gentlemen, Miss Eleanor Powell."

She holds a pose to show stopping applause then breaks into a soft-shoe to "Just in Time". She had a show stopping ovation every time. The first thing I did for my idol, and it proved to be a big hit.

I was doubly pleased with this success because when I first suggested this idea, she resisted by saying, "You can't open the show with a soft shoe."

I immediately countered with, "No you can't, but Eleanor Powell can!"

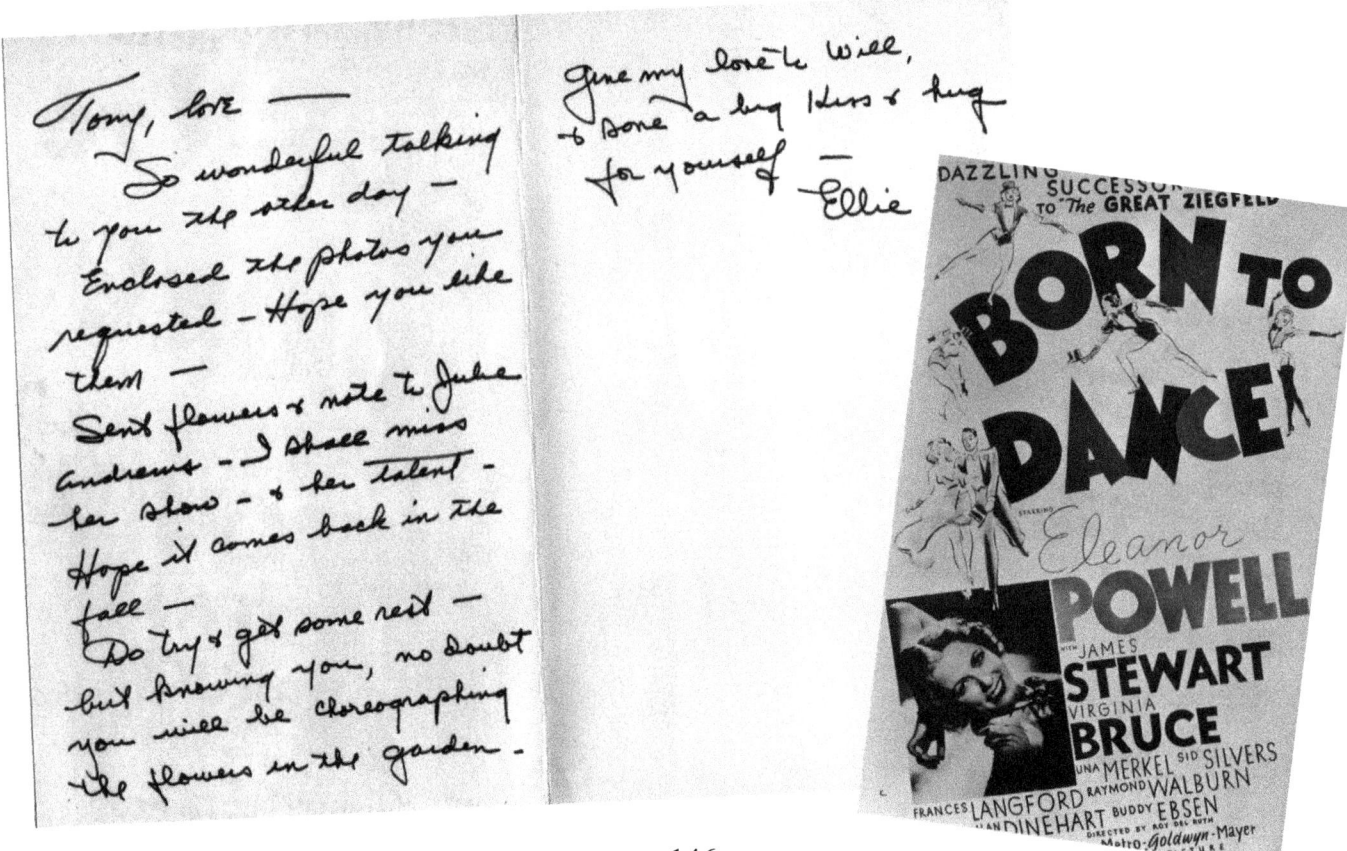

The rest of the show worked beautifully as well. We were both overjoyed and continued working together. With the club management, we had one more thing planned. Gwen Verdon was starring in a show on Broadway and she and Eleanor were great fans of one another, so we arranged a phone call from Gwen in her show on Broadway to Eleanor on stage in Las Vegas. Ellie took the call live on stage and it was piped so the whole room could hear. This had never been done before. So my first time out working with my first movie star turned out to be a fabulous and lasting affair.

Ellie had done the first part of her act in top hat and tails but a surprise was coming up to introduce the second part. The hotel had supplied an act called the Fontana Strings. It was comprised of about twelve violinists in black tuxedos who played semi-classical to contemporary music. Ellie had worked on getting her body back to performance weight and shape, so to show it off, we came up with wearing white semi high heel shoes with taps, a beautifully made white leotard, and over this a long to the floor black velvet cape.

The violinists started with a song and choreographed patterns of movement winding up into a diagonal lineup from upstage right to downstage left. On cue, Ellie made her entrance at the top of the diagonal wrapped in the floor-length black velvet cape down the diagonal of violins hardly moving her feet doing rapid machine gun taps. She seemed to be gliding down the row to the end, where she stopped and carefully opened one side of the cape punctuated by a violin chord, then the other side revealing her new lean dancer body to great approval from the audience. Another show stopper. Gracefully holding the cape open she slips into dancing to the strings. Another tremendous crowd pleaser. The whole evening turned out to be a fabulous "Welcome back Eleanor Powell" and my first time working with her. Her act received great reviews and she started performing it on the road.

Cut to the next performance in Florida where she went back on her word and spent twenty minutes of her act giving recipes to the audience. I was pissed and went knocking on her door after the show. She wouldn't open up for me, but through the closed door I heard. "I know, I know, I won't do it again." And she didn't. For my taste I just couldn't see her tap dancing while making pancakes. I kept reminding her she was a movie star, not Betty Crocker.

After this round of tours she pretty much hung up her tap shoes. This was a triumphant chapter in my career. It was the manifestation of a young poor boy's dream. My hitching a ride by hanging on to the back of a Greyhound bus to go see Eleanor Powell really paid off. Lesson learned, if you work hard and want it badly, nothing can stop you.

JOEL GREY

Fresh from his success in *Cabaret* on Broadway, Joel started work on a nightclub act. He was booked for the Fairmont in San Francisco so was anxious to get his club act together. He got Fred Ebb to do lyric's for fresh new songs and Marvin Hamlisch to do the music and little ol' me to stage and direct it. We all sat in my library and worked through the show. We had all worked with one another before so we dove in and seemingly in no time we had put the act together and were up in San Francisco.

I was familiar with the workings of the Fairmont Hotel Showroom so I knew what to expect. Our rehearsal with orchestra and lights went smoothly. Then came the anxious moments waiting to see how the audience would react. *Cabaret* was such a big hit and Joel was so good in it, that the minute Joel would start the song he'd get a big hand and usually a standing ovation. It certainly was a crowd pleaser. Having had the experience of performing to a live audience on Broadway certainly paid off in Joel engaging a night club audience. He was right at home with them. We were so happy for him, that those of us who drank went to the bar and toasted Joel after the show.

Right after this engagement he did a guest spot on *The Dinah Shore Show* so we had the pleasure of working together again. Being on the short side myself, I'm all the more pleased when I see another shorty succeed.

STANLEY HOLLOWAY

Stanley Holloway was famous in England and gained fame in the USA with *My Fair Lady* on Broadway with Julie Andrews, and then later in the film of the same name. He made a memorable impression as Liza Doolittle's dad, Alfred P. Doolittle who rocked the theater with his rousing rendition of "Get Me to the Church on Time." In 1960, Producer Martin Tahse, saw a one man show in him and asked me to stage it.

We called it *Laughs and Other Events*. Stanley had entertained in English supper clubs and theatres in London. When I asked why he wanted to come to play in America, he said he had just gotten tired of playing to the rattling of knives and forks in British supper clubs. He made the right move because American audiences loved him in *My Fair Lady*, and I found he was a hoot to work with.

We did our rehearsing in Canada and opening night went extremely well. The Canadian audiences ate him up with hoots and wild applause. Opening night in New York was also a thrill. The audiences loved him there as well. Stanley played out his limited run and moved back to England to be with his family. In all it was a fun and unforgettable experience.

CAROL LAWRENCE

Early one morning, in 1965, I watched the stage crew put up scenery and hang lights high up in the grid. One guy was on a tall triangular ladder on wheels, changing lights on the grid and as I stood watching for awhile an idea struck me. I asked the pusher if he could spin the ladder while the man was still on it. He assured me that it takes strength but very possible. I asked if I could give it a try. He obliged and started with a gentle turn and I said faster. It was tough but I hung on and raised one leg in arabesque until it got too hard to hold on and I said stop. It was great and the crew applauded me. I thanked him and immediately put a call into Carol Lawrence.

I was booked to do a nightclub act for Carol in New York.

I called and said, "Carol I have your opening number. Get a copy of 'Riding on the Moon' it starts with 'I walk under ladders.' I'll be in New York in a few days."

I got the ladder, had the wheels put on and had it delivered to the Mark Hellinger Theatre for rehearsal. Carol, Bob Lone, and Johnny Harmon, her two dancers, arrived for rehearsal. We were all anxious to try it. I told Bob and Johnny to grab hold of a rung on opposite sides and try spinning it.

When they got the hang of it, I told Carol, "Get on a medium high rung with both feet and start the song. Boys start turning walking slowly and speeding up as I direct you."

As the song progressed and the whole thing started to spin I told Carol, "Plié into arabesque!" As she did that I cued them to go faster and faster. I had forgotten *My Fair Lady* was currently playing there and the stage had scenery tracks. Too late! Crash bang, one wheel of the ladder got stuck in a scenery track causing the ladder to come to an abrupt stop and Carol went flying off - just missing the orchestra pit by inches.

On the ladder...

Brave girl that she is, she got up quickly, straightened up and said, "That was great let's do it again!"

By the end of rehearsal we had our opening number. Gwen Verdon came to see one of our rehearsals and was ecstatic with praise - which made our whole day.

Next the ladder was delivered to the Persian Room in the Plaza Hotel. We did a run through rehearsal and then it was show time.

"Ladies and Gentlemen direct from Broadway Miss Carol Lawrence!"

Bob Lone and Carol enter with Carol masquerading as missing Johnny Harmon and dressed in his tuxedo and top hat. After a brief interlude of Carol substituting as the missing chorus boy she makes a super quick change and in comes the ladder, Bob and Johnny pushing it with Carol midway up looking ravishing in a long white full-skirted evening gown.

Carol Sings, "I Walk Under Ladders." The boys turn the ladder simply at first but gaining momentum as the song progresses. The audience loves it. Gentle applause here and there. As the number continues, the turning gets faster and faster, Carol bends her knee deeper and deeper with the other leg sticking straight out behind her turning the dress into a huge sail. Now at the peak tempo and fastest spinning, the giant sail of a dress successfully whips two ringside guests off their chairs and on to the floor and all the drinks off their table.

The audience went wild with laughter and thunderous applause and an immediate standing ovation. This became the talk of New York and the Persian Room was packed every night. Poor Carol had to transport that ladder to every engagement she was booked after that - and there were many. It took guts and great strength to do this bit and she has both.

It is said of Carol that she is such a strong dancer she is able to do her own lifts and cook a five course Italian dinner at the same time and I'll not argue with that.

If you're ever invited to Carol's house for dinner, I suggest you fast for a couple days beforehand. The dinners tend to be loaded with umpteen courses and then some. She certainly is a true Italian with the portions. Once you are stuffed, you waddle from the table to the living room for dessert and entertainment. On departing, I'm very surprised she doesn't have a crane to hoist you into your car.

On another occasion, Carol was out of town with an act I had not staged for her when she called and said, "Tony I need your help, I'm having problems with my act. I am working like crazy and getting no response from the audience! Can you come and take a look at it?"

So, off I flew to Detroit to see her act. And she was right. After the show we sat down together in her hotel suite and tore the show apart. "You are working too hard at the start of the show. You start off with a can-can number. What if you lie back on the piano and do the kick in the air- that won't kill your energy like with a standard can-can kick." I suggested thirteen revisions and asked if she could possibly handle that many, I had to fly back to New York.

Her reply? "I've got to."

She called an extra orchestra rehearsal and that night she performed the improved show. Evidently the revisions worked because after the show she called me in New York and thanked me over and over and said "They were applauding even when I was sitting down! You're a genius! I even got two standing ovations." Our friendship solidified even further.

Robert Goulet was a handsome prick of a husband, violent and abusive. On one occasion in Lake Tahoe we were rehearsing a soft shoe number that he and Carol were going to do in their next engagement and he was simply rude to her through the entire rehearsal. My presence didn't stop him even though I objected and tried to stop his rude behavior several times. There were other occasions too tough to mention and it was a thrill to me when I heard that they were separating. I was glad Carol would be free of such treatment.

Her two sons, Michael and Chris, were very sweet to their mother and to me. One day, Carol's maid and the two boys picked Carol up at the rehearsal studio. Chris and Michael were in the back seat of the convertible. Carol sat up front and as they drove off her two kids yelled, "Thanks for taking care of our mother." Carol gave a big motherly smile as they rounded the corner and were on their way.

Carol wrote the following and insisted I put it in my book:

> *I've had the honor of working with many renowned Broadway and television choreographers over the years, but Tony Charmoli has remained my favorite not only because of his endless creativity and innovative concepts, but because he makes every day a joyous event filled with his charm, wit and love of theater. I am ever grateful to be a colleague and friend of this Renaissance Italian master.*

BOBBIE GENTRY

Around 1968, agent Jules Sharr brought Bobbie to my house one day with a "Tony this is Bobbie Gentry, she needs an act for Las Vegas."

She appealed as a good-looking girl in jeans carrying a small ukulele. I knew of her because she had a big hit at the time with "Ode to Billie Joe." She sang a few other songs to demonstrate she did have others in her repertoire. In fact, she was one of the first female country artists to find success writing and producing her own songs.

We agreed we should fluff up an act, so hired two boys, Richard Larson and Carlos, to support her. I went out with a camera and shot scenes supporting the lyrics of the hit song, but certainly didn't use a body floating down the river as some interpreted what the lyric's implied. I scattered a small bunch of field daisies floating down the river instead.

This little film seemed to support Bobbie well during the song. Other numbers were done by the Goose Creek Symphony and the boy dancers during Bobbie's costume changes.

She designed her own wardrobe and she often called me into the dressing room to ask my opinion.

In one case she stepped out in a costume that was very high cut and asked, "What do you think of this one?"

I responded, "Bobbie, if you wear it, I think you'd better shave."

She looked in the mirror, gasped and blurted out, "Oh! My God!" She quickly covered her crotch with her hands and darted back behind the screen. End of fashion parade. She did have a good sense of humor.

The Las Vegas engagement seemed to go well, and she moved the show to Harrah's Casino in Lake Tahoe. There she befriended Bill Harrah the owner of the casino who smothered her with lavish gifts of a car, jewelry - you name it. But, her marriage to Bill Harrah didn't last long. That's as far as I know. I haven't followed her career too closely. But we did put on a good show together.

Bill Harrah gave Bobbie a statue of a dandy cock, which she gave to me. It had such a fun sensibility I had to paint it. The statue is long gone the way of fragile things but its spirit lives on in the painting I called, "Bobbie's Cock." It now resides in the guest room of my friend Roger Case.

Ella, Tony, & Bernie Green who was involved with the show's music.

Chapter 9

SOME VARIETY SHOWS & TELEVISION EVENTS (1968-1990)

There have been a multitude of specials and variety shows that I have been involved with either as a choreographer, a director, or both. More than I can really remember, but here are a few stories that come to mind...

THE MAGIC OF ELLA FITZGERALD

In 1968, the producer Jackie Barnett called me to direct an Ella Fitzgerald special featuring the Duke Ellington Orchestra. Ella is one of my favorites so there was no hesitation in saying, "Yes!"

We met at her house and went over the details and the rundown of the show. During rehearsal I could see Ella perspired a lot under the duress of performance. That would present a problem when shooting close-ups so I suggested perhaps she could sing without the wig.

That was not an option, so I asked if she was good at lip sinking and yes she would do that - so problem solved. We recorded the entire song for performance excellence then went back piece-by-piece for some closer dried off close-up lip sync shots. It seemed to please Ella and everybody else. And all agreed the wig was necessary. Her lip-syncing was right on. The pick-up shots presented Ella at her best and as the star that she was.

I showed Ella the final result and she graciously thanked me over and over - she was so pleased. No pickups were necessary on the Duke and his orchestra. She sang some great songs on that show: "Satin Doll," "Things Ain't What They Used To Be," "Take the 'A' Train."

It was a marvelous show.

THE SHIRLEY BASSEY SHOW

Producer Jackie Barnett brought me in to direct Shirley Bassey in a solo concert style performance that would air in Sept 1968. He alerted me to a previous experience of trying to shoot a show with her when something had upset her and she walked off never completing the show. Obviously, this was a warning that she must be treated with kid gloves.

Prior to the day of the shoot I had a meeting with her and learned she started as a dancer who could sing, and had quite a career in Ireland and England. Right off the bat we seemed to feel comfortable with one another. I thoroughly described my ideas of staging with her, so rehearsals went very smoothly. She had elaborate costume and gown changes and when she got to her famous "Goldfinger" number, her gown was yards of gold chiffon.

On the shoot day, it was all going well until she made her entrance for "Goldfinger." I had set up a large black wall in front of the cyc, and Shirley entered through a door in the wall she was back-lit with vibrant gold light so that she practically glowed in the darkness. It was theatrical and lovely with panels of chiffon that she waved up and down on her entrance. There was no question this was a major star entrance, when her heel got caught in all that fabric and she slipped and fell flat on her butt, and wrapped in yards of chiffon - she just laid there.

Jackie Barnett gasped and said, "Oh my God. We lost her again!"

My instincts gave me a nudge and I quickly opened my mic and asked, "Shirley, is that in? If it is, I missed it, would you mind doing that again?"

Still lying on the floor all tangled up, she replied, "What? The fall on my ass?"

I said, "Yes!"

She picked herself up and played right along with me with, "I'd like to do it again but without the fall on my ass if you don't mind."

Our producer Jackie Barnett grabbed and embraced me until I couldn't breathe. He was so grateful.

Shirley turned in a great show. We somehow bonded and she invited me to come to see her show at the Persian Room of the Waldorf Astoria, in New York. I loved that idea, so Will and I flew to New York to see it. She was terrific and even introduced me to her audience and told them about the slip on her butt. She had them laughing and we had a good time all over again. After that she went back to Europe and I haven't seen her since. She is a unique talent.

THE KING FAMILY SHOW

In 1969 I was also offered the job to direct *The King Family Show* starring (naturally) The King family, who had an image of being straightlaced Mormons. I knew *The King Sisters* had a good reputation as a singing group, a Grammy nomination and a lot of hits during the Big Band era with the Alvino Rey Orchestra, but I was less familiar with the rest of the Kings who constituted the musical family group which numbered up to thirty nine members.

After a few meetings with Vonnie, I accepted. Vonnie (the lead singer of *The King Sisters* and producer of *The King Family*) was the whip cracker and could keep the younger

Photo courtesy of The King Family Archive/ Polly O. Entertainment

kids in order and on time. The quartet of Vonnie, Luise, Alyce and Marilyn were very professional and rehearsed as required, but when I called for the entire family to report to the stage it took them over half an hour to amble to the stage which was only five minutes away from their rooms. It was maddening. But, Vonnie stepped up. I'd tell her this delay was costing money and immediately she shouted Gestapo-style for everyone to hurry, "Alright everybody on stage double-time and I mean now! DOUBLE-TIME! MOVE IT!" They minded Vonnie. She was a great help.

The music for the show was pre-recorded at a studio in the Valley and I observed even in the long hours of work, that a few of the teenaged boys in the family seemed to get happier and happier as the work went on. They kept going in and out of a door which led to the parking lot. Finally, I took it upon myself to go out and see what was happening out there. A big party in Alvino's parked trailer-van. The men were drinking and I could smell something being smoked in the boys' dressing room…and I was surprised. But it was 1969 - all the world was exploring a bit at the time.

Alvino was mixing drinks and smiled, "Now that you know, what'll you have?"

I sighed, "Well, I still have work to do, so I'll take a rain check for when you invite me to your house."

That did happen in the not too distant future, and we all had a very good time. In addition to the 13-episode series, I also directed three TV specials for *The King Family* and one for King Sister Marilyn and her husband Kent Larsen. All in all, the Kings are a talented and closely knit family with great respect for one another and they always put on a great show. Truly good people who were fun to work with.

MAHALIA JACKSON

Mahalia had a great sense of humor. She came up with a few corkers that really need her to tell to get the impact. But, one day she had a finger wrapped with a splint and when asked, she explained that she didn't like flying so she always took the train. She had been asleep in the upper bunk and fell out and broke her finger. I'm sure it hurt, but the way she told the story it left us falling out of our chairs. She had a great sense of humor.

Groucho Marx was a guest on this special and was always on time for rehearsals. One morning Helen Traubel, who had just left the Metropolitan Opera Company in New York and was making guest appearances, was booked to guest on Mahalia's show. On this morning she was late for rehearsal. Soon the door opened and Groucho, seeing Helen, who was a large girl, called out, "Hey Helen! Pull up a couple of chairs and sit down." Helen shattered the windows with a burst of laughter and indeed pulled up a couple of chairs but sat on only one. Putting these two on the same show gave us one of the funniest rehearsal periods I've ever been through.

THE ANTHONY NEWLEY SHOW

Anthony Newley had a big hit on Broadway with *Stop the World I Want to Get Off* and he was to do a television special in 1971 called (of course) *The Anthony Newley Show*. I wasn't familiar with Mr. Newley, but what really enthused me were his guests, Diahann Carroll and Liza Minnelli. The initial get together went very well and we settled on the songs each of them would be doing on the show. But when I went over Liza's material with her, I had to put my foot down.

I asked Liza what she thought she would sing on the telecast she said, "I think I'll sing 'Swanee'."

I immediately replied curtly with, "Over my dead body! Your mother isn't even cold yet and you want to start with imitating her? I knew your mother and I don't think she would like that at all. You should create your own identity, and when you're established as Liza Minnelli, then you can include some of her songs." I was pretty strong.

Fortunately Peter Allen, the Australian singer, who came with Liza agreed with me and helped Liza to change her mind. Fairly quickly, Liza agreed and everything worked out just fine. She ended up singing an upbeat take on "I Wonder Where My Easy Rider's Gone." She definitely made the song her own. Now everybody knows Liza Minnelli as LIZA with a Z and not Judy's imitator. Now it's ok for Liza to include some of Judy's songs in her repertoire and not be slammed for it. Liza is her own star and has made her own indelible mark in the biz.

Diahann of course was already well-established, as was Anthony. I must say it was a very compatible cast and it made rehearsals fun. The run through of the whole show went just fine. They were released to get dressed for dress rehearsal and the first audience was let in. The dress rehearsal audience enjoyed the show, then the cast was dismissed to get ready for the "Black Tie" air show. Now the real thing was going to happen. The Black Tie audience arrived and they packed the studio. One could feel the excitement growing and now it was show time! Music and applause.

Anthony did his opening song and introduction, then introduced Liza, who also did very well. Next came Diahann - who had done better in her dress rehearsal performance. I heard a couple of notes I knew she wouldn't be happy with. When she finished after all the applause, I announced over the mic, "Diahann, this is Tony up in the booth, and we up here thought that you did a terrific job with that song, so we'd love to hear it again. Audience wouldn't you love to hear it again?"

Naturally they all yelled, "Yeah! Yeah!"

"Diahann, what do you say?"

With a big sigh of relief she replied, "I'd LOVE to." And she did and did a brilliant job, topped by a rousing standing ovation of approval from the audience. Then she supplied me with hugs and kisses after the show. She knew she had goofed on a couple of things and ever thankful I caught them and had her do the song again. The whole cast did a great job. That show should be run again. Particularly to hear and see early Liza.

I always liked Diahann. Years earlier, Diahann did a guest appearance on *The Danny Kaye Show* and arrived looking fabulous in a smart-looking suit. When she arrived the next day in the same suit, I just had to teasingly remark, "Diahann, I guess someone didn't go home last night."

She coyly answered, "Oh Tony, you're terrible!"

"Ah ha," I said," You see I'm right!"

But she never offered any other details - nor denials.

On the evening before Easter, Diahann and a friend were having dinner at Le Dome. Will and I were in the rear of the restaurant and had just finished at an Easter dinner party. On our way out we stopped at her table to exchange greetings and best wishes for Easter. As we were leaving, Diahann shouted after us, "Remember tomorrow when you're biting into that chocolate bunny think of me!"

JULIE ANDREWS

The world came alive with the sound of Julie and I had the good fortune of meeting and working with her. When I first saw her on Broadway in *The Boyfriend* I said, "Now there's someone to watch!" Little did I expect that years later I would be working with her. First, we had her as a guest on *The Dinah Shore Show* and Dinah and I agreed she was a talent.

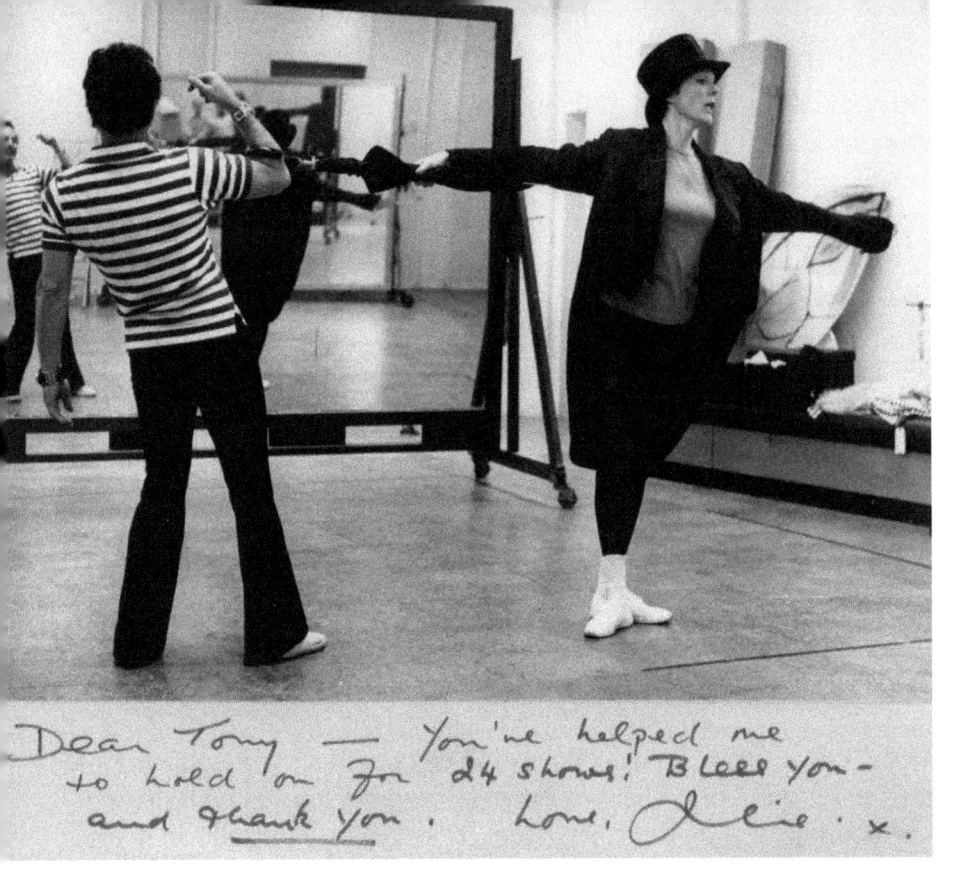

Dear Tony — You've helped me to hold on for 24 shows! Bless you — and thank you. Love, Julie. x.

The real challenge came when I joined her on *The Julie Andrews Hour* an hour special series she did from 1972 to 1973. I was hired to stage all the musical numbers. Julie did everything from comedy, to drama, to light opera, to you name it, she'll do it. That sweet charming princess image can disappear in seconds because Julie can get right down and still be fabulous. Julie was quite something to work with. Very talented and there were many sides to her. It was amazing to see the care and attention she got from the whole crew.

Sir Lew Grade put up the money for Julie to do an hour series of her own. No expense was spared. A private helicopter picked her up at her beach front home in Malibu and flew her to the ABC Studios in the morning and took her back after work in the evening, no matter how late it was. In fact that really was a necessity for it wasn't advisable for a girl of her fame to be driving those distances alone at night.

Working with the boy dancers was always a gas and often hysterical because Julie was not what you call a trained dancer but she moved very well and when the boys would have to handle her in some of the choreography it always wound up in gales of laughter.

Angela Lansbury guested on one show, and I staged a number in which they had to do identical movements. They were dressed in long, sleek, white satin evening gowns. When I thought they were ready, I cued the music and they did the number.

When they finished, Angela said, "Well how was that Tony?"

I said, "It was just ok. You have to be sharper and move those hips more aggressively. Put more umph into it."

Angela turned to Julie and said, "Come on Julie, let's do it again, this time move your bloomin' arse."

They did and they did. It was great. The audience and crew loved it.

One of her guests was Gene Kelly. They worked well together and in one of their dance numbers instead of hoofing, "Just In Time" was done in a more sweeping ballroom style with some hoofing thrown

Julie Andrews, Gene Kelly and I on the set of Julie's TV series.
Photo by Gerald Smith, used by permission of the Gene Kelly Legacy

in. They looked good together. It was great fun. In all the years I had admired Gene I had never done a major work with him.

In another show Julie played a toy doll sitting on a table in the toymaker's workshop. All was going along well until a little live pussycat came into the scene. It was supposed to lend atmosphere to the shop but once it discovered Julie's crotch it kept close to it wandering in and out but never leaving her crotch. Up on her leg then back into the crotch. Somebody yelled, "It's pussy on pussy!' Julie couldn't hold it in anymore and just burst out laughing and we had to start all over again until we finally had to do the scene without the pussycat.

On another show Donald O'Connor was the guest, so of course we had to do a tap number. I worked it out so I could give Julie some easy steps and Donald could do his own.

While putting it together I would say, "Julie, you do this," and demonstrated, then I said, "Donald you'll do some of your Donald O'Connor bullshit, and Julie ..."

Donald interrupted, "Donald O'Connor bullshit?"

I said "Yeah. Or what do you call that great tap stuff you do?"

He said, "Donald O'Connor bullshit."

I said, "There you go."

Donald was a favorite, a very talented favorite and a sweet person. The last time I saw him was at a party at my house then soon after he moved to Arizona.

On one show we worked late, well into the early morning hours. Julie was singing a swinging jazz tune and I stood next to the camera coaxing her to be more jazzy. We did the number over and over and she kept hitting those high notes seemingly effortlessly.

When finished I said, "Julie, I just don't know how you do it. It's two o'clock in the morning! We should all be in bed, and here you are hitting notes only people in outer space can hear."

She replied, "Tony darling, it's simple. I'm not wearing any panties!"

Everyone busted into laughter and we had the energy to finish the evening.

Besides her talent as a singer she had a great sense of humor. I'm sure it came from hanging around the theatre when she was a little girl. As the surprise at the end of her mother and father's act in vaudeville, this little girl would come out and wow the packed houses. The theatres were packed because everybody came to see the little angel. Julie told me they couldn't afford little slippers so they painted little black slippers on her white stockings. When you gotta do it, you find a way to do it.

Julie and I got along great. When 4 o'clock in the afternoon rolled around, without fail, Julie would announce, "Tony - Teatime!" And the whole studio stopped cold. Orchestra, camera guys, lighting, cast, dancers, everybody took a break, and Julie and I would go to her dressing room where her maid would have tea ready for us. Julie and I had a good time just talking and telling jokes many of which I can't repeat here. She is a treasure.

One thing that got me was a country medley Julie was going to be doing. The medley was all right but, unbeknownst to me, she had a costume made specifically for this medley. She told me how great it was going to be. When it arrived, I was appalled. The medley was of good contemporary country songs but the costume looked like something out of the musical *Oklahoma*. It just didn't make it for me. She loved it.

Fortunately her husband, Blake Edwards, arrived and I brought him in on the situation. He agreed with me, the dress just didn't make it. I asked if she had anything more contemporary that would work better. He assured me she had a lot and would rush home to get something. He came back with an assortment of boots, Levis and a simple long sleeved white silk blouse. She put them on and we all agreed they were much better. In fact they looked great. Thank God for Blake and the wardrobe.

Blake said, "Now there, I saved that number!"

I was in New York one-day shooting models for Eileen Ford when I got a call from Julie. She needed help with a duet she was doing with Tom Jones. Could I come and help? I asked her what the problem was (she just said to come over and look) I'd see the "it." I told her when I broke the girls for lunch I could come over. She allowed that would be fine.

I taxied over, walked into their rehearsal and after all the kissing and hugging Julie told me they were having a problem with this duet would I fix it for them?

"Okay, let me see what you're doing. From the top."

They started to sing and after about eight or sixteen bars I saw the problem and called "cut." I walked up to them and said "Tom, don't touch the princess. Don't embrace her or try to kiss her, keep your hands off her and just sing the song. Now once again from the top."

They did it just as I had directed and Julie said, "Thank you Tony, much better." I went back to my photo shoot and finished up with the Eileen Ford models. I think that turned out to be a Two Martini Day.

In 2010, the Professional Dancers Society honored her at their spring event at the Beverly Hilton Hotel. Julie's appearance absolutely packed the place with the biggest audience of any previous recipient of this honor. Fortunately I was able to get to her and spend some time reminiscing and catching up for all the time we've been apart. She is special. And what's more I still do tea at 4 o'clock.

THE CHER SHOW

When Cher separated from *Sonny and Cher* and started hosting her own show in 1975, I was called in to choreograph the musical numbers that needed movement or out-and-out dancing.

On the first episode, the guest stars were Elton John, Bette Midler and Flip Wilson. Billy Barnes was on board to do special material and we had two fabulous women to work with. When you pair Cher with Bette Midler you're bound to get something going if you just leave the two of them to fend for themselves. We didn't do that, however. Billy came up with a duet that would turn them loose and have lots of fun.

He came to rehearsal one morning with, "Tony how does this sound to you, a Trashy Ladies medley?"

Well I jumped with joy. To think what I could do with those two broads! We started rehearsals immediately. I wish I had some film of the rehearsals. To see one out trash the other was worth some air time as well, but unfortunately we were the only ones to enjoy it. Now that it's too late comes the idea we should have taped the rehearsals. When we did do the air show they did a great job with selling the number - even to the ending when Bette Midler fell out of the pose. It really perked up the ending instead of spoiling it. I laugh just thinking of it.

Before going on the air I always did a check to see if everybody was indeed ready. As I came to Elton John's dressing room, he stepped into the doorway and asked, "Tony, what are we waiting for?"

I said, "Elton, we're waiting for the ladies."

He put his hands on his hips and replied, "Well, I'm ready!"

I answered "Touché!" Indeed he was ready wearing a fabulous Bob Mackie outfit and oversized colored glasses and almost out-dressed Cher. He joined her at the piano and the two of them went into a fabulous treatment of "Lucy in the Sky with Diamonds."

Flip Wilson, who appeared as his iconic Geraldine, rounded out the cast to help make this special very special for Cher's opening show.

The second show for Cher had Raquel Welch and Tatum O'Neal as guests. Tatum was still a very young girl when she came on the scene, so she had to have a schoolteacher in attendance while she was working. The school area was usually in a corner of the rehearsal hall. Rehearsals were generally carefully conducted with no hard slang or swear words because of the young ears.

I usually start the rehearsal with the star. I was standing in front of the rehearsal mirror with Cher and describing what we would be doing when Cher asked, "Tony, am I alone in this number?"

"No. Raquel and Tatum are also in the number."

Cher turned and looked in the direction of Tatum and her teacher, and shouted, "Hey Tatum get your ass over here, you got to learn this shit too!"

I thought the teacher was going to faint. But Tatum came running to join her. It didn't bother her a bit.

The next day Raquel came to rehearsal and I had her join them. Raquel is a pretty good dancer so the number came together quite easily. I put Tatum between the two of them and it worked fine. Even the teacher was pleased.

Working with Cher was quite easy and pleasant. She seemed very secure with herself and knew what she could and couldn't do, and when she looked good and when she didn't. To do comedy she was comfortable with tarting up or dressing down anything to make it happen. She could laugh at herself in the comedy situations then to follow up with that tall slim body dressed to kill, how could she not look fabulous in a Bob Mackie gown?

It's amusing to see how things change in this world. I think back to Cher starting this show of her own and there was someone I used to kiddingly call her coffee boy - or at least he used to bring coffee to her. He was none other than David Geffen. I think that's pretty hot.

I went out to David's beach house a very, very long time ago and was impressed with his collection of paintings. On one wall was one of David Hockney's famous Swimming Pool paintings. I found it amusing that my perceived "coffee boy" could afford a Hockney, and one of the famous ones at that. Now, I wonder how many he has collected. Talk about coming up in this world. WOW!

Working with Cher didn't cover a long period of time but the time spent is still a fond memory.

DORIS DAY

My experience directing the *Doris Day Today* special in 1975 was interesting from the standpoint of Doris herself. Here was a woman who was astutely aware of the Doris Day brand.

One day the wardrobe guy came into the rehearsal with a number of gowns to select from for the show. There were several gowns we liked, but when Doris came in to look at them, she agreed that they were nice gowns but that we wouldn't like them on her. As a good sport she modeled each garment. A couple were passable, but she was right. None were a knockout on her. She offered to bring in some of her own at the next rehearsal. On that day we had another fitting. She was one hundred percent correct. Each gown was much simpler than what we had been looking at. She seemed to look best in clean, simple lines and she understood that about herself. It turned out that the wardrobe for the TV special would come from her closet.

There was another thing she never wanted to see playback of any of the stuff I had just shot. She'd always ask, "Are you happy?" and a "Yes" answer would always bring, "Then let's move on."

The guest for the special was John Denver and they got on just great. Their vibes just seemed to flow together. We did have a rather complicated shoot where I needed them to change many different positions after eight bars or so, but they never questioned and went right along with my direction. Over the course of the production, other actors from other shoots in the building stopped in to watch what was going on and often applauded something they thought extra special. Added to that was our producer George Schlatter's constant, "Fucking great, Tony." It all contributed to the circus atmosphere.

The warmth between these two stars was something outstanding. Plus the antics of Tim Conway in scene with a long flowing black chiffon evening gown playing the cello was very funny. Then the impressions by Rich Little made this an all-around wonderful shoot.

There was also an outstanding performance by Doris singing "The Way We Were." I told her that as she was singing the lyrics, I would slowly float past her the handsome faces of the many major male stars she had worked with and many were no longer with us. It was a warm and touching effect. This also turned out to be very emotionally exhausting for her. I had to shoot the song several times before she could get through it without breaking down.

With the shoot completed she asked if she could come to the edit. I told her I never allowed anybody to an edit. She said she would sit in the back and never say a word. Against my better judgment I said OK. She did what she said she would, so sat rather far back.

Just as I tested the first edit she said, "You're going to use that first close up aren't you?"

I slowly turned and raised an eyebrow. Immediately she got up and left.

She later returned with a big dog she had rescued just wandering the streets and a bag of lunch for the editor and myself and left, and never came back.

The night of the telecast I called her house to see how she liked the show. The maid answered, "Oh she's in bed. She never looks at herself. But I loved the show."

I said, "When she gets up, tell her she should look at this one, she was terrific. And tell her I said so. Also her songs with John were outstanding."

SHIRLEY JONES

Shirley was in a TV special I directed - can't remember the name of the special. But, one of the songs seemed to call for an outdoor location instead of a studio. The lyrics suggested a spring like setting. After much scouting of locations, I chose one of the grassy knolls in Griffith Park near Hollywood. Griffith Park is large with some areas developed like a city park, and others undeveloped and good for hiking. These varied areas curl around each other providing a lot of unexpectedly nice places to picnic that are private and also good for shooting a musical number in.

The weather was perfect on the chosen day so we gathered the camera crew and necessary equipment and set everything up on the mildly secluded location I had chosen. I choreographed some dance moves that Shirley could do on the grass, swinging on tree branches, in and out of bushes and all fresh spring like maneuvers. She looked lovely doing all of these things on the rehearsal shots so I called for makeup and hair for a touch-up and Shirley was ready to go.

I called "Roll tape, music, and action!" It started out well, but Shirley got caught on a twig so we had to start over. Shirley was beautiful and the moves were all one could want. The swinging on the tree branch was perfect.

But as the shoot started up again, we became aware of some half-dressed young men coming out of the bushes to watch, and one stark naked and unintentionally entering frame. It was annoying, but at the same time we were all amused. I changed the angle of the camera and had Shirley do a different entrance than planned and was able to exclude the men from the background. She looked lovely and the picture was excellent so I called a wrap.

The men applauded and in unison yelled, "Thanks for the show!"

I shouted back "And yours wasn't bad either!"

PAUL LYNDE

I met Paul while still living in New York. I had used his friend as a dancer in a production I was doing, and he invited me to their apartment to meet Paul who was starting to make quite a name for himself in the clubs and on Broadway. Paul seemed rather pulled together at the time so we had a nice visit.

Years went by and Paul found himself doing work on the West Coast and in film. We had a nice reunion meeting but it wasn't long before news was out that he was drinking heavily and becoming difficult. At a party at my house one evening he took quite a liking to one of my guests, Allan Zolezzi who was quite a handsome piece of meat, and invited him to go home with him. Paul was quite drunk when they departed and when they got up to Paul's front door, a very drunk Paul turned to Allan and sneered, "What are you doing here following me? Get lost." And slammed the door in his face.

Of course Allen returned to the party and told us the story. In 1975, Paul got an offer to do a television special and announced to his producers he wanted me to direct and choreograph it.

I was summoned to a meeting with the producers to discuss this project, *The Paul Lynde Comedy Hour*. From what I knew about his social behavior I made it quite clear to the producers I would accept the offer to direct and choreograph his TV special on condition that there be no alcohol in his dressing room and he comes to all rehearsals totally sober. I made the stage managers and dresser check his dressing room every day.

I must say Paul adhered to the request and we got through the whole production with an excellent TV show with Juliet Prowse and Brenda Vaccaro as guests. All parties were pleased. However at the cast party afterward which was attended by the whole cast and crew and quite a few film celebrities, late in the evening Paul staggered in drunk as a skunk and making a giant fool of himself. Naturally this killed the party. That was the end of this chapter and I don't remember if I ever saw Paul again. It's a shame to see a great talent wasted like that. I think he moved back to New York. At least we separated as friends.

SHIRLEY MACLAINE

In 1976 I was asked to direct and choreograph the TV special, *Gypsy In My Soul*, for Shirley MacLaine. The intent of the show was to celebrate the work of the theater gypsy - the chorus line that is so often taken for granted. Despite her success, Shirley has never forgotten her roots as a dancer in the chorus. The whole show explored dance and the dancer and judging by audience reaction the choices paid off great.

The finale was to choreograph the entire audience. We had invited dance schools to send a specified number of students to be the audience for this event. Shirley acted as the choreographer out front calling out the different steps and it was great to see a full audience dancing. The payoff? She would invite the whole audience to come to the stage and lead them in a high stepping grand finale. It was triumphant!

We had wanted Chita Rivera to be her guest but the Network and sponsor wanted a bigger name so they brought in Lucille Ball. We had nothing against Lucy, after all she's a terrific star but what do you do with her on a dancing show? Lucy might have started in the chorus line, but those years were long past and even then dancing was not really her forte. I racked my brain to come up with an approach that would use Lucy's natural comic gifts and downplay her need to actually dance. I had an idea to play Lucy as a major star headlining in Las Vegas backed up by a group of dancers. It was what was happening in clubs with celebrities with minimal dance talent. Lucy would sing/talk the song while the dancers danced full out behind her. Then she'd do an occasional small leg movement and an occasional shift of weight and fast arm flourish ending. The studio audience got it because Lucy received a big hand on the finish.

My assistant, Dick Beard, made an observation the morning Lucy arrived for rehearsal. She was wearing a mink coat with a scarf covering her head and most of her face. She spoke to no one and was ushered directly to her dressing room. She would reappear an hour and a half later in time for rehearsal all made up and coiffed looking great. Dick gathered Shirley and me and quietly said to us. "There is no Lucille Ball, there is just a little old lady who arrives in the morning and they paint Lucy on her".

We did have one major problem with her. Her memory was very poor. For example. I had staged a duet for the two of them with movement and lyrics. We had rehearsed this number for a week and then went to orchestra and recording session. That went well and the next day we did a run-through with the music tracks.

When we got to this number, the music came up and Shirley started to sing and Lucy just stood there bewildered. She stopped the music and turned to Shirley and asked, "Shirley, what is this? You know I don't like surprises."

I couldn't believe it and Shirley was totally surprised as well and answered, "But Lucy we've rehearsed this number for a whole week."

She replied, "Let me hear it again."

I sent the track out and she went right into it like nothing happened and did it in one take. Go figure. But I liked Lucy and besides, years before she came beautifully dressed in all her Hollywood Glamour to my first exhibition at the McKenzie art gallery and bought three of my paintings.

While we were working on this special there was something rather daring that Shirley would do. We rehearsed at the CBS-TV studios way on the West Side in New York City and Shirley was staying way on the East Side. To go back to our respective hotels I suggested we take a cab, but Shirley insisted on walking. From CBS on the West Side to her hotel was a very long walk and going through that part of town was a very dangerous drug traffic filled experience. We'd pass several suspicious groups of guys just lurking around and rather scary. Several times we would cross over to the other side just to avoid coming too close to them and she still would insist on walking. I'd stop at my hotel and insist she call when she arrived at hers. I guess she always made it. She's still here and doing just great.

Gypsy In My Soul was nominated for three Emmy Awards and won two; Outstanding Special - Comedy-Variety or Music, and I won the Emmy for Outstanding Achievement in Choreography. I also won the Directors Guild of America Award for best TV musical. That made me very happy. I immediately called Shirley and it made her happy too.

⁂

Later that year the producer, George Schlatter was putting together a TV special for Shirley about contemporary subjects in America, called *Where Do We Go From Here?* It featured the talents of The Electric Light Orchestra, and Les Ballet Trockadero de Monte Carlo, among others. I had been asked to direct and this time I had Alan Johnson help choreograph as he has a great relationship with Shirley and I was really busy in those days.

George called me into his office and said, "Tony, I have a problem, the comedy sketch the writers have come up with for Shirley just isn't making it." A few minutes later I went to him with an idea that sent him into gales

Shirley with Les Ballet Trockadero de Monte Carlo. You must seek them out - they are marvelously funny. CBS/Wikicommons

Shirley at a Christmas Party at my house, with Tad Tadlock - my assistant from the Miss Universe Pageant standing with us.

of laughter and he said, "You fuckin' little dago, that's fuckin brilliant."

My plan was to have Shirley in an old folks' home fixing her lunch. She'd be padded with beanbag tits, which could swirl and move plus a grey wig, and a medium long loose black dress. She would be making a salad to the music of "The Stripper." I asked the prop man to get me a head of lettuce, some hard-boiled eggs, celery and a strainer. I had Shirley sit down and watch. I put the music on and proceed to make the salad, first washing the lettuce at the kitchen sink swinging my hips, washing the lettuce, putting it into a strainer then spinning it round and around and bumping stripper style, then throwing it over my shoulder piece by piece into a bowl. Then I carry it to the sideboard doing bumps in time with the music on the way. Next the hard-boiled eggs - I rolled them back and forth to crack the shell, all with a sexually fulfilled expression and proceeded to peel them piece-by-piece. Then I tossed the salad and carried it to the dining table bumping all the way and finally sat and started to eat the salad with a sweet, demure and saintly expression. On applause I look at camera and daintily dab the corners of my mouth with my napkin and wink.

Shirley broke up laughing and said, "Tony, just great! How does it start?" She learned it in minutes and added a few Shirley touches that spiced it up and it was a big hit. George and the writers upon viewing it commented "that's just great!" It worked and the fan mail was proof of that.

That year I was nominated again for an Emmy for *Where Do We Go From Here*.

While working on another dance piece for Shirley, there was a dance number in which she had to do a quick sit on a building stoop and simply cross her legs. All worked well until we did it full out till where everything starts to get exaggerated, as was in this case. Instead of simply bringing one leg over the other she developed the leg full out to the side then folded it in a big fan over the other. It was great but revealed too much under her skirt.

When I went out to tell her how to modify the movement she asked, "What's the matter could you see Cleveland?"

From that time on I have always called it "Cleveland."

Shirley and I also took care of a former American Ballet Theater dancer Paul Godkin. Unfortunately Paul was an alcoholic and was terribly scarred with brutal bruises he contracted in an auto accident.

Shirley always gave him a hundred dollars a week, which unfortunately would go for booze. Will and I would shop and keep his cupboard and refrigerator full with provisions as often as possible. He was a good cook and sometimes would come to cook dinner at our house and have a few shots at the same time.

Fortunately he was good company when he was sober, but impossible when he was drunk. Bea Arthur was a good friend of his. They often got swacked together. For his own good, Paul left this earth and we gave him a big send off out in the garden, toasting him with his favorite vodka. Shirley brought a huge bunch of white balloons attached to a large bottle of vodka. The balloons were released with everybody saying "May Paul rest in peace!" We did what we could to make his life at least bearable.

Shirley was tapped to do her show at the Palace Theatre in New York. We borrowed numbers from different shows we had done with her and added new material as well. We were pretty confident with the material and spruced things up here and there to spark it up a bit more. On opening night we were honored with the presence of Jackie Kennedy, looking outstanding in a long silver satin evening gown. After the show she paid a visit backstage to offer her compliments. She certainly wore the title "First Lady" very well but we changed it to "Great Lady" we were so impressed. Incidentally, Shirley did her usual killer performance and wrapped the audience around her little finger.

The show got great reviews and was booked to play London. After the opening night show in London, Shirley called me with "Tony, what have you done to me?"

I said, "Why, what have I done?"

She gasped, "The theatre is packed and there are lines around the block for tickets!"

I said, "Congratulations! That should make you extremely happy!"

Elton John was there opening night and it made him happy enough to write, "Seeing is believing and this lady captivated me. The lady is quite simply a lesson in professionalism for any other performer. For once a genuine standing ovation."

I am ever grateful to Shirley for recommending me to Mikhail Baryshnikov to direct the television special of his ballet *The Nutcracker*. It was a triumphant undertaking and still can be seen on television at Christmas time.

I have always sung Shirley's praises. Definitely one of a kind! She's still out there in great demand. Bravo!

CAPTAIN & TENNILLE

The Captain & Tennille Show aired from September 1976 to March of 1977. I directed their popular TV series and we got on just fine. They worked very closely as one, but had very different personalities. She (Toni Tennille) was very effervescent and he "Captain" Daryl Dragon) was very laid back. One other distinguishing trait, they were both strict vegetarians. In one scene where the action took place in a diner, there was a table with the usual dressing of napkins, salt and pepper, catsup and mustard. Oops! The catsup and mustard had to go, lest someone think that meat might be served in that diner. Fortunately food was not part of their act.

We had one accident. At a party at my house the caterer had made a beef loaf covered in cream cheese. Actually it looked like a cream covered chocolate cake and tasted very good. Toni unknowingly tried it and thought it was delicious until somebody told her that it was meat. Upon hearing that she actually became ill and had to go lie down.

Of course, being a vegetarian was a minor quirk when you consider how great she could sing. They are a perfect combination together. Their ratings were excellent and the show would have been renewed for a second season but they decided to focus more on their music and asked to be released from their contract. They hadn't expected their show to be such a hit - but that's my job! They had a great show.

LIBERACE

Liberace was an excellent pianist, a great entertainer, and a big camp, but I knew him as Lee - a dear and funny friend.

In 1979, Lee had an offer to do a TV special for Valentines Day with Sandy Duncan and Lola Falana as guests and he asked me to direct and choreograph it. Bob Banner was the producer and since he knew I knew Liberace as a friend he kept his distance splendidly. I had a nice history with Lee and he trusted my directions. He knew I would make him look great - like the star he was. So, he went along with everything that Bob and I, and the writers had planned for the show. We were to start with Lee in bed and see him get up in his fabulous pajamas, do some simple runs on the piano next to his bed, and head for the shower. Since Lee was not exactly an Adonis undressed, we agreed to have him submerged in a sunken tub. When he got in and dipped all the way, the water rose up to his chin. It looked funny with just his head floating in the water - I thought it needed more. It came to me in a flash. I got it! For a Liberace bath we need soap bubbles. The prop man was quick to supply some mouth blowing bubble wands. I got the crew and anybody standing around, including myself, to blow bubbles just out of camera, while he accompanied himself on a small keyboard resting on the edge of the sunken tub just singing away. It was very Liberace.

Next we picked up Lee walking down the mirrored corridor containing a mirrored piano on his way to meet the girl guests in the breakfast room. It was a lavishly campy meeting but quite Liberace elegant at the same time. Breakfast was brief and they all piled into Lee's Rolls Royce with two white Russian Wolfhounds and his lover, Scott Thorson, in full livery as the driver. We are on the way to his little yacht for the birthday celebration. I had the camera guy shoot the Rolls head on, coming down the dock with the water on the right, then follow the car closely till the picture pulls back to reveal his little yacht to be the Queen Mary. It worked beautifully as over-the-top Liberace. The limo stopped at the gangplank lined with musicians playing their welcome. First the two elegant white Russian Wolfhounds on a leash and the chauffeur enter up the carpeted gangplank followed by Lola Falana and Sandy Duncan. Now in a huge red velvet robe comes Liberace himself with a long velvet train grandly sweeping the red carpet and the musicians following still playing as they all enter his yacht. You couldn't ask for anything more Liberace.

The celebration dinner was very elaborate and the wine and everything else was plentiful including the decorations sparkling up the dining salon. Everybody seemed to be having a grand time and ready for the evening entertainment, which was soon to begin. Lola was a knockout with her songs, and Sandy and the boy dancers really rocked the place. Lee did a few numbers which we knew would satisfy the guests and saved some for later on in the festivities. Next the balloons were released and dancing began amongst all the balloons on the floor.

To wrap the whole thing up there was a good night number played on the top deck of the ship with Lee seated at a white grand piano. To end the fantastic evening Lee, Lola, and Sandy piled into a helicopter waiting on the deck to fly them back to Los Angeles. Now really, how Liberace can you get?

On another occasion, Juliet Prowse and Cathleen Nesbitt were at a dinner party at my house and Lee also came. He went to the bar and over my bar are two big antique gold initials - a "C" and an "S" rescued from the remodeling wreckage of a dime store. They were meant to identify the hosts - "Charmoli" & "Sanders."

Ray Arnett, Lee's assistant asked Lee, "Do you know what those initials stand for?"

Lee matter-of-factly said, "Cock sucker."

Juliet screamed with her loud laugh and almost shattered some of the crystal in the bar. This party was shortly after Lee had recovered from a rather long illness so he was the first to leave with a parting statement "Now if you'll all excuse me, I have to go out and earn some fresh money."

Another shattering burst of laughter from Juliet. She was a great party guest and often after rehearsals would say, "Tony, let's go up to your house!" We often did to hash over what we had done in rehearsal. I never did do a show with those two together. Too late now.

On another occasion Will and I were invited to a New Year's costume party at Liberace's. I happened to have a sequined jacket that was worn on *The Danny Kaye Show.* There were two sparkly Liberace-style jackets made - one for Lee and the other for Danny. Danny's fit me perfectly so I took it home just for the next occasion of being invited to Lee's house for a costume party. I thought this would be the perfect time to dress as Liberace.

On the way up to his house I said, "Will, there are going to be so many people dressed as Liberace, let's go back and I'll get into something else".

He said, "We are almost there! What difference would it make if there are lots of Liberace characters?"

We arrived at his house and to my astonishment I was the only Liberace look-alike. Naturally, Lee with a giant smile was happy to give the prize to me. The Prize? His autographed cook book - which I have never used.

RAQUEL WELCH

In the 1980 TV Special I did with her called *From New York with Love,* Raquel could show her true colors as an actress, dancer, and comedienne. She is also a beautiful woman who is not timid about stepping out of her glamorous image for the sake of comedy.

In the opening to *From New York with Love,* she steps off the plane, and stands at the top of the stairway looking very glamorous. Paparazzi blinding flashes were going off like crazy, reporters asking questions, bright sunshine, picture perfect when suddenly a downpour of rain changes the whole situation. She starts rushing down the steps and by the time she hits the last step she is totally drenched destroying her whole glamorous look. For any other woman this would be disaster, but Raquel still looked amazing even when drenched with rainwater. Fortunately we had to shoot the scene only once.

One subway production number showed her off particularly well. While waiting for a train she meets up with a variety of dance styles. An urban crowd number leads into a nose-in-the-air number with well-dressed black tie, evening-gowned Eastside Manhattanites coming from a formal party. The uptown folks exit, then she has an exciting encounter amidst a Latino gang with an up-tempo feeling of two gangs clashing. One girl engages Raquel in a stylized bitch fight. Then another train stops and a gang of leather clad

Raquel, myself, & Betty White at my Christmas Party.

guys sweep Raquel on to a train car with them. Raquel is in a very short red satin dress with two large open holes on each side showing very lovely skin. Any undergarments would be visibly distracting, so there were none. They engage in a number with lifts and innuendos of a sexual nature that are quick to raise the temperature, particularly if you consider that she is not wearing any undergarments. It was a steamy number. Then this led into a final raucous disco number. This whole sequence showed Raquel's true star quality.

In the show, Raquel continues her tour of New York in a cab. Mickey Rooney played a mythical angel; an out of this world cab driver who drives Raquel to all the different locations in Manhattan. When he was good as this character, he was very good. But one time he really was a pain in the ass. We were shooting in Central Park and Raquel, the crew, make up, audio, everybody was on time and ready, but no Mickey.

Much later when he did finally arrive after all the greetings, he said. "Okay, what do I say?"

I couldn't believe it. A script had been delivered to him at least a week before this shoot. Now the whole crew and Raquel are stuck out in Central Park. We could do nothing until the prop man ran out to find an art store, get some supplies, write out Mickey's dialogue and have him read through it before shooting. I guess it was our good fortune this happened only once. Fortunately, after that Mickey really was great and embraced the character and delivered a smashing performance. In fact the whole special went very well and showed off Raquel's vocal, dance, and acting talents and physical beauty. A knockout!

LOU RAWLS

In 1980, Lou Rawls Parade of Stars was at the Tropicana Hotel Casino in Las Vegas to benefit the United Negro College Fund with all black talent donating their services. Lou opened the event with some of his wonderful songs and got things off to a great start. He told the audience what the event was all about and thanked the artists for donating their talents to this admirable institution.

He then introduced Sammy Davis Jr. who really got the place rocking with his wonderful energy and very upbeat performance of his great songs and dancing. Lou announced that Bill Cosby would be performing later in the show. Next came the Pointer Sisters and they too captured the audience with their stellar carrying on and sparkle.

Bill Cosby called to tell that he would be late, but he'd be there. In the meantime, Lou went on to do some more songs and entertainment. Then came another filler act.

Still no Bill Cosby.

So Sammy Davis said he would go out and do more. Then to help fill the time while waiting for Bill, the Pointer Sisters did a whole different show. Lou also went out and did more show. Since the audience was starting to thin out, Lou finally just wrapped up the show. Bill Cosby never did show up. I never heard why. I'm sure he had a good reason for not showing up, but we should have been notified. It was disappointing.

RUDOLF NUREYEV

In 1980, I directed Julie Andrews' *Invitation to the Dance with Rudolf Nureyev*. It was hosted by Julie Andrews and Rudy Nureyev and held at the outdoor Merriweather Post Pavilion in Columbia, Maryland.

The show embraced all forms of dance from Martha Graham to Broadway. Rudy agreed to do it if he could do "I've Got Your Number" from the Sid Caesar Broadway show *Little Me*. My good friend, Swen Swenson, had replaced Bob Fosse in the show on Broadway, so I found him on tour with a show in Detroit. I called and indeed he had a recording of the number and would teach it to me if I flew to Detroit. Of course I did and had a great time learning it. I immediately flew back to New York to teach it to Rudy. He was a quick study and good at it.

He was also quick to get out of his rehearsal clothes to go cruising the 42nd street movie houses. I warned him about the possibility of getting arrested and the possibility of contracting STDs, but he paid no attention. In his mind none of that could happen to the great Nureyev.

The day came for the shoot at the Merriweather Post Pavilion. All the cast was ready and anxious to get on with the show, but no Rudy. The audience was getting restless.

I told the stage manager to knock on his door, but he said he had done that several times.

I ripped my headset off and said, "I'll be right back!"

I went to Rudy's dressing room and I just walked in without knocking and there was Rudy sprawled out on the bed in just a dance belt.

I said, "What's going on? The place is totally packed with people over flowing the hillside and they're getting very restless."

He said, "I don't know which tights to wear."

Spread around his dressing room were twelve pairs of tights to choose from... and they were all grey.

I grabbed the pair nearest me and threw them at him and shouted "Here, wear these and get your ass out there double-time."

He did and the show was finally able to start. He co-hosted with Julie and she did well, but his reading of the cards was sporadic and lackluster. I don't know if the huge crowd paralyzed him or what. He had done okay in rehearsal. We went on anyway. Julie was wonderful.

We had an assortment of talents from the world of dance showing off its diversity. Ann Reinking in particular was great and showed off Bob Fosse's style of dance with "My Baby and Me." She was terrific.

Fortunately I had carefully camera blocked the solo, Ruth, that Martha Graham presented and danced by Peggy Lipton. Martha made a point of thanking me after she saw the Telecast. Rudy's turn came now and after he danced to "Shall We Dance?" He tore up the stage with a brilliant performance of "I've Got Your Number."

The crowd went wild and didn't stop applauding until I announced over the sound system, "Mr. Nureyev has agreed to do the number again if you agree to let him rest for a few minutes." More applause and whistles of agreement and Rudy did it again resulting in the same boisterous reaction.

His dance performance was terrific, but he struggled as an emcee. He just was not good next to Julie. Off camera, Julie gave me worried looks as he stumbled through his bits. I knew I'd have to fix that later.

When the show was over I told the stage manager to bring Julie back. She didn't know I had released Rudy, and when she arrived she asked, "Poor Rudy, Tony what are we going to do?"

I said, "It's simple Julie, I've dismissed Rudy and I'm giving all his lines to you. The cards are ready, let me know when you're ready."

Julie brightened right up. "Thank you, Darling."

Julie hosted the whole show without a hitch. I thanked her and dismissed the crew. We edited Rudy out of the hosting sequences.

Final touch? The show was awarded an Emmy but I forgot to enter my name as director so I missed the chance of getting another Emmy. Tough!

BOB HOPE

Bob could be the nicest person you'd want to meet, but look out when something rubbed him the wrong way. That happened to me once and I vowed never to let it happen again.

Bob did have a great sense of humor though. We surprised him one night in rehearsal with the football team for *The All Star Super Bowl*. Bob didn't know that they would not be rehearsing in football regalia, as I'd had a fun idea.

The staff gathered in the rehearsal studio to witness Bob's reaction when the football team skipped into the rehearsal dressed in Shirley Temple polka dot dresses and blonde Shirley Temple curls. Bob just doubled up laughing. Hooray! We got the reaction we were hoping for. It really looked silly and the more we rehearsed the funnier it became.

When we did it on the actual show, we got the same reaction only this time the studio audience was involved. The guys were all good sports to go along with the joke. If I remember correctly, the whole show came alive with guests Lola Falana, Ann Jillian, Don Rickles, and Merlin Olson.

BETTY FORD

The birthday of America's 38th president Gerald Ford's was to be celebrated in his home town of Detroit in 1981, with Bob Hope as the Master of Ceremonies. A surprise guest performer was to be the former president's wife Betty. The surprise was for Betty do a dance number with Bob Hope. Secret rehearsals were held at Betty's house in Palm Springs. Bob and I would fly to Palm Springs and have lunch with Betty while her husband Gerald was away tending to his busy schedule.

This was a whole new world to me to see how well protected a former president is. There were guards behind distant trees, close to the house, and everywhere. Betty and Bob certainly were two quick studies for they both caught on quickly to the routine, and Bob and I were out of there well before the president returned home. Fortunately Betty had studied dance earlier in her life. We did this preliminary rehearsal one more time before flying to Detroit.

Betty and I had another brush up rehearsal in Detroit on the day of the show. Our pianist and I were in the rehearsal room before Betty arrived and already there were four security guys in the rehearsal room. We were checked out and cleared, and soon Betty arrived with a couple more security agents all carrying brief cases. Betty remembered the whole routine. I asked the security if they would like to join us. Of course they politely refused except one who stepped forward then quickly retreated. At least one had a sense of humor.

We all went back to the museum theater where the dedication was to be and the place was packed with important dignitaries from Washington. In fact there were so many, another room had to be opened up to take care of the overflow. A Washington dignitary made some opening remarks and introduced Bob Hope. The place went wild with applause and the show was on. It all went smoothly. At one point, Bob starts to do a dance then stops to say, "I can't do this alone. I need a partner. Will somebody join me?" Then Betty walked out to a pleasantly shocked audience who immediately gave her a standing ovation. Even Gerald the President was surprised. They did the number perfectly together and received another standing ovation. The rest of the show went off very well.

At the dinner afterward, Gerald Ford came over and thanked me for making Betty look so good. It was very gracious of him and even that was followed by a handwritten letter thanking me. It was an evening I'll never forget.

Bob received quite a number of gifts on this occasion and wanted to get them all back to his home in Burbank without having to pay to ship them or deal with fitting them in his luggage. So, since he and I were on the same flight back to California, he asked if I would carry a rather large jar of nuts on my lap

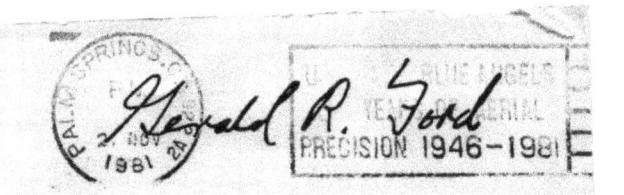

GERALD R. FORD

Nov. 25, 1981

Dear Tony:

This is a very tardy note of appreciation for the superb job you did on the Bob Hope Show at the Dedication of the Ford Museum in Grand Rapids. Everyone tells us it was one of the finest and Betty and I concur.

The "soft-shoe" with those two "hams" was fantastic. Congratulations on taking new talent and making it the hit of the show.

You have the heartfelt gratitude of Betty and me for making the show a tremendous success.

Thanks again for your many kindnesses and especially your friendship.

Best regards.

Jerry Ford

on the return trip. When we arrived at our destination he made it very clear he wanted those nuts back and that just because they were in my lap for five hours I was not to even think about keeping them.

JACK LEMMON

While I was directing *Musical Comedy Tonight* in 1981 for Sylvia Fine Kaye, I worked with a lot of great talent but I particularly remember working with Jack Lemmon. He had been up for the part of the Leprechaun in *Finian's Rainbow* in the revival Broadway stage production, but couldn't do it because he had a prior film commitment in Hollywood. Sylvia asked him to do it for her series and he was delighted - and delightful.

He was perfect in the part. I staged a dance for the deaf girl dancing around him while he sang, "If I'm Not Near the Girl I Love, I Love the Girl I'm Near." It's too bad we never got to see him do the role of the Leprechaun in the film. He looked so good just doing this little bit in Sylvia's lecture demonstration series.

Jack getting into character as Og the leprechaun

LILY TOMLIN

I had seen Lily do a lot of things from *Laugh In* to her Broadway show and concluded that this was one talented lady. When she asked if I would work with her on her upcoming 1981 TV special, *Lily Sold Out,* I was more than delighted.

I remember our first get together was a wonderful and beneficial meeting. The ideas were flowing and we came up with some fun things that cemented the fact we'd have a great time working together. Lily was already doing an act on tour with her principal character, Tommy Velour, a nightclub singer patterned after Jack Jones or one of those balladeers. She had a cucumber on a string swinging down the leg of her pants like a big dick. Tom Jones anyone? Very funny. We knew this character should be in her special, which was going to be taped in Las Vegas at Caesar's Palace with the character Tommy Velour as the headline entertainer. Lily suggested her character Ernestine should be sitting in a booth watching the show. I quickly added Ernestine should have a date and he should be Liberace.

Lily screamed with delight at the suggestion and asked, "Can we get him?"

The Emmy that Lily gave me next to one of my full size Emmys

I said, "He just happens to be a good friend of mine, I directed two of his TV specials and I'm sure he'll be happy to do it."

Liberace and I went out to dinner that night and I told him about her special and he loved the idea and immediately agreed to do it.

Getting Liberace had its price to pay. Bob Banner our producer was furious I didn't attend a little staff get together of no importance the same evening I had dinner with Liberace. The next day at the staff meeting, I told him I wasn't there because I was getting Liberace to be Ernestine's date for her special. The whole meeting erupted in laughter and applause. I think Bob was annoyed because I didn't invite him to dinner with Lee and me.

So Ernestine and Liberace, candelabra and all, sat in a booth enjoying Lily, I mean, Tommy Velour. It was the biggest camp of the season. We also had an overflow audience for this taping. It was fun to see Lily playing two roles at the same time. Everybody had a great time.

Lily was game to try many different things if she thought they had merit. "Born to be Wild" was another challenge. It required Lily to enter on a motorcycle, but she had never driven one. That day a driver came with his bike to show Lily how to operate it right there on the stage in the wings. I thought this to be dangerous and said so, but she said she was positive that she could do it. Music was cued and in she came on the bike and stopped right on her mark and did the whole number with dancers and all. Amazing and Bravo! The audience agreed with tremendous applause.

In this same TV special, there was another high point when Lily as a diving champion would dive from a high platform into a barrel of flaming water. When I suggested this idea to Lily I thought she would crush me with hugs she so loved the idea. Of course a professional diver did the actual dive. But Lily came up with the topper. After the pro did the actual dive she got out and Lily stepped into the barrel to do the clincher. I cued her and she ducked down completely submerged herself and let her falsies float to the surface then she popped up between them with a big smile. What an ending! I still laugh when I recall the picture and the whole TV special.

Not surprisingly the show was awarded an Emmy. Since there was only one statue, Lily had tiny miniatures made and gave one to each of us. An unforgettable experience and an unforgettable artist.

OLYMPIC GALA '84 GREEK THEATRE

Jane Fonda was one of several hosts of the Olympic Gala and did a very good job. She arrived with several choices of gowns and I chose one. She seemed to need to hear my reasoning, so I gave her a lengthy explanation of why that was my choice. It was all about lighting and location and she was very impressed with my lengthy explanation of how I came to my choice and went with it.

Johnny Mathis was one of the star performers and I tried one of the very new, at the time, hand-held cameras on him. I explained that the camera and the operator would be coming on stage and going behind him to see him in front of the huge packed audience he was performing for. That was okay by him, so I got my first-ever-done hand held shot with a traveling camera. I was overjoyed and have been using it ever since.

One camera guy way out in the woods amongst the trees and weeds on a hill shooting the whole audience and theatre quietly said over the headset, "Tony, there's a coyote sniffing at my heels what shall I do?"

I said, "Don't move and don't be afraid, they don't eat much."

Well, he was okay, nothing happened. I was glad it wasn't me back there.

The rest of the cast of the Olympic Gala was shot on location in various countries. We were in Spain to shoot Placido Domingo singing "The Impossible Dream" in the soccer stadium. We met and did a pleasant exchange of greetings and I asked if he was ready to sing "The Impossible Dream." He had known about this choice of song weeks before, so when he answered "Yes, but I don't know the words." I couldn't believe I heard what I heard.

Here I was in a huge soccer stadium with a world-class singer who doesn't know the lyrics to the song he had been assigned to sing weeks before this. He'd had plenty of time to learn it.

The manager of the stadium was right beside me when an idea struck me. In desperation I said, "Sir, could you please send someone out to get the sheet music for "The Impossible Dream," and call the guy who puts the scores up on the scoreboard and tell him to get here immediately."

This near fiasco became a plus, for when you see Placido singing - seemingly looking up to the heavens - he's actually reading the lyrics off the score board. It worked just great until clouds started to move in and as he was hitting the last note it started to rain and we cleared that soccer field double time. We got the song and gained an experience we'll never forget.

In Mexico City we were in front of the famous Palace of Fine Arts. For this occasion the Mexicans had decorated the Palace with thousands of lights and fireworks, which meant we had only one crack at getting this shot without a long wait to reload the fireworks. The TV truck was parked a block away to avoid being hit by the hot fireworks.

Cantinflas was on the sidewalk near the camera truck with the beautiful Palacio all lit up behind him. I was near Cantinflas so I could cue him for the shot and keep him pumped up to give a good performance. Everything was a go so I called, "Cue the fireworks!"

I waited until they were hot then cued Cantinflas. He did his speech, then sang beautifully. The fireworks were still flying so I cued him again and we got a second take. They were still going when I cued him the third time. As he turned to look they started to go out rapidly and Cantinflas slowly turned back to us looking like a whipped puppy with a funny sad face and said, "No mas."

He had a good time and so did we. With a "Muchas gracias!" we were on our way.

KURT THOMAS

Kurt had just won the Olympic Gold Medal in Gymnastics and was booked to appear on a TV Special I was doing at the time. To show the beauty and strength and the art of the various exercises which brought him the top prize, I was struck with the idea of having him do these marvelous feats to classical music. I thought the highbrow music would give it the class it needed. He agreed the music would not interfere with his concentration but perhaps even enhance it.

We tried it and when the music started with his acrobatics it was magic. Everybody stopped what they were doing and watched. The music really enhanced the beautiful, powerful movements. The whole room seemed to be at serene attention. This lasted for the entire routine. Pure magic! I asked for a few things to be repeated for different camera angles and he was quick to oblige. When he finished we all agreed he should have been awarded another gold medal.

AMERICA'S DANCE HONORS

In 1990 I directed *America's Dance Honors* for the inauguration of the San Diego Convention Center. The show opened with a huge production number displaying all the existing forms of dance starting with ballet to modern, then jazz, tap to Latin, then street/rap to the finale. This all took about five minutes. Then the large roster of participants gives you an idea of how huge this spectacular event was going to be.

First out was Shirley MacLaine who introduced dance on film. Kenny Ortega introduced Patrick Swayze who accepted an award for *Dirty Dancing.*

Next Cyd Charisse, looking great, honored Arthur Mitchell and Dance Theater of Harlem.

Next George Chakiris honored the dance in *West Side Story* and also Paula Abdul's choreography on *The Tracy Ullman Show.*

Juliet Prowse followed with clips of her dancing in films and introduced Broadway's top winning queen of the gypsies, Chita Rivera, who performed with dancers Tony Stevens and Robert Montano. They stopped the show performing "The Pain" singing "why don't they mention the terrible aches, the crack of the bone at the moment it breaks, the tendons you're certain to strain. Why don't mention the PAIN?" This dancers' lament got laughs and a well-deserved standing ovation.

Next came Ann Margaret, only to be a presenter for Walter Painter and Mickey Mouse to accept.

Next Onna White and Lester Wilson came to the podium to introduce an award-winning modern dance company. They sadly announced the loss of their leader Alvin Ailey but assured the audience that his company is still performing.

Chita Rivera came up next to award the Broadway musical choreographers: Jerome Robbins for *Jerome Robbins' Broadway,* Tommy Tune for *Grand Hotel*, Michael Smuin for *Anything Goes.* That night the winner was Tommy Tune.

Next the Nicholas Brothers performed. Betty Ford, the president's wife who had studied with Martha Graham, introduced film clips of some of Martha's works and closed with "I'm honored that she is my friend and I am thrilled to accept for her the honor of first place in the National Academy Dance Hall of Fame. Bravo Martha!"

Next Michael Crawford, the Broadway star of *Phantom of the Opera,* entered to introduce the dancers of the future, "They sing, they dance, they do chest rolls, cartwheels and they are adorable." And they certainly were. Tommy Tune entered to present the Choreographer of the Year Award to Paula Abdul.

Liza Minnelli presented the Hall of Fame award to Sammy Davis Jr., who then introduced and presented the Dancer of the Decade Award to Michael Jackson who was also given a well-deserved standing ovation.

Then, all the dancers and performers joined together into a giant kick line for a rousing closing to wild applause. It turned out to be the dance event of the year and a once in a lifetime event. I was proud to be at the helm of it.

Juliet Prowse and her dancers: (L to R) John Frayer, Bradford Craig, Lance Avante, Nick Navarro, & Norman Edwards

Chapter 10
Juliet Prowse

BOLERO

Juliet Prowse was a "no bullshit" girl. Honest, to the point, and a hard worker. Her agent Mark Mordoh brought her to me with a proposition to do a nightclub act for her. I knew nothing about Juliet as she had just come to this country from London, and had been dancing her way through Europe after leaving South Africa where she grew up. Small piece of trivia - she was actually born in Bombay, India. She had made a name for herself with the film *Can-Can* and was in a high profile romance with the star of the film, Frank Sinatra.

Upon seeing her for the first time in my house, I was quick to see this magnificent creature was really something. Tall, great smile, small waist, long fabulous legs, small butt, everything that says she just has to be a great dancer.

I did not hesitate in declaring, "I would love to do a show for you".

I didn't have to see her dance. I just knew she was capable and would be a smash in Las Vegas. Now it was up to me to make it happen. I thought we should start with something from her roots – Africa! With titian hair and alabaster skin Juliet is not one you'd expect to be from Africa. Here we are introducing a pure white goddess. Fortunately I had the time to prepare this act.

The gods were with me for when the time came; I had laid out the plan of how we would introduce her. We would dress the male dancers in native African costume including spears. They would do a tribal dance around a thatched column in the center of the stage. Lighting would be dark and mysterious with a bright golden shaft of light shooting straight down on the thatched column. The dancers are doing a ritual dance and as the music grows in intensity and tempo, the shaft of light blasts into a blazing white and the column bursts open to reveal a great white, half naked goddess - Juliet!

The audience stood up and applauded - something I had never seen in Las Vegas. A standing ovation and she hadn't done anything yet! The dancing proved she was born to dance, and even before the end of the piece the audience was on its feet giving her another standing ovation. Juliet was on her way... welcome to the USA.

Of course getting ready for that show takes rehearsal and a lot of work.

On Valentine's Day she asked if she could leave rehearsal early because she had a date with Frank Sinatra. Of course I let her go so she could get ready. The next day she walked into rehearsal and of course we all were curious to know how the evening went.

I asked, "Did Frank give you anything for Valentine's Day?"

She said "Oh, ya. It's here somewhere in my rehearsal bag."

We waited while she dug around searching and finally she held up a stunning wide diamond and ruby bracelet worth a fortune. She seemed unenthused.

We all gasped at how magnificent it was, "Don't you love it?"

She said, "No, I don't wear stuff like this." and threw it back into her bag.

After another date we anxiously asked how everything went and she said, "The whole thing is off."

We were in shock, "What do you mean?"

"I'd have to give up my career and stay home and be a housewife," she answered. "I wouldn't even be allowed to take dance class." She was a little afraid to tell him that she was breaking up so she just left the ring on the bedside table one morning with a note.

We all sympathized with her and agreed that she did the right thing. Imagine what selfish demands - he evidently was selfish in the bedroom too. She didn't see Frank again till sometime later when he came to see the nightclub act. I wasn't there, but there was quite a bit of nervousness backstage among the dancers knowing he was out there. But he didn't make a scene. Perhaps he could see why she could never give up the art of the dance.

Nicky, Juliet, & Tony at dinner

Rehearsals can be a bore sometimes. To watch dancers repeat and repeat dance steps is often a great joy, but when they do it over and over again and don't get better then it's up to you to change the choreography until every move clicks and all gels into something triumphant. Then your heart beats and a sense of joy fills your soul as a choreographer.

To watch Juliet go through this process was an absolute joy. That tall well shaped body was just made for the dance. Those long turned out legs, arms, and hands flowed and gestured and made your heart beat faster as you witnessed what was happening before your very eyes. It was if an angel had come down from heaven.

But her manner of speaking was another thing, and not that of an angel. Juliet attended all rehearsals whether she was in the part being rehearsed or not. She would bring knitting to keep her busy, but she'd keep one eye on what I was giving the boys to do and one on her knitting.

Nicky Navarro was also an excellent dancer with matinee looks to top it off. At one rehearsal while working with the boys in a very sexy part of the number, Nicky started to ad lib something that didn't set well with me, he kept changing my stuff into body rolls, he liked body rolls and I didn't think they were right for this part of the dance.

I stopped the rehearsal and said, "Oh, Nicky, you're so dumb."

Juliet, not looking up from her knitting said, "Ya perhaps, but he's the best fuck I've ever had!"

Upon which Nicky put both hands on his hips, leaned forward, stuck out his tongue and said, "So there."

It struck me so funny I called a ten-minute break.

Word has it that Nicky wasn't the only one to have visited Juliet's balcony. On the road she enjoyed many after-show conquests. It's not clear if there were three ways or not. I lean toward the affirmative. Also there were lots of letters between her and Elvis Presley (with whom she starred in *G.I. Blues*) confirming their wonderful sexual escapades. She told me she kept all of his letters and was very open about having had quite a roster of adventures with him and other star actors in the business - and a couple of other dancers in her act namely Norman Edwards and Lance Avant. It was common knowledge they were both very well-endowed. It certainly suggested she liked the large ones. She lived life to the fullest and got what she wanted.

There was a period during the mid- and late '60s when I was so busy doing a steady series of TV shows, I didn't have time to do any new shows for Juliet. But one day, Mark Mordoh, her manager, called and said "Juliet needs you."

A meeting was called and we met at my house. Just the three of us. It was great seeing Juliet again and we had a good time reminiscing until she told me what I already knew.

She said, "Tony, you have to do a new show for me. I'm working my ass off and not getting the reviews I did when doing your work, do you have any ideas?"

I said, "Yes, Juliet I know. I've kept track of you and I think I have a solution. You've been doing a lot of short snappy numbers with costume change after costume change when you're not on stage. The audience has come to see you, not your group of boy dancers. So, to correct this, I would like to do a number that will keep you on stage more than off."

She asked, "Do you have an idea?"

"Yes, RAVEL'S *BOLERO*."

"Oh!" she exclaimed, "I love it. How much of it?"

I said, "The whole thing!"

"But how long is it?" she asked.

"Fifteen minutes"

Mark said, "Can she do a number that long?"

I said, "She has to."

Juliet was ecstatic, "I'll do it!"

Rehearsals started a few days later. Boy dancers Ed Kerrigan, Eddie Helm, John King, Nick Navarro and girls Mable Robinson and Lorraine Field, were hired to round out the cast. Bob Mackie was hired to do the costumes and a set designer came in to do some things I needed to help give the dance that extra impact and allow Juliet to rest without leaving the stage. One important thing was a giant mirror covering the whole back wall of the stage with the ability to tip forward from the top.

When we had completed the main choreography, I said, "Now let's run it from the top and Juliet when you get tired, just stop and sit on the stage until you get your wind back, then get up and start the dance again."

I timed the rest period and told the set designer at what point I wanted the mirror to tilt so the audience could see Juliet doing a variation while lying on the floor. I worked out some sexy variations with Juliet writhing and doing movements close to the possibility of getting raided, but allowing her to catch her breath. When this so called rest period was over she was able to get up to join the dancers and resume the dance out to the end.

Once the rehearsals were over, the orchestra rehearsed, and the lighting, sets and costumes were ready, the dancers were more than ready to strut their stuff for a full audience. Juliet and the dancers could feel this work was going to be something spectacular and special for Las Vegas.

Juliet is in her very sexy revealing Bob Mackie costume looking like something out of this world and ready in the wings. I'm in the light booth ready to call the light cues. The crowded casino is packed and feels anticipation of something special about to happen. Finally we are on: "Ladies and Gentlemen. Miss JULIET PROWSE." The orchestra strikes up and we are off with a bang. Juliet and the dancers put on a marvelous show with singing and dancing, but I saved *The Bolero* for last.

For the finale, the stage is dark. In the darkness, the first strains of *The Bolero* whisper out of the orchestra pit as the lights come up to reveal that the stage proscenium is covered in a giant multicolored silk curtain shimmering in slight wavy movement. On the last climactic chord of the overture it whips away down a hole in the center of the stage floor to reveal a darkness and a spotlight tightly focused on an elegant hand moving high up and snakelike amid the blackness. Juliet is actually on Nicky's shoulders who is entirely in black. This gave her hands an inhuman height. Nicky slowly plies and invisibly brings her to the floor and he disappears as the spot widens to encompass a sparsely clad goddess.

The audience goes into thunderous applause and Juliet starts her magic. She is in top form. She is selling like crazy; sexy, sexy, sexy. The boys enter showing lots of firm flesh very sexy and available. The music is slowly building in intensity. Juliet is really turning it on. The audience absolutely still and transfixed seems to be holding its breath. Everything is working beautifully and as rehearsed.

Then Juliet slithers to the floor and is in hot form, as the mirror tilts to reveal some of the choreographed

Celebrating with Will and the cast

sexy gyrations. The audience seems to be holding its breath and is fascinated with Juliet's image in the mirror and applauds in approval. (This was before *A Chorus Line* used the same trick. In fact, Michael Bennett saw *The Bolero* and complimented me on the mirror effect... Just sayin'...)

The music is beating closer to the end as the boys prepare to catch Juliet. The music transitions to a higher key. Juliet and the boys are on opposite sides of the stage. Juliet makes a dashing run the full width of the stage and leaps like an arrow into the boys' arms. They catch and swing her forward then quickly backward and up and around into a high standing regal pose punctuated with a giant cymbal crash. This sends the audience into earth shattering applause and an explosion of "BRAVOS" and a standing ovation as the boys slowly carry this goddess into the wings.

The company returns for their bows and the audience continues with their applause which erupts into wild shouts of bravos as Juliet graciously bows, and bows, and throws kisses. After multiple curtain calls she finally waves good bye. Overnight Juliet became the new star of the Las Vegas Strip.

> Dear Tony & Will
>
> The act is a big success, everyone is raving about it. Thanks to your brilliant mind. However Juliet got tired of doing that french routine, and decided since I had the next best legs, I should do the part. I am sure once you see the enclosed potograff you will agree. Show it to Dick Beard and tell him to eat his heart out.
>
> Take care see you in Vegas
>
> Love Nick Navarro

It was a night of magic and the reviews reflected that, one stating:

> *"There are two stars of the Desert Inn's new offering which opened Tuesday night and as surely as Juliet Prowse is the absolute star of her act, the magician is Tony Charmoli, who staged, directed and choreographed the show. The happy blend of Prowse and Charmoli has produced this season's Blockbuster."*

Juliet came to many parties at my house and always seemed to enjoy herself. Even in a packed house you could always tell where Juliet was by her ear shattering bursts of laughter. She was very good at mingling and getting around to a lot of people.

She also was a dog lover. One night after a party at her house we were saying good night out in the yard when she said, "Let me show you something."

Her dogs were all cavorting and playing in the driveway and the garage door was wide open when she said, "Tony, here it comes." She clapped her hands and shouted, " All right, to bed!"

Another hand clap and all the dogs ran into the garage and each jumped into their own separate box. It was a delightful surprise. She proudly said, "I taught them." It was a wonderful evening.

Juliet is one soul you can't forget, but the time comes for everybody. One day, I got a call from her assistant who said, "Tony, Juliet would like to see you now. You know she's here in the hospital at UCLA."

I did know that. I rushed out there and into her room. Poor Juliet. She was a poor skin and bones image of herself. We talked and laughed and had a good time reminiscing about all the good times in our past and the wonderful accomplishments. For those few minutes Juliet seemed her old self again. Finally her assistant interrupted and said, "It's time for her to rest now."

My heart dropped into my shoes. It was over an hour I was there but it seemed like ten minutes. That was the last time I saw her. Goodbye FABULOUS JULIET!

Sid & Marty Krofft Productions

Chapter 11
Puppets and Muppets

SID KROFFT

I first met Sid Krofft when Will and I were living at the Chateau Marmont when we first moved out to California. He was living in one of the bungalows. Sid is an extremely creative fellow and we hit it off pretty quickly. He'd had a one-man puppet show that he had performed throughout Europe and by this time he'd settled back in the US, and was staying at the Chateau.

After we moved into our house - which was just a few blocks away from the Chateau, we built a pool and Sid was a frequent visitor. Sid has always been a handsome man with a good sense of humor. One day, while he was out by the pool I asked if I could paint a portrait of him.

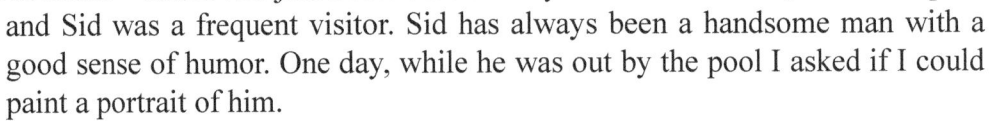

Soon after that, he and his brother Marty created a risqué puppet show called *Les Poupées de Paris* and had a fair amount of success with it. Ironically some of the show's success was from Billy Graham warning people about the show's topless puppets, which spurred ticket sales and gave a boost to publicity.

Sid did opening acts for my friends Judy Garland and Liberace. Then did eight episodes for *The Dean Martin Show,* but was let go when it became clear

Sid spending time by my pool.

that they were too funny and upstaging Dean. So I was happy for them when they had a hit with their own series *H. R. Pufnstuf* on Saturday morning TV. When they asked me to direct their next series I knew it would be fun and creative.

THE BUGALOOS

The Bugaloos (1970) was an excellent vehicle for the antics of Martha Raye, who was cast as the eccentric witch Benita Bizarre. To watch this pro was remarkable. She'd arrive for work without ever having read the script for the day's shoot. She would go directly into the makeup chair and have her assistant read her part to her while she was being made up. By the time she got made up and dressed for the shoot she would know her lines to the "T" without cue cards. The only time I had to do a retake was if one of the other cast members would blow it. This would annoy Martha to no end and I don't blame her.

The story line generally followed three teenage boy bugs and one teenage girl bug who lived in the forest. The pretty teenage girl bug lived in a giant flower. Upon rising each morning the huge petals of the flower would open up revealing her saying "Good Morning" to all the little creatures of the forest, then break out into a song. I would describe it as precious. Sid and Marty Krofft are experts in knowing how to engage the young audience.

The mail was fantastic and proof that the series was well received. After shooting the last episode, a large cast party was going to be given at the studio for the all those who worked on the shoot. I had an idea

Below and above Left: Wayne Laryea as the Bumblebee (keyboards), John Philpott as the Ladybug (drums), Caroline Ellis as the Butterfly (vocals/percussion), and John McIndoe as the Grasshopper (guitar/vocals)

Sid & Marty Krofft Productions

Martha Raye hamming it up as Benita Bizarre

on how to put a playful period on this series for the cast and crew, so I secretly pulled it together.

The evening arrived and the party was going full swing when I invited everybody to gather down on the set for a surprise. I cued the music, cued the spotlight then cued the stagehand to remotely open the flower exposing a beautiful stark naked girl who said, "Good Morning" just like the girl in the series. The boys screamed with delight applauded and scrambled closer to the flower for a better look - joined by Martha Raye. Then my stripper went into her dance punctuated with more salivating screams from the boys and the crew. The dancer did a great job. She ended in an artistic pose and the flower slowly closed around her. Well, those boys ran up to me and gave me big hugs of appreciation and even Martha was grateful. The boys all said we should have had the stripper in the show. It turned out to be a fun way to bring the series to a close.

Martha was a character. She had recently done marvelous work on the front lines during the Vietnam War as a nurse with soldiers. She'd be there as a performer but work as a real nurse during the day, prepping badly injured men for surgery, and also going around the beds, talking with the men and giving them a bit of Martha Raye cheer. But back in Hollywood, she could still be a little frustrating. She invited a group of us to dinner one evening, then mid dinner abandoned us for a young couple at another table and she propositioned both of them for sex. She then left the restaurant with them and we were left with the bill.

Martha came to a lot of parties at the house and would inevitably be walking around with poppers stuffed in both nostrils. I stopped inviting her to parties when she left one evening with one of my paintings. I'd been working on a series of oil paintings of children and she took a rather large one right off the wall and carried it out the front door when I wasn't looking. When I asked around I was told who took it. When I asked her she said she liked it and would "replace" it. She sent me a large velvet black-light painting of Jesus in recompense. (My maid said she liked it so I gave it to her). Needless to say, Martha was not asked back.

LIDSVILLE

Charles Nelson Reilly was a loud camp to work with on *Lidsville* in 1971. He played a green magician, Horatio J. HooDoo, the villain of the series. His character was always chasing a boy named Mark who has an incompetent "Weenie" instead of a Genie. Horatio J. HooDoo would try to get Mark's Weenie in each episode. Granted, the Weenie belonged to Horatio first, so perhaps the magician had cause. But generally speaking the most of the plots involved the pursuit of Weenie. Weenie was played by Billie Hayes.

Charles often could be heard yelling, "Who do you have to fuck to get out of this Polish prison?" In spite of all that yelling I know he was bored if he wasn't in every scene. He was excellent in the role. He could chew up all the scenery he wanted to, and did every episode. I think Charles would have blown up the studio if we took him at his word and replaced him.

Charles Nelson Reilly as Horatio J. HooDoo

Billie Hayes has always brought that extra touch to every project since I saw her as Mammy Yokum in *Lil' Abner* on Broadway. In the Sid and Marty Krofft television productions she always fits right in with the little people and brings a professional flair to the colorful and often very funny proceedings.

She was hysterical as Witchypoo in *H. R. Pufnstuf*, so it was a no-brainer to have her back in *Lidsville* as the incompetent genie. She's an all-round singer, actor, dancer, a true asset to any production and a good friend. She was a frequent guest at my Christmas parties. These days, I run into her at lunchtime on occasion at a neighborhood restaurant. Lots of good memories.

Thanks to Sid Krofft for the great photos of the productions!

Butch Patrick and Billie Hayes

Butch Patrick and the cast of Lidsville

FOL DE ROL

Fol de Rol was a TV variety special I directed for Sid and Marty Krofft in 1972. It was patterned after a 16th Century Renaissance Fair, and was lightly based on a popular puppet show the Kroffts did in 1968. The overall plot structure was loose and allowed for a series of songs and vignettes such as you might see at a festival.

Robert Shields opened with an excellent dance pantomime setting the mood and time for this elaborate production of a Renaissance Fair. With such a varied cast of characters, the days were unpredictable and loaded with many surprises. Surprisingly and fortunately it was more fun than not. The smiles on Sid and Marty's faces told me they were pleased, as was the cast and the reviews. I had a good time too.

Ann Sothern was the queen. Mickey Rooney was the Executioner and also played Noah, with Totie Fields playing his wife. Ricky Nelson was a handsome troubadour who sang as he wandered from scene to scene. He was a little stiff as an actor so I used the mime Robert Shields to give more life to his numbers.

Cyd Charisse did a spectacular dance to the song "Classical Gas" which was supplemented with Yma Sumac's unintelligible birdcalls. I wanted to choreograph something special for Cyd and came up with an idea she loved. She is first discovered as the centerpiece of two giant golden wings from which she emerges and then does a stunning pas de deux partnered by an excellent dancer, Swen Swenson whom I had flown out from New York. Their dance is cinematic in scope and other-worldly beautiful.

Mickey Rooney had fun over acting and chewing up the scenery as the Royal Executioner, but especially as Noah. Off-camera, Ann Sothern never stopped eating and you could find her by following the path of crumbs she dropped along the way. Totie Fields had a great time getting the most she could out of her multiple roles and she's amusing to watch. Totie was a true pro. She and Ann really sell one humorous dance number with four witches singing "Love Is the Answer." *Fol De Rol* needs to come to DVD - it is worth seeing.

It was always a pleasure to work with such a wonderfully creative man like Sid Krofft. He always had ideas, but at the same time he was not a micro-manager and gave me a lot of freedom when it came to shooting every show I did for him. We worked very well together.

I've known him for many years now and he is still just as creative and full of fun as ever. He has a waterfall coming off his roof into the pool and still has a tree house in his backyard.

Sid & Marty Krofft Productions

Fol De Rol with Robert Shields

JOHN DENVER AND THE MUPPETS

I thought a Christmas special starring John Denver and the Muppets was a great idea. I had worked with John when he guested on the Doris Day special a few years earlier, and I was very fond of the Muppets from the first time I saw them on TV. I grew even fonder of both of them when I got the opportunity to direct this wonderful TV Christmas Special.

There was a lot of holiday pageantry going on, and Miss Piggy was in her dressing room getting all primped up for the next scene. She was powdering herself vigorously and I thought it would look better from a different angle, so from the director's booth I said, "Miss Piggy would you turn a little more to the right while you're powdering yourself?"

She turned to Jim and coolly asked, "Mr. Henson, WHAT is the director's name?"

He replied. "Tony, his name is Tony."

Miss Piggy turned to me as directed, then in a crisp undertone added, "Anthony, you're treading on thin ice!"

It cracked me up. She was a handful.

John Denver seemed to fit in easily with the Muppets, as he did in a big number set in a town square. I surrounded him with real dancers and singers doing an up-tempo winter holiday production number. Having done so many appearances alone with his guitar, John seemed energized when supported with singers and dancers. It appeared he was fully enjoying all the extra help.

Later in the show, he sang "Have Yourself A Merry Little Christmas" with Rowlf the Dog at the piano and it was very touching and sentimentally slushy, but wonderful and deeply heartfelt. It's difficult to accept we will never get to see that combination in performance again.

The tableau of the holy birth done Jim Henson style was a treasure. I added some gossamer angels floating above the manger scene to Jim's approval and delight.

The topper was that the Directors Guild of America honored me with a Best Directors Award for this special.

That night we celebrated with a late dinner in Beverly Hills. Coincidentally John was also having dinner in the same place. I was still so excited from the win I went over to his table to show him the trophy. I was so disappointed with his non-reaction. He seemed so unenthused he didn't even congratulate me. I don't know what might have happened prior to my getting there, but even a slight acknowledgment would have been appreciated... but none? What a bummer. We had a good time at our table anyway. That was the last time I saw John and was shocked when I heard about his fatal plane accident. I still have my Directors Guild Award to remind me of the wonderful time we had working together.

I ran into Kermit a few years later while I was on a shoot for a pageant at a high end hotel is some exotic locale I can't quite remember. We had a shoot scheduled for the pool area that day and when I got there, Kermit was lounging on one of the pool lounges in the midst of another shoot.

I said, "Kermit! What the fuck are you doing on my set?"

Kermit was of course very polite and explained that their shoot was running long, but they'd be finished momentarily. He was much more respectful than Miss Piggy. He called me "Mr. Charmoli."

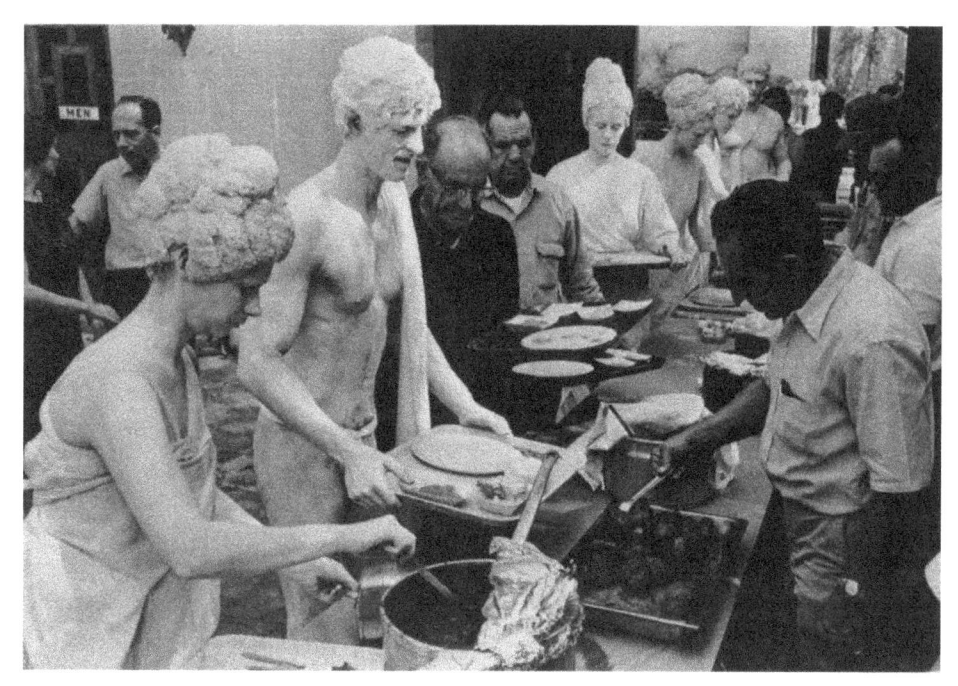

Even statues have to eat!

Chapter 8
Forays in Film

THE LOVED ONE

Tony Richardson called and said he needed some help with some scenes he was working on for the film *The Loved One*. It sounded interesting and I took the job.

The first scene we tackled was the one with Liberace as the Funeral Director. Lee is in a room surrounded by caskets and starts to sing a sales pitch when suddenly all the caskets fly open revealing scantily clad showgirls. This develops into a full-blown production number. The number became a big camp and suited Liberace's style perfectly. Tony, the director, was pleased so we moved on to the next scene that needed attention.

The next scene took place in the office of the director of the cemetery - a Dr. Kenworthy played by Jonathan Winters. On the walls of his office are large display cases, which hold life size all white rather naked statues of boys and girls in suspiciously sexual poses. At carefully selected moments with the flip of a switch these figures come to life and engage in all manners of copulation.

There were times during filming Tony would yell out to me, "Tony, more fucking! I want to see more fucking! I want the audience to see this gentle old man is a real Lothario!"

The crew always gathered to watch the filming of these scenes. The poor live dancers had to remain

Sally Mason poses by a pond.

in the heavy white makeup all day long. They were called in for 3:30 in the morning, stripped to thin gauze underwear then made white with rollers of Plaster of Paris white make up. They also wore Plaster of Paris wigs. It's surprising no one caught cold. The girls were offered more money if they exposed their breasts to be covered in white plaster and only one agreed. Jackie Gregory had reason to bare it all. Covered in heavy white makeup they didn't seem so naked.

The poor dancers endured another hardship. At the end of the day, the showers on site had only cold water. I understand the white plaster makeup didn't completely wash off, but eventually wore off. What dancers do for a paycheck!

The real payoff is that the statues looked terrific and were a major plus to the scene. Later I was informed the whole crew unanimously attended the rushes of these scenes. They were eager to see the copulating statues. I should have charged admission.

The Loved One was shown some years back at the *Hollywood Forever* cemetery and projected up on the wall of the mausoleum while the audience sat on blankets on the grass. I can't think of a more fitting place to see the film. Tyler Cassity, the handsome and charismatic owner of the cemetery has really transformed it into a place for the living as well as the dead. An interesting side note - Tyler was a consultant on the show *Six Feet Under.* You'll have to visit his cemetery if you ever come to Hollywood.

WHAT'S THE MATTER WITH HELEN

Singing In The Rain turned me into a big fan of Debbie Reynolds, so when I got a call asking me to choreograph a dance number for her in the film *What's The Matter With Helen?* I immediately accepted. I rushed down to Paramount studios for a quick meeting and learned she needed a dance partner.

My house guest at the time was Swen Swenson who had just hit it big on Broadway replacing Bob Fosse in *Little Me* with "I've Got Your Number." I immediately suggested Swen. They said they had contacted his agent and he wasn't available. I argued that was not true, I'll call him. I knew exactly where he was. He was at my house probably out at the pool with his feet dangling in the water. I called him and made the offer and had him repeat his acceptance to them, he was hired.

When Debbie was told she immediately said, "Isn't he too tall for me?" When I countered, "I'll have him dance in Plie", (bent knees) she agreed with pleasure. We went into rehearsal immediately and all went swimmingly. Debbie asked for the rehearsal to be extended. This was wise because in addition to doing the dancing she was required to do the acting of making her boyfriend, played by Dennis Weaver who was on the sidelines, quite jealous. This meant she had to know the dance routine perfectly without thinking about the steps. The extended rehearsal period did the trick. The shooting of this dance sequence was excellent and fun and all parties were very happy.

Working with Shelley Winters in the same picture was a whole different bag. First of the annoyances was the need to always have opera music blaring throughout the whole studio when they were not shooting. She said she needed it to calm her nerves.

Swen Swenson and Debbie Reynolds

On another day she had a medic wheel her onto the set because she had turned her ankle during the shooting of a night rain scene. Debbie was there also and verified no such thing happened. So Debbie not to be outdone countered by having two stagehands dressed as medics in white jackets carry her onto the set on a stretcher. The crew loved it and gave her a big hand.

Another time Shelley was heard to say, "Where is that little girl I'm supposed to work with, I want to do something like strangle her." And Debbie countered with "Wait 'til you see what were going to do to you Shelley when this is over!"

Shelley was constantly drumming up trouble and pulled a trick like this on the director, "Look at this dress, it's awful, It makes me look like an elephant!"

Debbie said, "No, it doesn't make you look like an elephant, Shelley you *are* an elephant." The truth about this dress was that it was designed and made especially for her. She had several fittings with the costume designer.

This was typical Shelley being a pain-in-the-butt - by extending the days of shooting it would make more money for her. Shelley was an instigator. She seemed to be happiest when she was complaining about something or when she was drumming up a problem of some kind.

Debbie and Phyllis Diller at my house

On the other hand Debbie was a dream to work with. Shelley constantly complained she was not lit properly. At the end of the shoot the crew gave her a light on rollers so she could roll it out to her car and just get out. She did that and got big applause and jeers on her exit. It was clear everybody was happy to see her go.

Shelley was a good actress. It's too bad that she had all this extra baggage that made her so difficult to work with. I guess we don't have that worry anymore, may she rest in peace. Shall we say, "When she was good she was very very good, and when she was bad she was a major pain in the ass!"

Debbie was a Tap Dance teacher in the film and I suggested Debbie borrow one thing from my tap teacher Miss Gardiner. Willy (Wilhelmina) never taught a class without her diamond earrings. She said they gave her an added sparkle. They worked fine on Debbie too.

❦

Debbie and I worked together another time. Lauren Bacall was to go on vacation again from *Woman of the Year* and again I was asked about a replacement for her and once again my suggestion was agreed to and Debbie was slated to cover while Lauren was gone. I also changed the choreography to accommodate Debbie's best dancing style. Debbie can tap. It was great working with Debbie again and she did an excellent job in the show and made the role her own. It didn't last very long however because New York suffered another of those huge snowstorms which forced the closure of theaters and brought New York to a virtual standstill forcing the show to close.

I think we all knew Debbie had been a collector for years, buying famous costumes from major film studios and creating a significant collection of Hollywood history. So it was great to hear see how she has turned this into a major source of income through several auctions. I think I can safely state we're all so happy for Debbie who has, in a sense, been paid back after having been ripped off by a couple of bad marriages. Bravo Debbie!

I had a celebration for my oldest sister Nell's ninetieth birthday at Le Dome Restaurant and Debbie Reynolds happened to be at lunch there the same day.

She came over to ask, "Tony, what's going on?"

I told her we were celebrating Nell's ninetieth birthday.

She immediately turned to the room and announced to the entire restaurant, "All right everybody. It's Nell's Ninetieth birthday. Now everybody together, "Happy Birthday to you..."

Immediately she had the entire crowd singing a rip roaring birthday song to Nell. It was a great never to be forgotten event.

But that is who she is - a down to earth girl with a big heart who is always fun to be around.

Kip Grimm, Jordan Randall, Paul Manchester, John Shaffner, & Tony.

Chapter 13
A Variety of Friends

I've made so many wonderful friends over the years, it is difficult to just pick out a few. But here are some who stand out in my memory...

EDWARD ALBEE

I formally met Edward at a party in Bel Air long after I had moved to California. When the host introduced us, Edward said, "I know who you are."

That surprised me, and I asked, "Have we met?"

He said, "Not officially, but I know you from having delivered Western Union telegrams to you in your apartment in New York."

I asked, "Why didn't you introduce yourself?" He replied, "I wasn't 'Edward Albee' then."

I guess that explains it. I admire Edward's talent as a playwright. He had me when he wrote *Who's Afraid of Virginia Wolf?* He had me with the Broadway stage presentation, then again with the film version. I believe I'd go see it again if it was playing nearby.

Not long ago, he got me once again with *The Goat*. Upon seeing it, I wrote to him, "Anyone who can

Edward Albee and Tony

write a play which can keep an audience laughing for half an hour by simply repeating the line, "You fucked a goat?" is pure genius. The audience wasn't simply laughing, they were roaring. Brilliantly intelligent and side-splittingly funny.

On a visit to my house on Easter one year, we were having a good time telling stories about nothing and everything and laughing and just having fun. Gordon Reagan and Paul Templeton from Berkeley were also visiting. We had shopped for dinner prior to Edwards's arrival so Gordon was making frequent trips to the kitchen to help with the dinner. After several cocktails Gordon announced dinner and we all responded with a wobbly sashay into the dining room.

We did a toast and wished everybody a happy Easter.

Edward remarked, "That's right, it is Easter isn't it?"

Gordon responded with, "Yes, that's why we're having rabbit."

Edward immediately dropped his knife and fork and asked, "Is this rabbit?"

When he heard "yes!" Edward cringed and said, "You mean we're eating the Easter Bunny? Well, I can't eat the Easter Bunny."

And didn't. He did enjoy desert. The rest of us enjoyed the Easter bunny and everything else. All in all it was a very good Easter Day and a very happy reunion.

Visiting Edward in his apartment in the village is truly an experience. His collection of various paintings and art objects is an eclectic treasure trove. As with any collection, some is amazingly wonderful and some questionable... there was a pile of sand and drift wood by a well-known artist in the middle of the room that begged the question "What is Art?" Which is just the sort of worthwhile conversation one is apt to discover in his home - always rewarding with a wonderfully talented playwright and person. He was also good at choosing a life partner. A visit with Edward is sure to be a memorable one.

I went to see Edward recently on his lecture tour at UCLA. It was a little long but enlightening. I then went backstage to visit him, but all we could do was wave "Hello" because a couple of powerfully buxom women plowed in and bumped me out of the way. Edward and I just smiled and shrugged a "What to do?" and I left. I called him the next day instead.

ROCK HUDSON

Not only was Rock Hudson a handsome devil of a guy and a wonderful Hollywood movie star, but he was also fun at private parties. Portia Nelson from New York was a singer-actress who famously sang "How do you solve a problem like Maria..." in *The Sound of Music*. She also gave great parties. Her guests usually were friends with whom she'd worked with in theatre or films.

One evening Will and I attended one of these and were pleased to see Rock Hudson was one of the other guests. We had attended parties at Rock's home and knew he loved to play parlor games. This evening at Portia's he suggested we all play charades. This game requires two teams. The members of each team write out different song titles, movie titles, famous people, etc. These are then put in a hat and one person from each team draws one folded slip, then without speaking a word, they act out in pantomime what they have drawn. Rock loved this game and was a whiz at acting out what he had drawn.

Rock also could be a mischief maker. This evening another guest was up acting out what she had drawn. Rock's team was to guess. She would act out something and somebody on Rock's team would shout out an intentionally wrong answer; even though the answer was totally obvious. Rock had primed his team to deliberately give wrong answers. She kept trying to act out the word and Rock's team would give another wrong answer. You could see she was going crazy that no one was getting it. This kept up until everyone finally busted up laughing and Rock admitted they were joking to see how long she would go on. Poor girl was exhausted but we had a good laugh on her creative and diverse ways of acting out the song title. Many of the guests were very funny in pantomiming the subject or title of what they had drawn. It is a fun game for actors and comedians. And Rock always had a great sense of humor with it.

JOHNNY MATHIS

Dick Priborsky was a pianist I used a great deal and one evening he called to say he was working just down the hill from me at The Interlude accompanying a new young singer. "I know you'll like him. His name is Johnny Mathis."

Will and I went to the club that evening and indeed Dick was right. We both thought Johnny was an excellent singer and a good all-around entertainer. We praised him in his dressing room after the show and offered to take them out to dinner.

Dick said "That would be terrific but where do you take a black man out to dinner in this neighborhood, and at this hour?"

It's hard to believe that but it was true. I offered that we live right up the hill and could go up and I could make sandwiches. They thought that would be just fine. Will reminded me that my sister, Nell, and her husband Camillo were up in the guest room and her husband was very anti-black. We took the chance anyway. I thought, what the hell, it's our house. We got to the house and in no time I prepared food and drink and we had a grand time, and my sister and her husband never woke up. We remained friends to this day and he actually is now one of my neighbors.

Johnny and Tony

At another party Johnny was the first to arrive and was sitting at the bar when two of my dancer friends arrived and went to the bar. Followed by another couple, but the next one to arrive was a good-looking blonde boy. You could see Johnny's eyes light up.

Soon the cute blonde was there at the bar. I introduced the two. Johnny whipped his arm around him and took him straight out the door. That was the last I saw of my young blonde friend until Monday morning when he stopped by to pick up his car to drive back home to San Diego. He said he and Johnny had a good time listening to Johnny's music all weekend. Johnny and I have remained friends, still hugging hello wherever we meet out in public.

I told Johnny when my last Christmas Party was going to really be the last - "so be sure to come!" He did and everybody was happy to see him again because he had missed a couple of years. He honks every time I see him on my morning walks as he's on his way to the golf course.

He's a sweet and talented man. And it was exciting to hear how he recently wowed the audience at a Grammy shindig and stole the show from much younger performers. He's still got it.

TOM TRYON

Tom was a physically beautiful man and a talented actor besides. I was happy the day he moved into the house right across the street from me. His success as a writer proved he was more than a pretty face, and he definitely had an introspective side to him. It was an added plus when his boyfriend Clive Clerk moved in as well. Clive was part of the original cast of *A Chorus Line* on Broadway and eventually had some success as a fine artist under the name of Clive Wilson.

Around that time, I was at my easel painting every day and I asked Clive if he would sit for me. He did, and the portrait turned out quite well - I did two of them. One went into the Mackenzie Gallery and was sold on the first night. The other still hangs in my bar.

My painting of Clive

Tom, not to be out done, said, "You paint Clive but you don't paint me?"

I said, "Well, sit for me and I'll paint you."

He did and the painting turned out well and he was very satisfied.

I sold it years later to Joe Stewart and John Shaffner.

Tom was a good host and entertained quite a bit. Frequently on arriving I found a host of naked bodies swimming and splashing in the pool and in and out of the Jacuzzi.

When he did some additions to his house, one piqued my curiosity. He added a large platform extension from his upstairs bedroom which went out over the outdoor Jacuzzi. A round glass window was put in the floor right over the popular Jacuzzi below. We found it to be rather suspicious. Was it there to allow the sun to hit the occupants in the Jacuzzi or for him to spy from above on the intimate goings on below. One guess! In any event, Tom eventually sold the house, moved and we lost track of one another. Tom and Clive are now long gone, but Tom's books live on and are a testament to the complicated and interesting man that he was.

Since then the house has been sold several times, demolished and currently replaced by a very modern 4 million dollar architectural box.

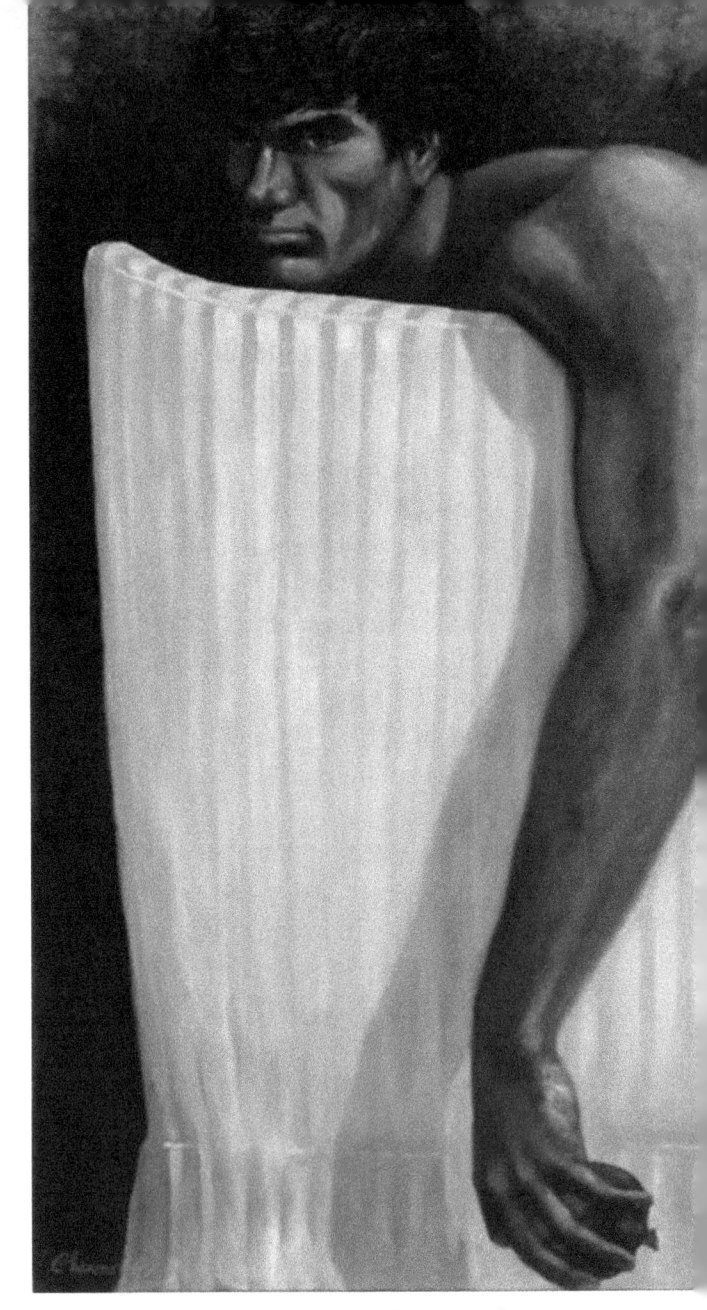

Tom Tryon by my pool.

MAURICE EVANS

I first met Maurice Evans when I worked on *Alice in Wonderland* in 1955. He played the narrator. Right after that in 1956 I worked with him again in the Hallmark TV Production of *The Taming of the Shrew*. Maurice was Petruchio and Lili Palmer was Katharine or "Kate."

I was staging a scene where the two are sparring with each other and we put them in a boxing ring. Symbolically they are having a fighting match - but with words. They would circle the ring and lunge at one another, then wave their arms and other physical gestures associated with a fight. It turned out to be a very effective scene.

Maurice, Tony, and Lisa Kirk

Dress rehearsal was next and when Maurice appeared in white tights, I jumped into the ring and quietly told him we should go back to the dressing room. We did that because in the tights he was absolutely flat through the crotch and not looking like the strong commanding character of Petruchio that the script calls for. I got wardrobe to get a decent jock strap and a ladies Kotex and in minutes we had a virile looking Petruchio. I think it helped in the acting as well. Maurice seemed to be much more in command and looked more like the virile character the part calls for.

Through these initial projects, we developed a lasting friendship. Martin Tahse was assistant to Maurice at the time and he and I continue to stay in touch with each other.

Maurice worked constantly. He appeared in more American TV productions of Shakespeare than any other actor I know of. He did memorable roles in the TV series, *Bewitched*, played the Orangutan, Dr. Zaius in the first two *Planet of the Apes* films, the Butler in *The Jerk* with Steve Martin... His career was always thriving, but he never spent his money if he could help it.

Maurice always was a frugal person and when he was getting roles in television on the West Coast, he would stay with Will and me. This would save him from paying for a hotel room and he'd cash in what the company paid him for travel expenses. My guest room was free. He also would save on his airfare because he'd fly regular fare and cash in on the first class ticket he was given. He did buy his own cocktail liquor. Stuff I had never heard of and you can bet it didn't cost very much either. He did fix dinner one night and announced it was going to be ham and I don't know what else. Dinner indeed was prepared in such spare portions one could say we had hors d'oeuvres of ham for dinner, and a glass of my own wine.

But, God rest his soul, he was a good friend and a very good actor. We're very sad to have lost him. He'll never be replaced.

PAUL ROSE

Paul Rose remains high on the list of dear friends of Will's and mine. He was not famous like many people I talk about in this book, but he was bigger than life. And he introduced me to Mitzi Gaynor when I moved to California.

He worked for Nancy's ladies clothes on Hollywood Blvd in Los Angeles and he was in New York for Market Week. Will and I were still living in New York and I was in dance class under the American Wing. Will was waiting for me in Franklin Coates' apartment on 51st street, next door to the famous Night

Club #21. Paul was also a friend of Franklin, who was the Organist and Choir Master at The Little Church Around the Corner and had come to see him.

When Paul Rose walked into Franklin's apartment and saw Will there, he extended his hand and introduced himself with "Hello, I'm Rose."

Will using his camp name replied, "Hello, I'm Gert!"

They clicked immediately and remained friends for an entire lifetime. Paul became such a close friend, he was the only person to have a key to our house in California. He quickly became friends with our entire social circle. Paul's outrageous camping was contagious. People gravitated to him. He loved to get into costume - or drag to be more specific.

Paul Rose

One evening he invited his boss and wife to dinner at his house and was very nervous for some reason and decided to welcome them with a practical joke. He got into a ladies' corset and garter belt, a wig up in curlers, mules, creamed his face and waited for their arrival. Peeking from behind the window shade he watched them come up the walk and ring the doorbell. He opened the door part way enough for them to see he was not dressed for company and gasped in mock horror, "Wrong night!" and slammed the door shut - then quickly put on his regular clothes, wiped the cold cream off his face and opened the door with a gracious, "Oh, Hi I'm so glad you could make it." Fortunately they loved it and also had a good laugh.

One Thanksgiving, Will and I decided everybody should dress as an early American. Several guests came as Pilgrims. Will was very convincing cooking and serving - dressed as a Pilgrim woman. I dressed as a Turkey. Danny Kaye was the turkey in his Thanksgiving TV show and the turkey costume fit me perfectly. I brought it home and wore it the day of our party but warned everybody it was me and I shouldn't be mistaken for the one on the dinner table. Swen Swenson looked great dressed as a drunken Indian. But when Paul arrived, he had us perplexed. He was wearing a very short tight black satin skirt, a flaming red silk blouse, fishnet hose, high-heeled black patent leather shoes, big hair wig and dangling earrings, along with huge ruby lips and long false eyelashes while carrying a silver clutch purse.

I said, "Paul, you aren't an early American."

He replied, "I most certainly am, I am the first whore who came over on the Mayflower."

At one of our 4th of July pageants around the pool, he was another hilarious character. These parties started when we put the pool in and always had a costume parade around the pool. These parades graduated into hysterical and outrages costume pageants, where guests dressed as all sorts of early Americans. Paul did not have a body to be seen in a g-string but that never stopped him. When it was his turn to circle the swimming pool, he came out riding a hobbyhorse with the stick between his legs and wearing a beaded jock strap almost hidden by an overflowing stomach, a beaded overstuffed bra, heavy makeup, high heel

Fourth of July insanity. Right: Paul Rose Below: Paul and Gordon as french maids

shoes, a huge frizzy red hair wig topped with a tricorn hat.

He was very wobbly in his high hill shoes galloping around the pool yelling, "Run for your muskets, the Yiddish are coming, the Yiddish, are coming!"

It was hysterical. He had the entire pool side crying with laughter. I think if he actually had done it in real historical time the British would have fled in droves posthaste back to England.

At the same Fourth of July pageant, another friend Chris Hersey, appeared at the top of the steps posing glamorously covering his theoretically topless figure, and when he raised his hands up, his tits unrolled down to his feet. It was a hysterical entrance and his parade around the pool was augmented by a shoe with a broken heel that gave his sexy walk that extra dose of comedy. What better way to celebrate the Fourth than to make those around us laugh? Laughter and friendship was at the center of all those parties.

Halloween was another chance for Paul Rose to stop traffic. On one particular Halloween he dressed as a bride. He always started with a nude false rubber pregnant looking stomach with large quite pronounced tits, but this time, he added white tights, a flowing veil, high heel shoes and carried a bride's bouquet grandly parading on crowded Santa Monica Boulevard. I think he was the most photographed that Halloween.

The avenue was packed and we soon lost track of Paul along the way. Will and I realized we hadn't seen Paul for quite some time. We looked everywhere for him and it was getting rather late. Finally we gave up and went home without him. When it became very late we called to see if he went directly home. We called several times and never got a reply. When it was almost three in the morning we became really worried. We had called his home again, the hospital, the police station, but no Paul.

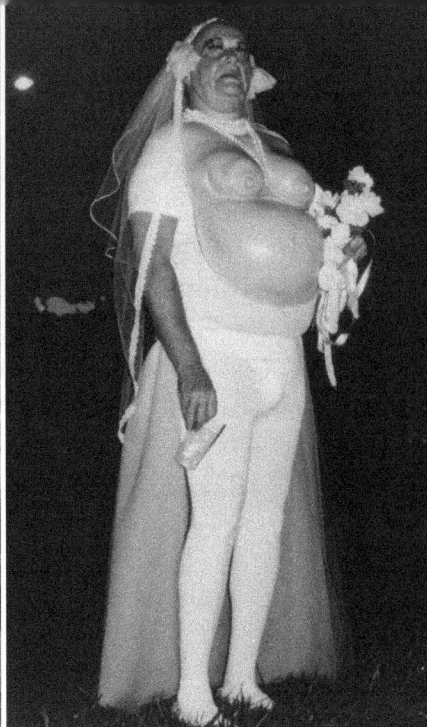

Left: Pageant and Show by the pool, Right: Paul in his wedding attire.

    Will and I decided we should take another look down on the Boulevard. We had done that twice before, but low and behold this time did it. I'm sorry I didn't have my camera. Finally at almost four in the morning there was Paul, sitting on a Hydrant in front of the Bank Building. He was still in costume but it had rained and he was drenched with a rather sick looking bouquet and wilted veil, turned in high heel shoes really looking like something the cat dragged in. We mildly scolded him for disappearing on us and he explained some photographers whisked him into their black curtained booth to photograph him for a calendar and he was there for a long time. There was no way on earth we could have found him. We never did see the calendar with the photo but Paul gave us the picture here in the book. I still keep it out as a treasured remembrance of that Halloween night.

    At an Easter party with my sisters, Paul came dressed in one of his over the top drag outfits. It was garishly Easter in color and drag. The lips were twice their regular size, the lashes like fans and of course carrying a purse shaped like an Easter egg.

    My sister Al commented, "Paul I love your outfit."

    He said, "Thanks! You can get away with wearing anything if you're pretty enough." He was quick with a comeback.

    Paul was also good at keeping the service boys at Camp Pendleton happy. He advertised on their bulletin board at camp, "Free bed and shower with overnight stay." Then he would drive all the way out to Camp Pendleton to pick them up, take them to the cheap bars, then to his apartment to spend the night. After they had spent the night fulfilling Paul's desires he would drive them back to camp. I know all this because as an added bonus if they stayed the weekend, he'd bring them up to our house for a swim in the pool. Paul got great pleasure out of telling how the weekend went and how well hung his tricks were. Of course we knew when Paul was exaggerating actual dimensions since the boys were frequently laying naked around our pool. He kept the boys happy for years - or at least until they were reassigned. I guess you could say he was our local USO.

Not long after Will departed this earth, Paul left us too. I took care of Paul in his last days, bringing food to him, cleaning up after him until he had to have serious medical attention and go into a hospital. He passed away in a private care facility. I honored him with a reception for the remainder of his family from Florida and all of his friends who could make it to my house. Mitzi Gaynor being close to him, gave a lovely tribute. Then as Paul would have it, we all got pretty smashed. His sister Nancy in Key West and I still keep in touch.

BOB RICHLEY

Bob Richley was a classmate of Will's and they both graduated from South High in Minneapolis. Bob decided to go to New York with us and we arranged for him to have the room next to ours in the hotel Bitsey got for us.

Bob was one of the cleanest people I know. I mean why else would he spend hours in the baths - and sometimes the entire night? We never asked questions but we knew what he was up to. He was very free in telling of his sexual encounters. Often in vivid detail and sometimes stuff you didn't care to know. It seemed strange that he was very big into religious history and went to work for Morehouse Gorham, supplier of religious items, and still frequent the sexually driven steam baths.

Back in Minneapolis Bob had an aunt who was heavy into Victorian fashion and had quite a wardrobe, which Bob inherited on her passing. It proved to be rather useful.

Bob, Will and a group of their friends liked to rent a weekend cottage at Lake Minnetonka just outside of Minneapolis. But, the rental agreement stipulated that there must be a woman present at all times. So each morning, the neighbors would see a tall elderly lady walk through the garden and poke at the various shrubs with her cane. The sight of this mysterious woman ensured the neighbors that the young men renting the house would behave in a civilized manner.

He brought that entire wardrobe to New York and on weekends in the country he would wear it to play croquet. Later at our house in California he always played English Royalty visiting us Americans on the 4th of July to see, "How we were doing in the Colonies!" He and Paul Rose as Pauline Revere really livened up the Pageants.

Bob also was a cat lover and brought Cora Ann Louise Charles the Second to NY with him. She was the damnedest little creature. The bathroom in our first apartment was tiny. If you were sitting on the toilet you could count on Cora to come in and jump up into the washbowl, which was eye level to you when sitting on the toilet. Cora would squat to pee right over the drain hole. She always looked at you while she was in action and never splashed a drop. She had perfect aim. She also loved living in the barn with us in Westport. She was not familiar with the creatures in the wild and one day wandered too far and never returned. It was a terribly sad day when we lost Cora.

Television moved to California and when Will and I moved with it, Bob was not far behind. He found an apartment not far from our place and managed to find a replacement for Cora who we continued to call Cora 2. They looked very much alike. He continued his drinking and one night we followed him driving home to see if he might need help. He was driving about 5 miles an hour the entire way. The cops also began following him. As he pulled in front of his apartment the cops stopped right behind him. One cop got out and walked up to Bob's car. He asked Bob to step out and when he didn't budge the cop opened his door and Bob just fell out. He was passed out and dead to the world.

Bob didn't last very long in California. He eventually moved to an affordable housing place but too far from us to look in on him very often. A friend in his building took care of Cora. I guess one day he just gave up. We lost a longtime dear friend and also contact with his former friend Reggie Adams. I do have the painting I did of Bob in his Elizabethan English Royalty drag. It's a favorite. A painting in the same costume sold. Fortunately we have memories or it would be unbearable losing dear friends.

ERIC UNDERWOOD

Will and I met Eric when he was 23, and he came to a party at the house many years ago. His genuine nature and ready sense of humor quickly made him a very dear friend.

Eric had already worked at the Lido de Paris, Las Vegas, several commercials, and performed around the world at that age, and had worked with many of the same people I had worked with including Nick Navarro who had been doing quite a bit of choreography by then.

Soon after I met Eric, he was hired to work at the original Chippendale's in Culver City. Soon he was cast as Nicky in *La Cage aux Folles* and performed with the show on Broadway. He has kept pretty busy over the years as a professional dancer with a long list of credits.

Eric continues to be our favorite Santa Claus at Christmas. Since he is blessed with - and works hard at keeping - a great body, he is a terrific sexy Santa.

*Eric Underwood-
Master of Disguise
Some of his costumes at our
4th of July Parties have been
absolutely hysterical.*

He also is the model in many of my paintings and often came to model for me on very short notice. He's worked with animators at Disney and his dance background makes him an excellent model for the animation industry.

These days he and his handsome husband are living on an island in the Pacific Northwest. Truly a piece of paradise and I am very happy for them.

PAUL TEMPLETON & GORDON REGAN

Will and I did many trips to the Wine Country and Mexico with these two dear friends from Berkeley, California. Our first visit to the Napa Valley was unforgettable. Our plan was to spend a little time at several wineries each day. On our first stop we tested champagne. The location was beautifully landscaped and the winery was comfortable and beautiful. Soon we were served a glass of their champagne and we all agreed it was delicious and required a second taste. You can guess what came next and after that the only thing we could do was stay and have lunch and another bottle of champagne or two. On our first day, we managed to only visit that one winery.

We spent the night in a lovely highly recommended hotel and were able to diligently get through several wineries on our second day.

The Robert Mondavi winery was a must because Robert comes from Virginia, Minnesota, and I'm from nearby Mt. Iron. He was very gracious and invited us to stay for lunch. Lunch was served in an outdoor pavilion in the middle of the fragrant grapevines.

A beautiful vase of flowers graced the center of the table and as Michael Mondavi placed it in position, I kiddingly said, "I like the centerpiece in the main lobby. It's much bigger."

Minutes later I saw the Lobby centerpiece bouncing above the grapevines on its way to our table.

I said "Michael I was just kidding."

He replied, "Ask and you shall receive, besides it looks better out here."

It turned out to be a beautiful and delicious afternoon. We continued our visit to the wine country and hated to leave. I can report that everywhere we went we were treated with the kindest hospitality and the finest wines. We felt everybody should make a trip to the wine country. We did load the car with cases of wine. In addition to the wine we said we could heartily recommend the restaurants for various menus of delicious food.

Later in the year, Robert Mondavi and I attended a celebration in Eveleth, Minnesota, honoring Italians Who Have Made It. The third person was the coach for the Hockey Team that won the gold in the Winter Olympics. I believe his name was Mariucci. The evening was great, but one thing struck me as strange. Robert had supplied the wine for dinner and there was a bottle of Mondovi wine on each table that was never opened until late in the evening. When I asked why it wasn't opened so guests could enjoy it with dinner. I was told because they would quickly chug-a-lug it all right down and get drunk immediately and ruin the show. In all, it was a very Italian celebration. I was given an Italian chef's hat and apron and I dressed in them for my acceptance speech. How much more Italian can you get? It was a pretty fun evening and I stayed a few days more to visit relatives and friends.

On a trip to Canada with Gordon and Paul, Gordon, who comes from Canada, showed us how annoyed a Canadian from Quebec can get if you mispronounce words in French. He stepped up to the front desk in our hotel and asked the girl in very incorrectly pronounced French, directions to "Rue St. Annie."

She quickly corrected him by saying he meant "Rue St. Ann."

Gordon kept it up saying, "That's what I said, "Rue St. Annie."

This kept going back and forth and got pretty hysterical until he finally gave in and pronounced it correctly. The clerk was exhausted. Poor girl. She never seemed to know she was being put on.

Our trips to Mexico were great fun and the beaches were great. To watch the guys dive off the high cliffs into the ocean was always a must. It's pretty awesome to see how daring they really are. The temptation to buy lots of stuff because of the cheap prices never seems to leave you and you always wind up loading the car with stuff you'll probably never use. On our return to the States we were always stopped at the border to have the Border Customs check our purchases.

I love the story about two American queens stopped at the border in their convertible with the top down and the car loaded

Gordon and Paul

Gordon sharing a moment with Carol

with lots of stuff. One thing they had was a carved wooden figure of a woman with only the upper half of her sticking out of a bag with both arms stretched out to the side and her mouth wide open.

The custom officer asked, "What's that?"

Without hesitation the driver answered, "Oh that! That's Ethel Merman."

Customs waved them on through.

SALLY MAE JONES

Once we were settled in our California home we had to get a maid to help with all the chores necessary to keep it together. It wasn't long before Will hired Sally Mae Tucker Jones, which she said was her "eagle" (legal) name. To say she was quite something is putting it mildly. She was quite a character.

We had put a pool in the backyard and used the maid's room as a change room to get into bathing suits. (Though we called it the "maid's room" she didn't actually use it - she didn't live with us and we used the room as a secondary guest room.)

One day Will was getting into his swim trunks when Sally walked in on a stark naked Will.

She exclaimed, "Oh Mistah Sandahs excuse me! 'Ahm' so Sorry. Ah didn't mean to walk in like this! Ahm so sorry! Please Ahm soooo-"

Will said, "Oh come on in Sally, I don't have anything you haven't seen before."

She quickly replied, "Diffrent collah!"

One day Sally arrived and was singing away at the top of her lungs when Will commented, "Sally, you're certainly in a cheerful mood today. What brought this on?"

Sally replied, "Mistah Sandahs, in church yestahday I was asked to sing a solo and I was scahhhed, really scahhhed, but when the time came the Lord possessed me and I sang like a bird! And I think I still feel a little possessed today."

Petula Clark with my Petula

Many times Sally would serve drinks to friends using the swimming pool, and one year they decided they should give her a Christmas gift. A friend who worked in the fur business decided a fur stole would be nice. Sally was overjoyed to get it.

She came to one of the TV Shows I was working on and when she saw me crossing the stage before show time she stood up and shouted "Mistah Tony! Mistah Tony! Look I'm wearing my fur strole," Then she turned to the audience, posed and said, "His friends bought me this fuhhh strole!" The audience burst into applause.

On another occasion I got an urgent call from Sally in a panic because she couldn't find Petula, our little white poodle. I told her to look again because I knew she had to be in the house somewhere.

About ten minutes went by and another call came in from Sally saying, "Mistah Tony, I found Petula. She was under the bed. Before, I looked everywhere and called her over and over again, and she never said nuthin!"

I'm sad to say Sally became too frail to work any longer and had to leave us. She did call one day near Thanksgiving holiday to tell us she was having a some friends in to celebrate Thanksgiving and said, "It sho would be nice if I could serve them some turkey."

Will replied with "Okay, Sally, I'll send you a turkey."

She quickly came back with, "Better be a big one! There's goin' to be a lot of them."

Soon after the Polaroid camera came out, Sally was out in the garden when I said "Sally just stand there and I'll take your picture." She hit a pose, I snapped the picture and pulled it out of the camera and showed it to her and she exclaimed, "OOOOH! Look at that Big Black Face hangin' out!"

I've looked all over for that photo to use it here - and just can't find it anywhere.... she was a dear soul. In all my years I've never run across another SALLY!

BARBARA LAZAROFF

Barbara is one of the Beverly Hills wonders who, along with her former husband Wolfgang Puck, established the world famous Spago Restaurant and a host of other restaurants. Because of this and her extraordinary philanthropy she fits into the title of my book as one of the STARS IN MY EYES! Though she hobnobs with the most famous people in the world, she is one of the most down to earth people you might meet... she just wears more diamonds than most folks.

In the early 80's I heard of a fabulous restaurant called SPAGO and Will and I gathered a few friends and decided to try it. We were ushered to a table with bench seats and slid into position when a great looking lady came by, bumped me over a notch and sat right down beside me. I said, "Excuse me, do I know you?" She said "No but I know who you are because I see your work on television. I'm Barbara Lazaroff and I own this restaurant." Touché! That's all it took and we became friends ever since.

Barbara Lazaroff, Tony, & Stephanie Powers

They feed many of the stars of stage and screen and Spago's is "the place to go" for a fabulous dinner. One year, Barbara arranged for a celebration at Spago for my birthday and typical Barbara pulled out all the stops. From a royal crown hat to a multilayered cake with small cards stuck all over in gold paint telling of my theatre and television accomplishments. It was pretty fantastic.

I was amused a few years back at a party thrown at the Hollywood Forever cemetery by Tyler Cassity. There is a lake with an island in the midst of the grounds, with a large Parthenon sort of tomb in the center of it, and this island is normally not accessible to visitors. For this evening, Tyler put a bridge across the water to the island and opened up the giant bronze doors of the tomb. A harpist played serenely nearby on the grass, and champagne flowing freely. Barbara arrived in a full length sparkling beaded gown, a wide brimmed black hat with a veil, black opera gloves and on her back was a large pair of feathery wings. It was wonderfully fitting for a cocktail party at a cemetery.

It was a marvelous event. The inside of the crypt (which is rarely seen) is tiled in gold mosaic patterns and the candlelit interior was magical once you closed the bronze doors to shut out the daylight. The flickering light sparkled off the mosaics and the marble coffins. In the candlelight, Barbara's dress glittered even more fabulously. But of course, the diamonds couldn't compete with the twinkle in her eye. She's a good soul.

At my Christmas parties she is a very busy woman photographing all the celebrities and being photographed with them. At a large garden party at her house I was overwhelmed when I learned she did all the wholesome and wonderful cooking. The only help she had was in the kitchen was for cleaning up and seeing things stayed hot. Oh yes! Her boyfriend, John, did the outdoor grilling. Pretty Fabulous.

Recently, I learned another great facet to this unusual woman. She was honored at a wonderful dinner event at the Beverly Hills Hotel for her extensive philanthropy and support of medical research. It was there I learned she is quite a public speaker. Furthermore, she has seen to it that a dear friend of mine is getting the best care to surmount his health issues. All of these wonderful traits seem to come so very naturally to remarkable Barbara! Angel wings have never been merely a costume.

JOE STEWART & JOHN SHAFFNER

I met Joe and John on *Star Search* and we quickly became the best of friends. They created all the fabulous sets for that and many other projects I've done. In fact they do many of the most popular shows on television. *Friends, The Ellen Show, Big Bang Theory, Two and a Half Men, Dharma & Greg*... more shows than I can list. On top of that busy schedule, John has served as the Chairman and CEO of the Academy of Television Arts and Sciences. John was even listed by a crazy blog as one of the most powerful Jewish men in entertainment - which is quite an achievement as he isn't Jewish. It was pretty amusing.

John and Joe called to say they were booking a trip to Russia on the Seabourn line - would I like to go along? Would I? Absolutely!!! I asked Paul Templeton to come along as well, and he was thrilled. Working with Mikhail Baryshnikov on the filming of *The Nutcracker* inspired me to learn more of his background. A friend of mine at Ballet Theatre in New York contacted the dance school in St. Petersburg to notify them of who I was and my visit. John, Joe, and Paul Templeton were elated when I told them of what would be waiting for us in St. Petersburg. We booked suites across from one another on one of the yachts of Seaborne Line and were off to an unforgettable summer experience. Just socializing with the passengers was great fun. When they learned of our professions we had even more attention and cocktail time always turned out to be a rather grand party. The photo speaks of our freedom on the boat. The ship's photographer was lining people up like a vocal group when I said to our group "This is dull. When I count to three hit a pose." We did it and wham! The result is what you see. We got applause and laughs from the passengers. Poor photographer had to put his foot down because the other passengers, seeing what we did, wanted to do the same thing.

When we arrived in St. Petersburg, I immediately contacted the ballet school and we were invited to come the next day to attend a ballet rehearsal. Next we hired a driver named Kolya who spoke English and proved to be a jewel. He stayed with us for our entire visit and helped tremendously in getting us to all the right places. At the school, we were met by the ballet teacher who had worked with Baryshnikov and Nureyev. I was rather formally introduced as an American choreographer who had worked with their Mikhail Baryshnikov and Rudolf Nureyev. They seemed genuinely pleased to meet us and proceeded to have the students do a whole class, barre and all. The teacher kindly asked if I would like to join in taking the class. Graciously I declined by saying I was on vacation. After class we had an informal question and answer get together followed by an invitation to lunch right there with all the students. Of course I got a lot of questions about Rudy and Misha. They were especially interested in their film and theater work.

After lunch we had a tour of the storage room containing the costumes for all the different ballets in their repertoire. It was mammoth and took a long time to go through the history of the Russian Ballet. Next we paid a visit to the upper floor where a ballet was in rehearsal with full orchestra. The dancers were in top form and really put on a fabulous rehearsal on a stage with proper lighting. It was a magical transition. I told our theater escort we couldn't leave until I saw the mirror in the wings where the ballerina's checked their tutus and toe shoes before going out on stage. Sure enough after many historical years it was still there in the same position leaning up against the wall. Everyone couldn't have been more gracious and welcoming. For the evening we were given seats in a prominent box in the Marinsky Theatre to see a ballet and the current opera, which was endless.

I guess our restlessness became obvious when Kolya said, "It's all right to leave at any time. People do it all the time."

John Shaffner, Joe Stewart, Tony, and Paul Templeton on our way to Russia

We took him up on it and went to a nearby restaurant for an excellent Russian dinner. This day alone was worth the trip.

After many adventures, we finally were back in the US and I was back in my own trundle bed. The

Tony and the great dancer Alicia Alonso on another trip of ours - this time to Cuba in 2002

overwhelming surprise was a gift from John and Joe of two huge photo albums loaded with photos documenting the entire trip. Those two, John and Joe are indeed A TREASURE, and they continue to prove how important they are to me.

SCOTTY BOWERS

Scotty has been a part of my life for many years. He still tends bar at my family Christmas parties and is great to my sisters and to all the guests. He even knows their drinks by heart. He can serve up a drink garnished with the funniest ribald tales of his adventures in Hollywood. He is one of those very capable people and can pretty much do anything. He has done my garden tree trimming and is especially great at fixing my plumbing. You can take that both ways. He became famous for stirring people's drinks with what nature provided him - to the delight of many laughing guests.

It seems around the holidays the first question from the family is, "Will Scotty be there?" Not only is he here, he has their drinks ready for them when they arrive. After dinner, David Streets plays the piano and Nick plays the sax and we all go into the living room around the tree awaiting Santa's arrival. One year Scotty was our Santa and to this day he remains one of our favorites. He was extra special with my sisters and would give each a box of chocolates as a Santa gift. He's definitely one of a kind.

For years, people have been telling him he needs to write down all of his adventures with acquiring sexual experiences for the rich and famous. Tennessee Williams took a crack at telling Scotty's story many years back, but Scotty wasn't happy with the result. Now it is finally out and his "tell all" book, *Full Service*, has become a best-seller. Proof that sex still sells and Scotty is the king. Since Scotty has been a good friend for so many years and still is, a follow up camera interview for a documentary about his life was conducted with me at my house just yesterday, Aug. 28, 2012. The interviewer seemed happy to collect some added information that I could supply.

I am happy to see him discover such great success (as long as he still has time to check my plumbing).

PAINTING

The creative spirit frequently finds many ways to manifest itself. I have always loved to paint. From that painting of the Indian when I was six, to now I have always made time to paint and to hone my skills.

It might seem that painting a canvas and staging a musical number are entirely different disciplines, but they are flip sides of the same coin. Arranging shapes, color, story, and movement within a frame are integral to both. Challenging one's self to excel in multiple disciplines increases what you bring to every project.

Dancing and choreography took up much of my time in New York and not until I moved to California and met up with Dinah Shore did I get hit with the painting bug. Painting in oils just seemed to flow naturally and I would occupy any free time at my easel painting pictures.

While on *The Danny Kaye Show*, I joined a group of painters at the McKenzie Gallery on La Cienega Blvd which was right on my way home. It was owned by Don Cook and Richard McKenzie, who later married Ava Astaire, daughter of Fred. We would gather in the room at the back of the gallery where Dick McKenzie would give us brief instructions on how to paint the model of the evening. I had a great time. You might be surprised at how many celebrities spend their free time in front of an easel.

Phyllis Diller painted with us in the workshop, which made all our classes particularly entertaining. We laughed a lot. Over time I developed a significant body of work and Richard thought it was time for an exhibition at the Gallery. After a star studded opening night, sales were so successful, we later mounted a second show. It was very satisfying to see the great reception my paintings received. It is even more satisfying when they sell!

The opening parties were full of people I had worked with and many of my paintings went to good homes. Danny Kaye bought a couple, Julie Andrews bought one, Stephanie Powers bought one, I've lost track of where they all went to - the Gallery burned down with all of its records of who bought what. An architect friend designed a studio to be built over my garage, so now I paint at home. Since then, I've shown my work at various events and it always gives me much pleasure to see a positive response.

I decided to do a portrait of Juliet Prowse - she was such a dear friend and I wanted to capture the Juliet I knew. She came by the house one day to model for it, and I thought since she was

Lucille Ball at Tony's first gallery show. She bought three paintings. One was a painting of an old lady who always sat on a nearby shady street corner selling maps to star homes.

221

Juliet Prowse as painted by Tony Charmoli

so famous for her legs, I would feature her hands which were every bit as spectacular in their ability to move and communicate. She was delighted with the result, and to this day it remains one of my favorite paintings. I have had many offers to buy it, but this is one I just can't be parted from.

Juliet and Nicky Navarro both modeled nude for a painting I called *A Portrait of an Apple* - though out of discretion, I did not use Juliet's face. Originally it was a dyptych with a painting of a snake positioned below - but that part was lost in the fire at the gallery.

I painted whatever interested me and worked in many styles. Sometimes I painted the world of dance - dressing rooms and dancers in motion. Sometimes I'd paint from photos of my travels, or people who have come by the house and sat by my pool, or flowers or still life.

As a director and choreographer, I always chose a style to suit the story or project, and I try to do the same thing as a painter. Not every story wants the same approach. Some stories are best told with ballet, some with modern or tap, some stories want to be abstracted, and some want details. It is always important that the method supports the story. There are choreographers and artists whose work always

Left: Nanette Fabray considers an apple martini at the gallery show. Right: With the wonderful character actress Reta Shaw.

looks the same. And that just gets boring to my mind - it becomes a gimmick even if it was clever at the outset. Your signature should be good work, not the same steps used in everything you choreograph. I believe in telling the story. If you do good work consistently, if you know how to tell the story, people will know who you are and you will stay busy. Do not rely on the same thing over and over.

This is just a sampling of paintings I have done over the years. Since painting is an integral part of my life and creative process, it seemed worthwhile to include it when I look back at my life. I encourage anyone to explore many avenues of creativity - it will make you a stronger artist over all.

Below: My sister Nell and my mother came out and stayed with us at the Chateau Marmont while Nell was waiting out her divorce. My mother is knitting my rehearsal socks. I've always liked this painting of her.

Above, Debbie and me having fun in front of a stage scene I envisioned.
Left: Clive Clerk
Below is one of two quite large floral pieces I've done. One was sold for a beautiful home in the Midwest somewhere, this one is in my entry stairwell.

223

L to R: Peter Stone (Book), Lauren Bacall, Robert Moore (Director), John Kander (Music), Fred Ebb (Lyrics), Tony Charmoli (Musical Staging) & Harry Guardino

Chapter 11
Woman of the Year

LAUREN BACALL

Lawrence Kasha was instrumental in getting me involved with *Woman of the Year* with Lauren Bacall. He had talked about it with me when I was at his home here in California, so when the call came I was not too surprised.

I practically moved to New York to start auditions immediately. Ed Nolfe was to be my assistant. This was a big help because he had worked with Bacall on a previous Broadway show. He was a big help - when he wasn't passed out on drugs. I had auditions for dancers and all the preliminaries. Meeting Bacall was pleasant and I must admit, I had a very nice time working with her. She was game to try stuff, and as long as I worked within her limitations, she was okay. She liked to do as little as possible, but that was ok. She is not a dancer, but she can move. And when she's moving in tempo, I call it dancing. This was not a dance show. It was a stretch to get some dancing into the show.

One novel way we added dance to the show was a dance duet between Harry Guardino and a projected dancing cartoon character named Katz. I think this was the first time that a cartoon character sang and danced with a live actor on the Broadway stage. I worked with Michael Sporn, the animation director, in plotting out the big dance number. I danced out the part of the character and they filmed me. They then used my dancing as a reference for animating the cat. There were more than 12 minutes of animated duets between Harry Guardino and Katz. The original plan was to have three pieces totaling about five minutes, but the animation was so successful in the tryouts in Boston, we kept adding more material. An additional short number was added with more animation, but it never made it to New York. Harry never quite got it in Boston and he was too nervous for the Broadway opening to learn it. So the number was cut. But the cat's movement was based on my dancing.

Lauren Bacall was not known as a singer, but she did her best. Early in the show, her big *Woman of the Year* number called for her to sing a note that she consistently struggled to reach. I told Fred Ebb and John Kander that they needed to change the note because she just couldn't hit it. But Fred insisted that he had to have her hit that note.

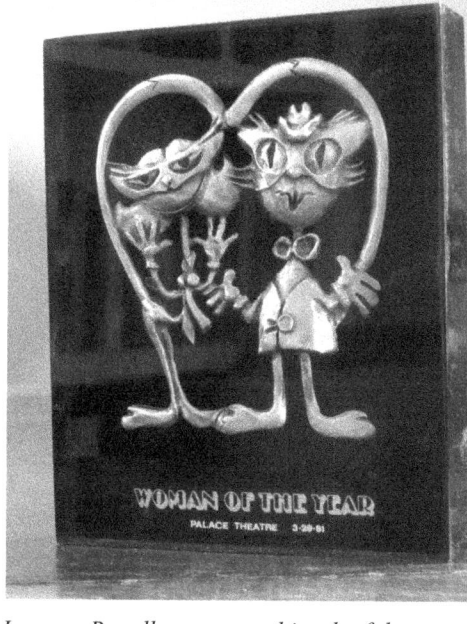

Lauren Bacall gave me this playful memento of the show - a pewter version of Katz in an acrylic block, with a thank you note on the back.

After the tryouts in Boston we opened at the Palace Theater in New York. The theatre was packed and I was happy to see Ethel Merman at the opening with my friends Lee Roy Reams and Carole Cook. They sat right down front.

After the initial applause subsided, Bacall launched into her opening song. Bacall reached for the climactic big note Fred Ebb insisted on, and missed dreadfully.

Then the entire theater heard Merman burst out with "JEEESUS!" It was funny. Leave it to Ethel.

I never understood why that note wasn't changed to fit Bacall's range. I always changed any dance movements to what her limitations were, which often meant she didn't do very much. But I never made her look ridiculous. I've always seen my job is to make stars look like stars.

Much later in the run, I was on a visit back to New York and I met with some of the dancers and they all seemed to have complaints about Miss Bacall not being very nice to them. In fact they had a new slogan for her BOB, (Bitch of Broadway). It was a surprise to me because I never had a problem with Bacall - in fact she always was very nice to me and we got on very well. But of course, she knew I was entirely focused on making her look good.

225

Dancers: Michael Gorman, Robert Warner, Dwight Baxter, Richard Larsen, Gene Montoya, Michael Kabala, Sergio Cal, Daniel Quinn

I had a problem with my assistant Ed Nolfi. He was hired because he had worked with Bacall in a previous show and she liked him. I also liked him when he was sober. But he was into drugs and sometimes passed out on the floor in the dressing room for long periods of time leaving me to do the work alone. Then when he came to, I'd have to teach him all the stuff he had missed while he was out cold. Neither Will nor I have ever had much interest in drugs. Not that I was particularly judgmental about drugs other than from a practical standpoint. A martini always seemed more civilized - not that we've been big drinkers either. There is too much to do in life to waste it under the influence of something.

When we were in Boston at Christmas time trying out the show, I tried to think of what Ed would want most for Christmas. It seemed obvious. I decided to give him a small silver box from Tiffany's filled with cocaine. Very early the next morning while I was still in bed, there was a knock on my door.

It was Ed asking, "Tony, do you have any more?"

I couldn't believe what I was hearing. He had used up the whole Christmas gift load I had given him not ten hours prior. It was sad to see this happening to such a nice guy, but I never used him again.

RAQUEL WELCH

When it was time for Bacall to go on vacation I was called in to the producer's office and there was a group of backers there.

I was greeted with, "Come in Tony, sit down. It's soon time for Bacall to go on vacation. You've worked with a lot of these women, who do you think could replace her?"

I said, "Mitzi could do it, but she won't because it's not written for her, but Raquel Welch could do it."

Immediately one spoke up with, "But can she sing and dance?" I countered with, "Can Bacall?"

Raquel was hired.

Putting Raquel into the show was a whole different ball game because Raquel really could move and really could dance. We still had the limitations of the music and the arrangements. We couldn't change those but having worked with Raquel before, I knew I could do a lot of fluffing and rearranging to perk up the numbers because Raquel is a pretty good dancer.

One rehearsal when she had danced something extremely well and liked what she saw in the rehearsal mirror, she complimented me on the choreography.

I responded with, "Stick with me kid, I'm never wrong!"

She snapped back with a smile, "That makes two of us!"

Stepping into replace Betty Bacall in *Woman of the Year* was quite an experience. When word got out that Raquel was replacing Bacall, almost immediately giant glamorous pictures of Raquel graced the sides of buses all over the city.

One of the dancers told me, "When Bacall heard this, she said, 'They gave her the buses! They never gave me the fucking buses!'"

Used by Permission. All rights reserved, Playbill Inc.

Lauren had opened the show in a silver sheath, and Raquel wanted to make her own statement at the top of the show, so she spent a good deal of focus on finding the perfect opening dress. When she announced she had found one, it was not to be seen until opening night.

When she appeared in the spotlight, it blew all of us away, as well as the audience. Norma Kamali had created a masterpiece in the form of a slick body hugging sparkling gold column. It echoed the trophy being bestowed on her in the play at the celebration she was attending. Raquel looked like a storybook Goddess and simply brought the house down with an ear shattering, standing ovation - just posing there like a curvaceous shimmering column of gold. A knockout! Never before have I seen anyone stop the show before they had done anything.

This was a great relief to Raquel. She was not known as a Broadway performer and was pretty nervous stepping into the lead role of a hit Broadway show. It had always been her dream to be in a musical on Broadway and to start out as the star who has to carry the show is a daunting task. While standing there in front of that thundering applause, she later said that she almost broke down in tears, "They like me!" It was a big moment. It is so easy to forget that celebrities get nervous too - but one of the things that makes them special is that they've learned to work through that fear and deliver a knockout performance.

This show landed Raquel a two-page color spread in LIFE magazine. She looked fabulous lying on the roof of a shiny black limousine with the sparkling night-lights of Manhattan in the background.

I was extremely pleased to see that my recommendation of Raquel worked out so well. Raquel had come in to replace Lauren for a two week vacation, but when Lauren finally left the show, Raquel returned to play to very good houses in an extended run. And I understand she was very civil to the rest of the company. She is a class act. Since she was a good dancer, I was able to pump up the choreography a couple of notches. The dancers were quite happy about that.

In *Woman of the Year*, she would often get applause on just her wardrobe and of course the way she looked in it had a lot to do with it. This always happened with the little red dress she wore in the opening of the second act. Raquel was a hit and had almost sold out performances for her entire run. We all liked Raquel and hoped she would run for a long time, but alas her contract was for only six months and she had to leave because of prior commitments.

DEBBIE REYNOLDS

Again I was asked about a replacement for her, and I suggested Debbie Reynolds. They agreed to it and Debbie was hired. I also changed the choreography to accommodate Debbie's best dancing style. Debbie is a great tapper, so I brought some tap numbers into the show and adjusted the choreography to reflect Debbie's strengths. She was rehearsing *Woman of the Year* by day and appearing at Harrah's in Reno at night. She was a busy gal.

It was great working with Debbie again and she did an excellent job in the show. Her run didn't last very long however because New York suffered another of those huge snowstorms which forced the closure of theaters and brought New York to a virtual standstill forcing the show to close. But she was wonderful in the role. Entirely different than either Lauren or Raquel.

Used by Permission. All rights reserved, Playbill Inc.

Circus of the Stars photos courtesy of Bunny Stivers and Tim Kettle

Chapter 15
Circus of the Stars

Circus of the Stars was the brainchild of Bob Stivers who dreamed up an extravaganza which used the talents of as many celebrities as could be interested in joining the Circus - and there were many. He already had a built in writer with his lovely wife Bunny Stivers. She did a great job. The quick response from so many celebrities willing to go through the rigorous training of various circus stunts was amazing. Celebrities spent weeks training on the high wire and trapeze and all kinds of circus stunts. Many of the stars realized long held dreams on the show. Performing in a circus is an amazing experience and held genuine danger. To step into the cage of a wild animal took patience and a lot of guts. Juliet Prowse was mauled twice when dealing with the cats.

Bunny and her assistants spent hours observing the training to be able to write stories and accurate introductions for the ringmasters. I also watched closely to learn what was facing me when capturing these stunts for television. All of this took place in a two ring circus tent but most of the stunts required only one ring. A new and different world of shooting challenges opened up. It was a great adventure.

There were more stars than I can possibly remember here, but here are a few that stand out in my memory.

BEA ARTHUR

Bea Arthur was wonderful on *The Golden Girls* with the other broads, but to work with her on *Circus of the Stars* was a different story. On this occasion we were doing the show at *Universal Studios*. I had parked in the lot and was walking to the stage door and hesitated when I saw her limo arriving. There were several "Do Not Enter" orange cones about 8 feet from the stage door and the limo stopped as per the law. I waited out of sight to see how this was going to play out. Bea apparently insisted that the driver get out of the car and remove the cones, so he could drive her right to the door so she wouldn't have to walk those few extra feet to the stage door. I smelled trouble with this woman right away.

It didn't take long to prove I was right. On the very first day, Bea was doing her job as the ringmaster wearing a long black gown but it didn't cover her bare feet. When I said it's not proper for the ringmaster to be barefoot she complained her feet hurt. I insisted she put shoes on for the wide orientation master shots, then she could remove them because I would focus on tighter shots. She begrudgingly acquiesced but didn't have her shoes with her. Instead of having her assistant bring them to her, she left the ring and was gone for a very long time. I learned quickly to never let her leave the set, and insisted that her assistants come to her.

Through the day the more difficult she became. We worked it out however. When I had to do a shot big enough to show the ring and the act she was introducing, she would put shoes on. I had someone standing by with her shoes and when necessary they would dash into the ring and put them on her. It often destroyed the tempo of the event because each time we stopped, she had to have a drink, fix her hair, touch up her makeup and review what she had to say. In the meantime the animals and performers impatiently stood by, the trainers working their butts off to keep their animals from going crazy till her highness could put her shoes on and do her job.

Bea with Dick Clark and Merv Griffin

One act was a group of dogs sitting on different levels and the one sitting eye level right next to Bea's face was the tiniest, funniest spiked hair almost hairless little creature, and I said to Bea, "Coming out of commercial I'd love it if you'd look at that little dog next to you and ask, 'Who does your hair?' Then turn front, and go on with the script."

The whole crew on headset laughed, but Bea in a bullish, negative kind of way asked, "Why am I saying that?"

I said, "Because we all think it's funny."

She just wouldn't do it. Bob Stivers, the producer, was standing behind me and everybody in the booth agreed that she was no fun and she would not be asked back.

230

I went to see Bea's one woman show and liked it. When it was finished she acknowledged many of her friends in the audience who had worked with her on *The Golden Girls* but totally ignored Betty White who was sitting right in front second row center. Such a talent but unforgivable manners.

MERV GRIFFIN

Merv worked with the large trained cats and it turned out that the small house cat was much more vicious than the big ones. It really put up a big fight. Scared the shit out of Merv.

I met Merv one night back in New York at the apartment of two of my *Hit Parade* dancers Tad Tadlock and George Vosburg. He was just plain Merv at that time and was working when he could as a singer in any club that would hire him. How things change in time.

The memorable thing that evening was Merv's wife, who was introduced to Will and me as a very good singer. After dinner she was asked to sing a number for us and after a great deal of coaxing and prodding she agreed. She very feebly started with, "Whenever I feel afraid, I whistle a happy tune" then she would try to whistle but only blew wind and her knees started to shake. This continued through a great part of the song. Will and I felt so sorry for her believing she really was so nervous singing this song until she broke up laughing seeing what it was doing to Will and me. She was really very convincing. We didn't realize all the coaxing was part of the act. She then belted out the tune full voice and impressed us all. We all had a very good laugh afterwards. Of course we all know what a great tycoon Merv turned out to be.

BROOKE SHIELDS

Brooke Shields appeared in five of our shows. In one she was the Ring Master in another Horse Dressage, then Rings, Dogs, and Aerial Acrobatics. She was a great sport beyond the call of duty. Name it, she did it. Sixteen-year-old Brooke even walked on broken glass.

JANE POWELL

Jane managed the pretty Liberty Ponies and put them through their paces, which is more difficult than it looks as they all looked alike. She fit right in.

Jane and I already had a great history with her special and with *Feathertop*, so it was wonderful working with her again and seeing her trying something new.

Chris Atkins giving a lift to a lion

BETTY WHITE

We were always happy to have Betty on *Circus of the Stars*. We were guaranteed something funny would happen. On one occasion in the ring Betty was given a camel to work with and she talked to it as if it was her agent. She scolded it for not getting any jobs for her then she fired it in the end. Her delivery was always spot on and would bust up the tent.

Betty is one of those performers who is truly great with animals. On another appearance she worked with an elephant and all went very well until at the end of the act and the elephant snatched off her wig with its trunk. It was hysterical. Even the elephant had a sense of humor.

MARTY ALLEN

Marty was on the show quite a number of times. He performed with seals, orangutans, elephants, horses, cliff divers, and wrestled a 450 pound brown bear.

Marty didn't believe in rehearsing his act much as he thought the impromptu of the moment made things funnier. He did spend a few minutes with the bear beforehand just to make an acquaintance - but evidently the bear would have liked a bit more rehearsal. The bear kept trying to bite his neck during the taping. But he kept the bear's chin up and his fingers out of his mouth.

LAUREN BACALL

With that stage voice of hers Lauren Bacall made an excellent Ring Master. Only a couple of years later, I would be staging her in *Woman of the Year* on Broadway. She has a strong personality but we always got along just fine. Her presence certainly came through in the ring. When she commanded an act to appear she made it sound like it was the best in the world. Then when the act was finished and she re-entered the ring, you didn't know if the applause was for the act or for her. She was a great showman.

She had one request from the management - she required a fresh bottle of vodka in her dressing room each day. It must be

Left: A mix of celebrity and professional trapeze artists. Right, a young Ricky Schroder ready to leap.

fresh whether any was used in the current bottle or not. The old one should be removed and another put in its place. I was curious to know how she could tell if it was a new bottle or the same one returned. It didn't matter as long as it didn't interfere with her work.

She still remains one of our best ringmasters.

Above, Marty Allen monkeys around.

233

One female celebrity I'll not name, though a beautiful woman, cost us a lot of time and tried our patience to its limit. She had no regard for when the trainer would say the cats were ready. Which means we must roll tape immediately or the animals become restless and can become dangerous. Each time she was called to the set she'd arrive - but not ready to shoot, she always had a mirror and spent a long time checking herself, then complain that something was not right. One time her earrings didn't satisfy her and the costume designer had to run to her dressing room to get others. By then the cats would be too dangerous for anyone but the trainer to enter the cage. That meant the cats would have to be taken out of the cage and returned to be taped the next day. Another time she didn't like the shade of lipstick and that threw that shoot over till the next day.

I never understood what she was doing with all the time she had between acts. She had lots of time to sort this all out way before she had to introduce an act. She was never asked back. I only include this story as it is an important lesson for any performer to remember to be aware of others beside themselves. It will help your career in the long run.

WHOOPIE GOLDBERG

Whoopie introduced the Aerial Acrobats. I had the camera positioned at a very low angle and she called my attention to it with, "Tony is that camera going to be down there?"

I said "Yes."

She said "Ugly!"

I agreed, but I explained to her I was not doing a close shot of her but a wide master to see her and the act she is introducing way up there on the high wire. After the introduction the camera would be raised to do the close up of her completing the introduction. She understood completely and was happy and I proceeded as planned. I showed her the playback and she was thoroughly satisfied. As expected, she did a very good job.

She is a good example of how successful artists are frequently interested in camera angles and lighting - some might accuse them of being difficult, but the reality is that knowing what makes them look good IS their business.

And that is one of the reasons why I was successful. I always made sure that stars looked like stars when they were on camera and they trusted me.

Left: Whoopie Goldberg; Upper Right: Lana Turner

LANA TURNER

The celebrities always knew what their act would be before showing up for rehearsal and the show, but clearly Lana hadn't expected it to be as difficult as it was for her. Her job was to thread a needle through a balloon without popping it. Lana was frightened to death of what was going to happen when she threaded the needle through the balloon. She would react to the bang before it happened and over and over would pop the balloon instead of threading it. And of course each time the balloon popped in her face, the more terrified she got of the balloon popping.

She was a nervous wreck before we finally got a take that worked.

RICHARD SIMMONS

Richard did the Spinning Plates and was pretty expert at it but he was never asked back. Once he finished his act he wouldn't leave. In his standard uniform of shorts and tank top he ran all around the arena singing and talking - presumably entertaining the audience. But his actions were ruining audio and camera shots and made the shoot much more difficult. But, one has to hand it to him, he's still out there fearlessly running around in the same old costume of shorts and a tank top.

Richard is a prankster. One time I was called into his office to discuss a project. I was ushered into a room with a desk and a large chair with a high back. I was told to wait there and he'd be right with me. The chair behind the desk was turned towards the wall. It was obvious that he was sitting there - but evidently it was supposed to be a surprise for when he turned around. So, I waited for what seemed like forever. By the time the chair turned to reveal Richard sitting there any joke was lost. It was intended in fun so I laughed. He is a bundle of energy who has inspired a lot of people to exercise, so I applaud him for that.

PHYLLIS DILLER

It was hysterically funny watching Phyllis in a pig pen managing pigs over hurdles and bumping through barriers. She managed to get through it with a lot of crazy antics. It was exhausting pushing and shoving those pigs through their barriers. Plus at the very end, we were exhausted from laughter. It was a "strenuous but worth the work" act.

Phyllis Diller working her magic.

In another event, she had to guide a seal through its tricks. We were laughing so hard it was hard to tell which was winning. She was always a lot of fun. Once she did a magic act on the show and pulled a skunk out of a hat as only Phyllis could do it.

She always was a welcome guest in my house and didn't have to do any tricks there. That loud cackle laugh of hers could always tell you where she was at a party. Phyllis always was a treasure at my Christmas parties or in any company. She also was mad for Will. When going out together she always wanted to sit in the back seat with him. I don't know what went on back there but she insisted. They had a great time together and she always teased about taking him away from me. Fat chance!

Surprisingly, her paintings are quaint, and her home-made greeting cards with humorous captions were always something to look forward to. One of her Christmas cards read, "The fourth Wise Man was not admitted to the stable because he brought a fruit cake.' Holiday wishes and Love from your Nutty Little Fruitcake!" That's one of many over the years.

Not too long back I was having dinner at a posh restaurant with a small group of people including Rip Taylor and Phyllis. After eating and drinking, and more drinking and a lot of laughter, Rip pulled off his hair piece, and not to be outdone, Phyllis pulled off her wig and the entire table screamed with laughter. I suspect the restaurant wasn't sorry to see us go home that evening. But, truly a good time was had by our table.

GARY COLLINS

Gary Collins was absolutely fearless. He was standing on the wing of a single engine airplane flying at a pretty good speed and I was in the plane with the cameraman flying alongside recording him. All he had was a rope to hang on to. He was smiling and waving and seemingly having a grand old time. I have to praise anyone who would do a stunt like that.

We stayed aloft for quite some time doing other maneuvers until Gary had had enough. He indicated this by pointing down meaning let's get back to old mother earth. On the ground he seemed very buoyed up and exhilarated. I had to congratulate him for this daring stunt.

Left: Gary, Marty Allen, myself and Mary Ann at my house. Right: Gary poses in position on the plane all set for take-off.

Gary and his wife, Mary Ann Mobley, would come to the Christmas party at my house. Very good people and I am sorry they recently left us.

Left: Elke Summers plays with a seal. Right: Nell Carter delighted the audience with a dog act.

Left: Loni Anderson walked on hot coals. Right: Greg Louganis on the Wheel-of-Destiny.

GREG LOUGANIS

Visualize two wheels attached to a long derrick-like apparatus in the center that is three or four stories high. Spinning and turning in the Wheel-of-Destiny, Greg handled it like a pro. He seemed totally comfortable bouncing around in all that turning. I think it takes an athlete like Greg to do that. It was one of the tougher acts on *Circus of the Stars*.

LYNN REDGRAVE AND DICK CLARK

Lynn and Dick were great sports to get into an elaborate clown makeup and costume and have to stay in it for such a long period of time. The payoff was one had to guess who was in the clown makeup and costume. Rarely were the clown's identities guessed. I'm sure Dick was much happier being the Ring Master.

Probably one of the most fun aspects of *Circus of the Stars* was working with so very many stars who were stepping outside of their comfort zone and who were willing to try something new. And it was a challenge to direct in the best of ways. With such a great number of acts requiring unique locations and preparations, I am proud of what we did and how much fun we had doing it.

Many thanks to the wonderful Bunny Stivers and Tim Kettle for the photos from the show.

I.B.M. Photography

Chapter 16
Mikhail Baryshnikov

THE NUTCRACKER

Baryshnikov... hearing that name meant *fabulous* in terms of dance. When I got a call saying Shirley MacLaine had suggested he get in touch with me to direct the television production of his ballet, *The Nutcracker* with Gelsey Kirkland, it seemed like the gates of heaven had opened up. The cab ride to where he was staying seemed endless even though it was a very short distance. There he was with a very charming lady who I gathered was instrumental in getting him over to the United States.

All seemed to go very well and that simple get together clinched the deal that, indeed, I would direct his *Nutcracker* for television. I think I started preparations the very next evening by attending a performance of *The Nutcracker*. I met the principal dancers afterward and everything seemed to go quite smoothly. We continued this routine for nine consecutive performances till I got to know the dancers, and what I'd be working with quite well.

I wanted this to be a magical event that would fit into the eye of the camera so audiences could enjoy it for years to come. In translating this work to the camera, one has many choices from wide shots to close ups from high to low etc. As director I knew I must be careful to enhance the ballet, rather than over use a lot of camera tricks and muck it up.

I.B.M. Photography

After all the evenings of attending the ballet, we were finally in Toronto in the actual studio for the shoot. We would record in sequence starting with the overture, which in the theatre is with the curtain down, dull for television. I had told Misha and Gelsey I was going to do something to fill during this overture. If they had any ideas they were welcome. None were forthcoming so I went ahead with my ideas.

I had them get into ballet rehearsal wardrobe and let me know when they were warmed up. Misha and Gelsey were ready so I asked Misha, "Do a grand jeté' and get as high as he could and extend the legs as far as they will stretch and don't worry about how you land because I'll freeze the leap at the highest point on the first note of the music and we'll never see the landing."

I continued, "Next, Gelsey, do a fast series of chainés on a diagonal and Misha from the opposite diagonal do a series of coupé jetés etc. and in postproduction I will cut all of these together to fill the music of the Overture. Now the Television audience will be treated to some special dancing rather than just looking at a blank curtain. And perhaps more importantly, Misha, the audience will see you rather than the character you play. Otherwise they don't get to see you until the second act."

The same consideration was given to Drosselmeyer and his puppets to help understand his character. All of this met with grateful approval from Misha.

The recording was moving along quite nicely, but I couldn't resist doing one thing in the battle scene. To review, at one point *The Nutcracker* does a series of fast coupé jetés in a huge circle. The first time Misha did them I thought they were great.

He caught his breath and said, "Tony, one more time."

I said, "Misha those were great. I got the shot but if you want to do it again they're your buns, when you're ready".

He did the series of fast leaps a second time and I didn't think it possible - but they were even better, in fact more than perfect.

I couldn't resist the joke so I opened my mic and said "Misha, one more time."

Huffing and puffing, he waived his hands saying, "No, no, no more, no more." I left my control booth ran down to the stage to congratulate him on the fantastic job he had just done. Spectacular!

We met with a giggly bit when in "The Waltz of the Snowflakes" I asked all the ballerina's, in their tutus to lie on their backs on the floor and to do changéments, full leg beats, and a high camera was going to pass over them and after it had passed them they could stop the beats. Fortunately the giggling recorded as smiles. This shot I explained to them would be mixed with the snowflake falling shot, opening the second act which was recorded earlier.

This explanation changed their minds from thinking, "What kind of crazy director is he, putting us on the floor in our tutus?" The rest of the shoot went nicely and I had Gelsey stay for a closing shot I had in mind. In the stage version the ballet just ends and the curtain comes down. I wanted a more memorable and fulfilling period to the story of the whole ballet, so I put this innocent young girl seated in a window looking up into the future through a partially snow covered window. A young girl dreaming of becoming a woman. This ending gave the ballet a heartfelt touch. I thought this to be more interesting and moving than just bringing the curtain down. Gelsey did it perfectly. She gave it that "Je ne sais quoi" look it needed.

I wrapped the shoot and taxied to the restaurant where they all were at dinner and I told Misha about the closing shot. He was very pleased and embraced me with "Have a drink!" Which I certainly needed. I don't think in my lifetime I'll ever see a better-matched couple fill the roles in this ballet than Gelsey and Misha.

I am also grateful I got out of Canada without anything tragic happening to me. The TV Studio was quite a drive from the hotel through desolate barren snow-covered country and each morning I noticed I was being followed by a single driver and it became quite nerve-racking to be driving alone way out in the snow covered desolate prairie with a suspicious car following you. I know the Canadian union was not happy to have an American TV director working in their studios, though it seemed it was okay for them to work in our country.

I brought my concerns to the Canadian producers and I guess they got right on it because the next morning I had no one following me. What a relief that was. Now I could think about what I had to accomplish on the next shoot.

The following days were extremely creative, fulfilling and joyous for everyone. We were able to produce a work we could all be proud of. Occasionally, Misha took a ballet class and once he asked me to go with him. I said I would be glad to join him but I wouldn't take the class. Be in class with one of the greatest? Are you kidding? I joined him in the cab and on the way he pulled out a cigar and lit it. One thing I really can't stand is smoking in a car. After the first puff I said, "Misha, it's either me or the cigar!" He put it out immediately. Observing him in class was a great joy. He's pretty intimidating and it convinced me I did the right thing by being just an observer. I could pass doing the barre work if it stopped there, but the rest would be shameful. I was never meant to be a classic dancer. I enjoyed taking different classes but half way through I'd always give the steps a Charmoli twist.

I saw Misha perform in a play *In Paris* just last year. He has become a very talented actor. It has been a pleasure to see his career travel to new places. After the show we visited a little backstage and it was very good to see him again.

Tony with Star Search producer Sam Riddle and his wife, Adrienne.

Chapter 17
Star Search

Bob Banner, the producer who years before had hired me to do *The Dinah Shore Show,* called me into his office and handed me a videotape of a show they were pedaling which was eventually called *Star Search*. Would I look at it and report back to him. I did that and went to his office and reported all the things I would do to change and enhance the show.

We stepped into the hall and coming out the opposite door at the same time was Sam Riddle.

Bob said to Sam. "This is Tony Charmoli our new director for *Star Search*."

That's how I found out I got the job.

Star Search was a talent show with several categories of talent produced by Sam Riddle and hosted by Ed McMahon. To maintain impartiality I had no part in advising, or training the talent. They had to come prepared to do whatever their talent was and hope to win. The talent was given a stage, proper lighting and a full orchestra rehearsal prior to performing before a staff of professional judges.

At that time there was no phone or audience voting of any kind. Prophetically enough even way back then Al Massini the originator of the show said someday he would like to engage a wider audience for judging by initiating phone voting from the public.

Star Search was a highly-watched show and introduced what turned out to be some highly employable talent still operating in today's market. The judging was made up of a panel of professionals in show business and the decisions were made at the end of the competition, with the winners announced just before the wrap up of the evening.

John Shaffner and Joe Stewart designed scenic elements to enhance a barren barn-like stage. It gave the talent a bang-up element of professionalism. John also sat behind me in the booth during the show and every time I was about to do a wide shot of the stage to show off the scenery I'd say, "John, this one's for you."

John also supplied sets and props for the model shoots to help the girls project an aura of feeling professional and special. It helped them achieve that extra model glow.

One day I walked into the theater for the model shoot and there was a blue drop with several big wads of cotton just hanging there in front of the drop. John was standing by and I asked, "What is all that supposed to be?"

He said, "Those are clouds." Then he looked at me crinkling up my nose then back at them and gave me another evaluation "They are kind of schlumpy aren't they?"

I still like that word "Schlumpy." It's so descriptive. Of course the so-called clouds were immediately replaced with some dramatic and imaginative lighting.

Blake McIver - Young Star Search winner - lately on Bravo TV's The People's Couch, and now a talented singer/songwriter. Blake and many other Star Search performers would come to my Christmas Party each year.

On another occasion, when we were doing a show in Hawaii, Joe had to rush back to the states and left me with a pile of various sized platforms and I asked "What is all this?"

He replied those are your sets, you can do whatever you want with them."

I teased, "How about toss them out?"

He quickly said, "That's one option..."

One more little item. Victoria, Ed McMahon's wife had to be seated so she could easily be seen on camera wearing a new dress which was part of her clothing line. I guess getting a little advertising in on her husband's show was acceptable.

The show seemed to run along beautifully and smoothly during the taping except for our host who would goof up names and introductions something awful. I'd have to ask Ed to stay after to do pickups. Ed's driver informed me that prior to a show, Ed would consume a bottle of wine on his way to the theatre, and then Ed would consume a bottle of white wine in his dressing room, which left him with only part of his senses during the taping. He made many errors like mispronouncing names of contestants and what they were doing and whether they were male or female. Things, which couldn't go out in the telecast. The wine also caused him to fall asleep during the show and the stage manager, Kenny Stein, would have to wake him up after each contestant's performance before I cut to him. His speech sometimes seemed impaired like a drunk which of course he was, but it meant I'd have to have him repeat things several times

Tony, Sam Harris & husband, Danny Jacobsen at my Christmas Party.

in pickups after the audience had cleared. That could take some time. Not a picnic to say the least.

In the beginning the contestants would bring their own wardrobe, two costumes, so we could choose what would be best on camera. As the director I had to remain impartial to all contestants, but I did make a casual but useful observation to one contestant. Sam Harris brought one outfit consisting of a pair of Levis and a Wally Berry shirt, which was the popular item of dress at the time. The other was a heavy sparkling sequined, very Liberace, very Las Vegas looking outfit. He was a young good looking clean cut sort of boy and I suggested the jeans and Wally Berry shirt. It looked clean and very young and in style. Not only would it be better on camera but it would be better on him. He really wanted to wear the other. But when the time came he chose the Wally Berry Shirt, and he won. I said nothing and he kept on winning. Of course he was very good. Late in the competition I had to leave to do another show and in my absence the director allowed him to wear the sparkly outfit and he lost. I was tempted to say, "I told you so." But didn't. Fortunately in the final event he won and became our first *Star Search* Champion, and I was happy about that. Sam Harris is still out there performing today and raising a beautiful adopted baby boy.

Another time there was a talented singer who was pacing back and forth on the stage as she sang, and I hinted she just stay still and sing the song. So often performers get distracted by trying to "perform" instead of just being in the moment and doing what they do best. Singing the song simply and honestly is always a safe bet to fall back on. She sang the song simply and beautifully - and she won.

Britney Spears competed as a child and won the first round. When I saw her on camera in the first round I remember remarking, "That's a cute kid." Unfortunately she didn't do well in the second round and lost.

Another child came along and after the first round over on the side stage I said, "That kid is great - move her to center stage for the next round." It was LeAnn Rimes.

Both these girls are way up there today and still going strong. Others who had a crack at *Star Search* are Sharon Stone, Justin Timberlake, Christina Aguilera, Rosie O'Donnell, Chris Rock, Beyoncé, Margaret Cho and quite a few comics and many others. I take great pleasure in reminding myself I worked with these talents at the beginning and I congratulate them on their great successes.

All in all we had a lot of fun doing the show. We had a great crew and a lot of very talented people come through to share their abilities and get good experience along the way. Some of the winners went on to great careers, and some didn't. And some of the losers went on to great careers and some didn't. It is a great lesson to enjoy the adventures that come our way and to pay more attention to the fire in your soul than the judgment of judges. I certainly never paid attention to the naysayers.

As a director it helps to know about all facets of production.

Chapter 18
Pageants

Entering the world of the beauty pageants was a whole new trip. Sid Smith, the producer, pulled me in to direct a *Miss USA Pageant*. Tad Tadlock, who was one of my dancers on the *Hit Parade*, who was the choreographer also encouraged me to come on board. Kiddingly I told Tad she could use all my old dance steps in the production numbers. Michael Onofrio, Alfreda Alridge, June Wylie, Katie Jones, to name a few were also on board when I joined the group.

My first *Miss USA Pageant* in 1986 was a pleasant experience, and the biggest thing I remember about that show was Halle Berry, who was the first runner up, I thought should have been the winner. However the winner, also very pretty, was Miss Texas. Visiting the different states to do the pageants was a great way to see America. It was not long before I was doing a lot of pageants for *Miss USA*, *Miss Teen USA* and *Miss Universe*.

In August of 1992, we had been rehearsing for the 10th anniversary edition of the *Miss Teen USA* Pageant in Biloxi, Miss.

We were preparing to air live as usual at 9 PM on CBS-TV but the morning of August 19 started with blustery, windy and stormy conditions. The word was that Hurricane Andrew was on the way, scheduled to hit Biloxi about the same time our invited audience would be coming to the auditorium. The question of course was would the audience be endangered by coming to the auditorium and could they get home after the show?

As the hurricane approached, getting closer all the time, a decision had to be made. After much consultation, our producer, Sid Smith informed us that we would record the Dress Rehearsal that afternoon. This was the first time a pageant had been pre-recorded. Of course, where would the suspense of the show be if the winner, *Miss Teen USA* 1992 was known that afternoon? The media would be all over it. Plus it would be known by the control rooms in New York and LA who were recording it. So, the decision was made to tape two endings. One ending had the legitimate runner up winning and the other had the real winner crowned. Even the contestants themselves didn't know who won until the show aired that night.

I understand that Dick Clark, the host of the show invited the runner up, the winner and their families to his suite to watch the show and that's when they learned that Jamie Salinger, Miss Iowa Teen USA was crowned *Miss Teen USA* 1992. Her runner up was a disappointed Angela Logan, Miss Oklahoma Teen USA. From our hotel we could see this dark gray weather wall from the clouds to the sea ominously moving toward us. Later on the strong winds and stormy conditions forced us to sit on the floor in the hallway of our hotel for fear of shattered windows in our rooms. That night seemed never to end. Perhaps if the bar had been open a delicious cocktail might have helped. After a long never-ending night we were bused to the airport the next morning, happy to have been spared a horrendous killer hurricane. I chalk it all up to a harrowing but otherwise great "hope I never have to go through that again" experience. Once is quite enough.

One doesn't have to go to a foreign country to find beautiful locations for the girls modeling sessions. In the good ol' USA, I found the White Sands in New Mexico to be rather fabulous. The only negative that day, although the girls don't show it, was that it was pretty cold for bathing suits. We had heat lamps and blankets standing by which the shivering girls welcomed every time I called "cut!"

June Wylie represented the company for the swimsuits the girls were modeling and always checked each girl to see the fit was perfect. June was famous for the various fantastic hats and jewelry she would wear especially to my Christmas parties. They never failed to be less than spectacular. She looked great on the location shoots as well.

Leeza Gibbons was our commentator on several *Miss Universe Pageants* and a very good one. I just couldn't get her to modify her makeup. Especially at fault was her heavy use of lipstick and heavy eye makeup. Compared to the contestants it tended to give her a hooker look and that wasn't what the pageants were all about. I solved the problem by not giving her too many close-ups. Medium wide shots were fine. After all these were young clean cut all American girls, or were supposed to be.

Another year we did a pageant in Mobile, Alabama which had an added plus. My dear friend, Miss Dixie from New Orleans came to visit and had the time of her

Tony with Miss Universe 1985, Deborah Carthy-Deu

life meeting and mixing with all the pretty girls. Miss Dixie is New Orleans personified. She owned, and ran, and was the bouncer for her Dixie's Bar of Music in the French Quarter. We had lots of memorably entertaining times in that place. Miss Dixie's sister was the cashier You haven' been to New Orleans if you haven't been to Dixie's Bar of Music. Too bad Miss Dixie left this earth. I don't know what's happening with her bar.

The *Miss Universe Pageant*s took me all over the world and gave me a great many amazing experiences - too many to list all of them. But here are a number of the most memorable ones.

PANAMA

Many years before the *Miss Universe Pageant* came to Panama in 1986, I was the designated escort for Margot Fonteyn to a celebration honoring Jerome Robbins in the Rainbow Room in the RCA Building. I picked her up at her hotel and we got to the celebration without incident. We had a very pleasant time talking dance of course. When we arrived she was inundated with people asking for autographs.

Dinner went off just fine and speeches were the usual self-aggrandizement speeches and when they were over, dancing started. When I asked Margot to dance she said, "Oh, no Tony. I just arrived from London this morning and I'm still tired from the long flight. If I dance with you I'll have to dance with everybody in this room." I honored that and got her back to her hotel.

Many years later, the Miss Universe Company picked Panama for the next *Miss Universe Pageant*. I thought how great, I'll get a chance to see Miss Fonteyn because I knew she had married some gentleman from there and they were living in Panama.

One day I was photographing contestants on the beach right in front of Margot's house. I was upset that I wasn't told her house was right where we were filming. There was no sign of her the whole day we were shooting.

I said I thought she would like to come to the telecast. The show came and went but I saw no sign of Margot. I asked about her and I was informed that she indeed was there to see the telecast, but didn't want me to know, because she was terribly crippled in a wheelchair and didn't want me to see her that way.

It made me very sad, but I understand. The pride of a world class Prima Ballerina came to the fore and I totally understood

Above: Dining with Margot Fonteyn

her point. I certainly would have fallen apart upon seeing this brilliant ballerina in that crippled condition. I'll live with the memories of enjoying her on stage at the peak of her career.

While on location in Panama, Katie wrote, "I remember attending a gala event in the Royal Palace hosted by Noriega himself with our main group you, Michael, June, and Alfie looking sharp dressed in evening clothes. As we entered the Grand Royal Ballroom and turned the corner we ran right into two women, both very large in size and dressed in bright Caribbean floral prints. Right at that moment we were at a loss for words, all except you. You whispered, 'They look like an ad for Miracle Grow!' I've never since been able to think of these ladies without a smile." The did give the impression of very large, healthy walking gardens.

SINGAPORE

The year we did the Pageant in Singapore in 1987, myself and some of the crew took a side trip to colorful Bali beforehand. What an experience that was. The countryside is very interesting and the people are quite exotic and lovely, but one can't help notice that everywhere you turn you see simple things like door knobs, door knockers, flying angels, you name it, all carved in the shape of a large penis or sporting one. In spite of this distraction we were able to come up with a very good pageant.

Dick Clark was our host and our regular crew remained the same. As a souvenir of Bali, the crew gave me a long necktie painted in the shape of what else, a large penis. The topper was they all autographed it to me including Dick Clark!

Prior to the telecast there is always huge tension in the air while waiting for the cue from New York to start televising the pageant. I typically liked to break that silent tension with humor, and Dick asked the perfect question so the entire crew could hear, he asked, "Tony, what happened to that tie we all gave you?"

I said, "I'm sitting on it."

Well the explosion of laughter nearly blew my headset off. I called the cues and we were off and running. That certainly broke the tension and became the talk of the whole company. Everybody was up and we had a good show.

Sometimes I'd have to have my stage managers stand in for the girls. It's easy to see why they aren't wearing a sash and high-heeled shoes. They always had a lot of fun camping it up. They stuffed huge carved wood penises down their pant legs and paraded around the set while I set camera shots. Singapore was worth the trip.

1992 Miss Universe Michelle McLean with Tony and Tad Tadlock

Sid Smith and Tony camping it up with the local dancers

CANCUN

In Cancun (1989), the pageant experienced a bit of a disaster with one producer who did not listen to me. The girls obviously came from a variety of foreign countries and many didn't speak English as their first language, so we created cue cards to help them with their speeches.

The show started and I cut to the girls individually where each introduced herself, but I was surprised when they had such a terrible time with the language. I couldn't understand why as they were so perfect in rehearsal. But here they were stumbling terribly on the live telecast. I sent a stage manager backstage and he reported that our new producer had ordered the cue card boy to leave and take the cards with him. He wanted all the girls to ad lib their speeches without cue cards. The poor girls were struck with fear and had a terrible time. They managed to stumble through their names and their country but were at a loss to say anything else. It was a mess.

When this was reported to me, I told head of cue cards to ignore any request or changes from the new producer for the rest of the show, and told the stage manager to keep the producer away from the contestants.

The next day I was called into the producer's office and scolded for delivering such a sloppy show. I certainly wasn't going to take the blame for the huge mistake they made in hiring this new incompetent producer. I told him what caused this heartless disaster and I didn't hold back any punches. I said I would resign if the new arrogant disaster of a producer wasn't kicked out immediately. I stayed. The producer was fired. It had also become quite clear to the whole company that the producer was making out with girls in every port. Not the contestants but the locals. The staff had become rather disappointed in him.

Angela Visser, the 1989 Miss Universe winner from the Netherlands.

THAILAND

In 1992 the *Miss Universe Pageant* was in Bangkok, Thailand. We had a tremendous welcome and on the first night we were introduced to royalty. We were escorted to the front of our hotel and there all the men were lined up in formal attire on one side of the red carpet and the women were lined up on the other beautifully dressed in very long elegant evening gowns.

Soon, the limo of Queen Sirikit arrived. The minute she set foot on the red carpet, the women dropped to their knees and bowed forward touching their noses to the red carpet. It was amazing and a turn off at the same time. I couldn't see an American woman doing that. Standing next to me was the gentleman of protocol and I asked him if I had to do that. "No," he answered with complete seriousness, "You will shake her hand only if she extends hers."

She did extend her hand, so I took her hand and all went well. When I complimented her on her dress, she told me that Bob Mackie had made her gown. She was even more gracious when she learned Bob was a dear friend of mine.

We went in to a lovely dinner and immediately after were escorted into a small theater and were seated right behind Her Royal Highness. Soon various singers began entertaining and I complained to our escort, "These singers aren't very good." He informed me they were all amateurs who pay the Queen for the privilege to say in their resumes that they had performed for her Royal Highness. I then told our escort I had to leave because I had a very full day ahead and had to get up early. "It's okay," he said. "We can leave now, she'll never know. She's collecting money and that will keep her here for a while." We were gone in a flash.

The next day's trip to Chiang Mai was interesting to see more of Thailand. On arrival we were met by the owner of the hotel where we were lunching with the director of our location unit. The second unit director assured me all was going well and hoped we were enjoying Thailand. He assured me he got some good stuff for the telecast. Lunch proved to be rather good and since it was on the house it was even better.

After lunch, our car was waiting for us and when we stepped up to it our very young driver snapped to attention, clicked his heels and bowed. I said "My! My! To what do we owe this?" He said, "I was born and raised in Bangkok and I've never even seen the Queen." Then he handed me a newspaper and there on the front page was a photo of me shaking hands with the Queen the night before. It looked rather regal.

Later that evening at our hotel in Bangkok, several of our staff decided to have a cocktail in the rooftop bar. As we stepped into the elevator, we observed it was beautifully decorated with huge white flowers and ribbons. I asked the elevator operator what the occasion was. He said "It's a secret but the Queen is coming to visit with the bartender in the penthouse bar." It appeared humorous to me. All this elaborate decoration would certainly make it obvious that the Queen was coming - so how could it be secret? I wouldn't blame her, the bartender was one great hunk.

Well back to our reason for being there. The pageant went off without a hitch and the Queen looked radiant from the supposed previous night's escapade and was pleased with the pageant as well. We were asked to come back and do the pageant again the next year but had to decline. We were already booked to go to Mexico City.

Tony meeting Queen Sirikit of Thailand

While doing the *Miss Universe Pageant* in Thailand, Katie Jones, one of our staff recalls that one day we were in rehearsal with all of the contestants when I lost patience with one of the girls.

> "You climbed down from the remote truck," she wrote, "jumped cables, ducked props, strutted about two to three hundred feet through the theater and climbed up on the stage to confront her face-to-face.
>
> She looked down at you as only a beauty queen can in her 5-inch heels and says, 'Sir, in my country I am referred to as a Princess!'
>
> You responded, 'Yes, and in my country they refer to me as a Queen! Now get this straight....'
>
> That kind of comic relief got us through all the insane rehearsals we go through in each country."

Katie Jones at my Christmas party

MEXICO CITY

The *Miss Universe Pageant* certainly gets around. In 1993, we were at the lavish Fiesta Condessa Americana Hotel in Mexico. Nearby, there was a giant pyramid of steps which seemed like a good location for the girls. They looked lovely in long black evening gowns up along the pyramid. We shot in several locations and it was pretty hot.

To cool the girls off, I asked them to gather around the hotel swimming pool. I then directed them to acknowledge the camera as it passed by them. They had fun doing all sorts of gestures as the camera went by when something struck me to say: "Now everybody jump in the pool!"

With screams of joy and laughter all the girls jumped or dove into the pool and came up laughing hysterically in their very wet long black evening gowns. The big clincher to the whole thing was my stage manager's Kenny Stein and Dency Nelson picked me up and threw me into the pool.

It was a wild ending to a fabulous visit to the Fiesta Condessa Hotel. Pete Menefee is still speaking to me even after my commanding all the girls to jump in the pool and ruin all those lovely black gowns. I couldn't help myself, it was one of those spur of the moment things.

PHILIPPINES

In 1994 the *Miss Universe Pageant* was held in the Philippines. On arrival we were invited to a breakfast to meet her ex-Royal Highness Madame Imelda Marcos.

In the foyer of her building there were several guards and we had been given special permits to go up to see her. I found her well pulled together and we seemed to hit it off right from the beginning. The meeting was great and breakfast was traditional - juice, eggs, bacon, toast and a great exchange of conversation.

Madame Marcos invited us to come back for dinner. Some of the staff that had been there before and had experienced a full evening declined but those who were new accepted. Upon arrival we had to go through the same routine with the guards in the foyer. This time the butler received us at the door and escorted us inside and then announced Madame Marcos. She appeared dressed all in black with diamonds everywhere - earrings, a bracelet 2 inches wide and a huge diamond ring. She was aglow.

We were informed that she had prepared the dinner herself. She seemed to favor me for some reason and took me to the kitchen where she cut two pieces of cake she said she had baked. She and I had that in the kitchen before going in to mingle with the other guests. I guess she liked her dessert, but we hadn't had a cocktail yet. After that big piece of cake, I was not hungry, but she managed dinner just fine. I skipped desert but she had just a touch more of her delicious cake.

Coffee was served and we all retired to the living room in anticipation of the next event, Madame Marcos sings! Her singing was okay but one song by Madame Marcos would have been quite enough. To go on for at least an hour and a half, made it seem like the end would never come. All in all I can call it an "unforgettable experience."

I thought as good guests we should invite her to come to the *Miss Universe Pageant*, but was immediately reminded by one of our staff that she was not allowed to leave the premises.

The pageant went off without a hitch and the celebration afterward was pretty fabulous. I'm sorry Madame Marcos wasn't there but had to remain cooped up in her lavish apartment. I do have a souvenir from that evening. I was wearing a necklace given to me by the choreographer of the dance group we had on the show. It was an antique men's necklace and Imelda commented on it. She said it was a precious Philippine necklace. She disappeared for a short while and not to be outdone came back and presented me with another native beaded necklace. Both necklaces are in a silver box beside silver framed photos of Imelda and Queen Sirikit of Thailand.

Visiting with these two women reminded me of how far I had come from growing up a child of immigrants in a mining town. Traveling with the *Miss Universe Pageant* gave me some truly unique experiences.

Will visiting me in Singapore

WINDHOEK, NAMIBIA

The last *Miss Universe Pageant* I worked on was in 1995, from Windhoek, which is on the west side of Africa. It energized the whole staff to know we would be in a new unfamiliar place. Upon arrival at the airport everything looked rather contemporary and normal. The hotel accommodation was civilized and all seemed okay. Our visit to the theater was a shock. During their preparations for the *Miss Universe* telecast they were working on the scenery when disaster struck. It started with a huge fire causing major damage to the stage and theater. It had burned a big hole through the roof and it was still smoldering when we arrived. We were assured everything would be restored repaired and in place for rehearsals and the telecast. We forged ahead.

We wanted to set the location of the Pageant by starting with a big production number with many varied tribal dancers. The call was honored with a huge assortment of natives from different locales in various tribal attire. Some clothed, others practically naked. Many colorful women with exposed breasts in all different shapes and sizes. Some huge and bare and others covered. The women from one tribe had their hair all done up in mounds of dark mud like substance, which turned out to be cow dung. REALLY!!!!! The men wore at least a tiny G-string or flap of some kind. It was indeed a *National Geographic* cover personified. Pete Menefee our costume official took over and covered naked breasts and any other dangling parts of the predominately naked bodies. Through diligent cutting and pasting he was able to put costumes together that would pass the censors. This certainly was going to let you know we were definitely in Africa.

Scott Grossman was the choreographer and did the best he could with such a varied group to work with. To choreograph a whole number with so many language and tribal limitations he asked if we couldn't pre-tape the opening number bit-by-bit? I met with our producer with this problem because in our opening announcement we say, "Live from..." wherever we are. He understood the problem and said go ahead and pre-tape. We'll handle that problem when and if it arises. Stop and start, bit-by-bit we got the whole number done.

It was a joy to see the local dancers have such a good time. I wanted to see their reactions when they would see themselves dancing on television so I played back a bit of the pre-tape. They giggled and pointed and laughed at themselves and obviously had a fun experience.

The live telecast went off rather smoothly but it seemed strange because of the major time change to be telecasting the show in the morning. Even at that early time the theater was packed with a lively audience. The windows were blacked out and all seemed like an evening show. The telecast went smoothly and the locals loved seeing much of their local scenery and color on TV.

The Governor of Windhoek had invited the Pageant girls and staff to lunch at the Governor's Residence. It was a great day and we all arrived at a lovely mansion on a hill and many locals were also there. A mixture of black and whites mingled around cocktails and hors d'oeuvres. Soon lunch was announced buffet style and we went up to the tables loaded with a great looking assortment of different and unfamiliar stuff. Their prize was springbok, a form of deer, which was rather delicious. We loaded our plates and went to our tables.

As we sat down I happened to look around and noticed a change. I said, "Sid, have you noticed something?"

He said, "What do you mean?"

I said, "Look around."

He said "What? I don't see anything different."

I said, "Don't you see? All the black guests have gone."

We were told that Windhoek was well integrated. I guess they should have said, "Sort of integrated!"

On a day off, members of the staff were treated with a visit to nearby places of interest and ended up at a resort where dinner was served. The scenery was lovely and the surroundings were nature at its African best. A large table was set up outdoors to accommodate us for dinner. All seemed very exotic and lovely, then they announced that there would be some entertainment with our dinner. We were enjoying the hospitality and the dinner was quite good - although I can't tell you clearly what it was. The wine glossed things over and made everything palatable.

Soon the entertainment was announced. It consisted of a couple of guys throwing out a dead zebra to several lions who immediately pounced on it and started tearing it apart and feeding on it. You can guess our reaction. I'm sorry we didn't leave earlier. I get sick just recounting this.

Other trips and locations were quite lovely. The red desert sands were miles wide and a series of rolling hills. Well worth a onetime visit. Our guides were white and quite interesting. They also expressed a desire to move to the United States. Did we have any work for them? We got that same wish from various visits to several different locations.

BANGKOK POST THURSDAY JUNE 4,

SPECIAL FEATURES

Not all glamour at Miss Universe Inc

by Mimi Lee

TONY Charmoli and Ms Tad Tadlock, exhausted, have fled to Thailand on holiday.

He has just finished directing a multi-million-dollar show that was beamed to roughly 600 million viewers worldwide in 56 countries.

She is still suffering anxiety attacks waking up too early in the morning, in anticipation of ten, maybe fifteen — if pressed, twenty hours of song and dance rehearsals with 68 nervous, home-sick girls.

"Somebody has to make it happen. First you have to have the concept, the sets, the costumes, music and everything all planned out — then you gotta get it going," chime the duo, without whom the recent Miss Universe pageant in Singapore might possibly have flopped.

Tony Charmoli (right) and Ms Tad Tadlock at the Oriental Hotel Bamboo Bar. Both of them are going to push Bangkok as the ne venue for Miss Universe.

and aggressive charm displayed by her partner, Tony Charmoli, for whom she has worked earlier as professional dancer.

"We speak the same language," she grins. "Tony in-

favouritism. Even if we thi one is prettier than the oth we can't let her feel that w. because we have to be fair bo to her and her country."

Judges to the pageant, ad

Cultural differences have made for some funny moments with the Miss Universe winners. The outgoing Miss Universe from India was at a dinner party one night, and in full voice at the table told the chaperone that she had to use the "shit box."

Everybody gasped. This coming from a crowned Miss Universe was totally unacceptable. When corrected she explained that was a very common expression in her country. She was surprised to learn that it was not the best term to use in the English-speaking world.

CAMERA OPERATORS

I am ever grateful for creative camera operators. They were quick to understand what I wanted - though at times we had to talk in code as there were too many ears on the headsets. When I wanted the camera shot to include the girl's breasts, I could not say "Pull out and show me some tits." So the code words became "More Dairy Farm!" I think they still use it to this day.

Dan Webb was a great camera guy to work with. In a shoot in Taiwan the location was a traditional Chinese garden. Checking his viewfinder the garden looked beautiful but rather sparse. I told him I thought it needed something in the foreground. In a very short time he came to me with. 'Take a look now Tony and see what you think." He had clipped a small flowering twig from a nearby bush and held it up close to the lens so the garden seemed ablaze with blossoms. Pure magic and I told him so. Just one point of criticism, I said "the bush is quivering." In seconds he put the twig in a clamp to steady it and it was perfect. He said, "You don't miss a thing do you?" With Dan on the crew I always knew we'd be guaranteed a good shoot.

In a studio shoot Mark Hunter the crane camera operator also had a keen eye. He could get his operators to move that camera into any and many creative ways. He confided that he always wore shorts on shoots because when he was way up in their on a high shot he liked to have the girls in the audience get a good look at his legs. They were always creamed and groomed to lush perfection. The rest of him was not bad either. David Irete and Sam Drummy were also creative cameramen who could make the camera shot worthwhile.

On a Miss Universe shoot in Mexico, David was shooting some Miss Universe girls up in a cable car and all was going well, but I wasn't satisfied with the sight for the Master Shot.

We moved down to the main street and as I looked back to the mountains where we had been, I saw way in the distance a beautiful master shot, the cable car between two buildings.

I said, "David, look! What a great Master Shot!"

He replied, "I already got it."

That was typical David, always one step ahead. Priceless!

I was in another location in Bali surrounded by water and too far away to cable. Marty Kip, who was in

Down front is camera man, Dan Webb

charge of the technical production, said, "Hang on, I'll take care of it."

In not too long a time, there was Marty Kip stripped to his shorts walking towards us with the water up over his armpits carrying a battery operated camera straight in the air above his head. We got the beautiful shot and all agreed it was worth the trouble and applauded Marty for saving the day.

Sometimes camera operators are treated to an unexpected revealing shot. In one TV special, the dancer was in a tight very short dress with openings showing lots of flesh. At one point in the dance she leans backwards as the guys lift her flat out high over their heads causing her short dress to ride even higher giving the camera man looking up at her a view which caused him to exclaim "Holy shit can't wait 'til I tell my wife!"

Only those of us in the control room knew what he was reacting to. The same dancer gave an unexpected shock to one of the boys dancing with her. In another move a dancer was flat on his stomach on the floor in front of her. She did a passé where she brought her foot to her knee raising her skirt and gave the dancer a view which made him forget all his choreography. Fortunately he was quick to recover and the TV audience had no idea of the extra show they were missing out on.

I was asking people who worked with me what they remembered. Michael Onofrio wrote:

> *"Sitting next to Tony in the Control Room when we were 'On Air' was like being on stage. Tony's body rose with the action, creating a living, breathing ambience in the control room equal to what was happening on stage. It was glorious and it kept everyone on his toes and in the moment. I was Tony's AD with the pageants for many years and will never forget the exhilaration. What described Tony's team? Loyalty. Tony never forgot the honest, tireless, and excellent output of all the talented members of his production team, such as his cameramen, stage managers, choreographers, producers and AD's who were so important in externalizing his creative ideas. He rewarded his team with applause, high praise, and remembered and requested their presence for his next project. Stage Managers Ken Stein, David Wader and Dency Nelson's availability was also always sought. They in turn were highly motivated to produce the best for Tony who admittedly relied heavily on their diligence and returned loyalty."*

Well, the affection and admiration was quite mutual. I worked with a great many wonderful and talented people.

Alfreda Aldridge, Michael Onofrio, Tad Tadlock at a party chez moi.

It was an amazing experience to see how many foreign countries are having their own beauty pageant. In Taiwan in 1988, they were holding a pageant in a coffee shop using the customer counter tops as runways. Not as glamorous as the real thing, but the enthusiasm for these pageants in these countries is so much more than we are used to in the USA. While in Taipei Michael recalls we were invited to an official dinner gala and were served native food so foreign and undelectable that we considered throwing the dessert at the dining room wall to see if it would stick there. Frightening! No, we didn't do that, but it was so unappealing that it did cross our minds. Sometimes you just have to smile and swallow.

There was a small group of our staff that always had lunch together. Sid Smith, our producer, Michael Onofrio my assistant, Alfreda Alridge, Katie Jones, and various others. We were all quite compatible and respectable except for one thing, our producer, Sid Smith always ordered at least two Bloody Marys and you could count on at least one of them being spilled. We always wound up with a messy table and several of us splashed by the spilled drink. A big mess. However in spite of all that we always wound up having a good time.

Tony having fun with the girls.

Mitzi... A Tribute to the American Housewife

Chapter 19
Mitzi Gaynor

I met Mitzi on my first visit to California. Will and I had known of Mitzi through our very dear friend, Paul Rose who was in the clothing business and often came to New York on buying trips for Nancy's Dress Shop in Los Angeles. Mitzi was a very young celebrity at the time, and Paul dressed her in clothes from Nancy's to promote the shop's fashions - which of course looked great on her.

Paul invited us to come over and meet Mitzi at her apartment. She answered the door and immediately said, "I have your replacement for *Hit Parade!* This is Ernie Flatt." I didn't ask questions I just called New York and informed the producer of *Your Hit Parade* about my suggested replacement and he hired him. This pleased Mitzi a great deal. Mitzi, her husband Jack Bean, and I had a great time getting to know each other and the rest is fabulous history.

Will also thought Mitzi and I were meant to be, but it wasn't smooth sailing for Ernie doing the *Hit Parade*. Not long after he took over, I was in New York staging new numbers for some big female star and rehearsing in another studio right across the hall from Ernie. Suddenly he angrily stormed out of his studio and slammed the door shut. I was standing right there in the hall and said, "Ernie, you should never storm out of a rehearsal when you're angry. You'll only have to go back and apologize to them. They're still loyal to me but they'll get over it. Don't let them get your goat." I think that worked. Ernie managed to stay on the *Hit Parade* for awhile.

Mitzi and her dancers

There was a long period of working on *The Dinah Shore Show* and many others before I was called by Jack (who was also Mitzi's manager), to do a TV special for Mitzi. I had seen her do some films and several TV specials and was always pleased to see her perky and jubilant personality shine through. First, I was hired to do a new nightclub act for her. I had seen a couple of her shows and I was struck by the similarity, which anchored them - but not in a good way. They always had the same number of boys supporting her, which led to a tendency to appear similar in nature and construction only with different costumes. To remedy this, we did our version of a minstrel show, which had a number of boys and girls sitting on stage most of the time. We called this, *Mitzi and a Cast of Thousands.* It certainly looked different from previous shows and stretched the performance.

When I first started doing shows for Mitzi, we opened them in a rather beat-up dive called The Cave in Vancouver, Canada. The clientele was typical of the dives one would see in B movies and the characters seemed left over from old Hollywood casting offices. But they loved their beer, a good show, and Mitzi. When they didn't like something they were quite vocal about letting you know it. This playing field gave us a good opportunity to test and workout any problems.

One thing stood out as being very strange. The very elegant costumes by Bob Mackie looked great but were too classy and so out of place in a dive like The Cave. Of course, we knew we were going to be playing in classier places so we didn't let it bother us. Fortunately, we weren't there for a very long time. All in all the Canadians were a good audience. I'm quite sure the "lovely" Cave is no longer. I still think of the memories that were lost when that dive was torn down.

I suppose I helped tear it down when I needed a special lighting effect for Mitzi. I told the lighting guy I wanted an overhead spot to shine directly down on her. He said he could do that so proceeded to climb up into the uneven cave-like rafters and I could hear him clumping along.

He'd stomp his foot and say "Here?" I'd say no and keep guiding him to the center until he was right where I wanted it and on the correct spot he yelled, "Here?"

I said, "Yes." and his foot came smashing through the ceiling. The light was just the right touch. I don't think they ever repaired the hole but left it as a souvenir of when Mitzi performed there.

I have discovered one principal thing about Mitzi. She is at home on the stage. She can wrap an audience around her little finger in seconds. She is radiantly alive when confronted with a packed house. One night I shall never forget. I believe it was Detroit. Mitzi was already on stage and into her opening number when a late couple came walking down the aisle to their seats in the second row front. Mitzi cut the orchestra off and in silence just stood and watched this couple walk down the aisle then sidestep their way into their seats. When they were seated in this hushed theatre. In a gentle manner Mitzi said, "You're late! I'll tell you what you missed." Then in rapid abbreviated talk she tells what she did so far, takes a deep breath and says, "Can I go on?" The audience went wild with applause. I suggested, perhaps we should plant two people every night so we could repeat this wonderful touch in the show. Mitzi thought not. She was right, the spontaneity would have been lost.

The touring nightclub act seemed to work, for this led to opening of the new showroom in the Tropicana. The new room was great and the new show was very well-received for the reviews were excellent.

This success led to another step up in Mitzi's concert career. Soon a major change came when I was asked to direct and choreograph a TV special for Mitzi. The title was, *Mitzi... A Tribute to the American Housewife.* This subject seemed underwhelming to me until I started thinking up ideas to make the special a special.

I immediately called some of the technicians I had worked with in New York to ask about new technical tricks recently developed for TV. I was thrilled with the new technology. One told me TV was capable of shooting three images of one dancer at the same time on the same tape. They were also capable of stopping action in a "freeze frame" then releasing it. This and slow motion all piqued my imagination. This technology is what I wanted. I wanted to show Mitzi off to the best of my and television's abilities.

Tony, Mitzi, & Barry Manilow at a party at my house.

Then, I chose music that would reflect and caress her position as a film star. It just jumped out at me, "Rhapsody in Blue." Mitzi loved the idea and the music. It turned out to be the perfect cookie and I was able to use all these marvelous new technical tricks to bring new life to a great old standard. In the special I presented it as a dream of the average American housewife. I wanted to do justice to this piece so I took my time and got Mitzi at her best and squeezed everything out of each effect that I could. Jack was up in the booth with the client and was reassuring me at regular intervals the client was very pleased with what they were seeing. I would show Mitzi just snips of what we had shot and she too was very satisfied. When I finally did the last shot of the "Rhapsody in Blue" number there was a shattering burst of applause and bravos in the studio.

Staying with the housewife theme we did a number in a housewife's kitchen. I saw Nancy Walker do this song in *On The Town* on Broadway and it just stuck with me. It was just what I needed for this Mitzi special. It was called "I Can Cook, Too." When I saw it on Broadway, Nancy just sort of sang the song out to the audience. No production, she just sang the song. My way was to embrace it and choreograph it in a way to show Mitzi doing common household chores quickly, magically and effortlessly. I danced the number for Mitzi describing what I was doing along the way and she was ecstatic.

She asked, "How does it start?" She learned it in no time and added her own little flourishes, turning it into something unforgettable. She was fabulous. It was an audience favorite. She's still doing it in her act, pared down quite a bit, but it's still fun.

The toughest thing with Mitzi was to come up with the subject of the one-hour specials. One day, I was on my way for a first meeting on a new show and had no idea of what I was going to pitch as the subject. However, I was struck with inspiration en route. I parked and hurried in.

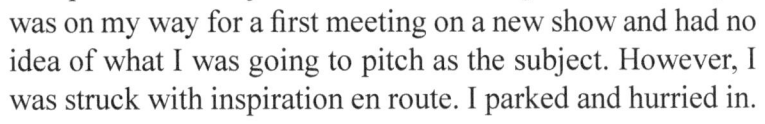

Jack and Jerry, the writer, were waiting for me expectantly.

I exclaimed, "Good morning, I have it! *Mitzi and a Hundred Guys!*"

They both perked up.

Jack asked, "Sounds great, who are all these guys?"

I said, "We get all the name guys who are performing on television shows and fill in with an all-male marching band to make up the hundred!"

Next it was Mitzi's turn to hear the news. Mitzi also flipped over the idea, so we immediately recruited all the male TV celebrities we could get and without hesitation all the guys flipped at the chance to do a show with Mitzi. It's fantastic how many accepted.

Bob Hope and Mitzi Gaynor

262

On the day of rehearsal and record they all arrived either in their tuxes or carrying them on a hanger. (Not only did they do the show for free but they supplied their own tuxes) During the shoot, I would run down to the stage and teach them eight bars of choreography at a time, and run back up to the control room and shoot those eight bars. Then I would repeat that until all the number was done. The guys had a good time doing it and it was a very happy day on the set. They all loved Mitzi and would have done anything for her.

Bob Hope arrived and I shot his bit after I dismissed all the other guys. Bob seemed

Mitzi and a hundred guys.

disgruntled about something and it showed in his performance, so I went down and talked to him. He took my advice and bucked up a bit and even managed a smile for the retake. This brought Bob's performance up 100 percent.

The USC marching band brought our "men" quota up to a hundred and they and Mitzi blasted their way through to a grand finale. This made a tremendous farewell and wrapped the finish of the TV special *Mitzi... and a Hundred Guys*. Everybody was still so charged up, the band stuck around and graciously did a mini concert which sent everybody out even more charged.

Bob Mackie has done well for Mitzi. But the design process is always a process with back and forth. There was one night at dinner when Bob brought sketches of the wardrobe for the next special. Mitzi looked at them first and passed them to me. I thought they were okay but they were exactly the same dress we'd had many times before, only in different fabric and I told him so.

Bob blew up, he became furious, picked up his sketches and left the table and went home.

Mitzi was taken aback and said, "Tony, what are we going to do?"

I said, "Not to worry, he'll be back with something better."

A week went by before we heard from Bob. He called for a meeting at Mitzi's and we gathered. He presented the first drawing to Mitzi and she gasped. She then passed it to me.

I stood up and declared, "Bob this is one of the best gowns you have ever designed for Mitzi."

All peace was restored. It was a simple long white gown with a big brass buckle pulled to one hip holding stretched fabric outlining the shapely body. It was one of the simplest and greatest gowns to come from Bob.

On one of the specials I was having a time shooting a close-up of Mitzi. The makeup was all-wrong. I had the makeup man with me while pointing out all that I thought was wrong. It just wasn't what I thought it should be - when Mitzi said, "Ton, what's taking so long?"

I flipped open my switch and said, "Mitzi, the lights have gotten older."

She straightened up, "Oops, I'll stay here as long as you need me."

This reminds me, that often Sonja Haney acted as her stand in and also her "dance in" to save Mitzi from exhaustion. Sonja has been a loyal stand in and worked with me as my assistant for years, also appearing as a dancer in many of my shows. She and Mitzi get along just great. Her energy is always positive. She is a gem.

On another Mitzi special we paid tribute to many nations by singing and dancing in their particular styles. Roy Clark and Wayne Rogers were guests on that show and word got to me that they were out binging all night on the night before the shoot. When they arrived in the morning, they were still wobbly. I didn't know how they were going to get through the show. I guess the magic fairy paid them a visit because by showtime there was no sign of two drunks performing. I don't know how they did it, but I don't think Mitzi knew any of this. Why bother her with their problems, she had a show to do?

Mitzi Roaring in the Twenties! was another, totally different, side of Mitzi. I think a "total camp" says it all! There were always surprises in Mitzi's capabilities as an entertainer. In one number she did a Tango with Carl Reiner. It was very high camp and they did it very well but kept breaking up every few steps. They did steps where they had to look away from each other but the minute they turned back to face each other they'd break up. They had the whole crew laughing and we all heaved a great sigh of relief when it was finally completed. We really weren't sure they would ever finish it.

Sometimes funny things happen in the rehearsal hall. In one number I had Mitzi in the center with three boys on either side. They were in locked arms with each other and seemingly glued together. All would do the exact same movements and never separate from one another. The number was "Boogie Down." By the end of rehearsal they seemed to have the number down perfectly.

Now here's the strange part. The next day at rehearsal not one of them, including me, could remember any of the choreography. They all, including Mitzi, had a mental block.

Bob Mackie designs not only spectacular gowns, but also garments that move beautifully on camera. That is one of the things that make him a truly great designer.

I said "Maybe it just wasn't good enough."

They all responded with a "No, no, no, we loved doing it."

I started all over again and came up with something similar. They did it well and said they thought it was better than the first one. Well in any event that's the version that aired and they looked good doing it.

In all my years of working with dancers, if I thought they had done a good job they were rewarded with a loud "GORGEOUS" from me. John Frayer said if he got a quarter for every time I said "GORGEOUS" he'd be a millionaire. On the other hand if I didn't say "Gorgeous," they'd shout, "What happened to GORGEOUS?" Sometimes you just can't win.

We did experience one shoot that nearly ended in disaster. It was during the shooting on a location of the opening for *Mitzi... Zings into Spring*. We had scouted a field of flowers and thought it would be great to do a helicopter shot of Mitzi standing in the middle of the field and acres of flowers. It certainly captured what we think of as spring. We did a practice run but I thought she looked too buried among the blooms. She had to be raised up a bit. The prop man found a box to put her on and that worked until the shoot. I was in the helicopter

Jack and Mitzi - a longtime team

guiding the camera guy and when I wanted him to get closer he said he was at the end of his lens. Well, the helicopter will have to get closer. That worked until the high wind caused by the helicopter blew her off the box and into the flowers. Fortunately the flowers acted as a buffer so she was not hurt and we got the shot.

Next she had to drive a tractor. One of the farmers started it for her and, fearless girl that she is, jumped on and sang and drove it like you'd think she knew what she was doing. When I got what I needed the farmer jumped on and brought it to a stop. We got the shot and Mitzi looked fabulous doing it. We all agreed we had another great opening for her special. Jack poked his head into the booth and laughingly said, "Tony, you're crazy but it was great!" It gave Mitzi a laugh to see herself on the tractor in a beautiful long chiffon gown.

The idea came to me while visiting friends on their ranch in Pennsylvania. Early one morning I was awakened by the sound of a tractor and got up to see what it was. There dressed in a long chiffon gown hiked up to his hips exposing bare legs and feet, a big picture hat and singing at the top of his lungs was Jack Barnard, our host, driving a tractor plowing the field. It was a hoot and when I talked to him about it he said, "Oh I always dress to plow the field." I loved it. But Mitzi was a little bit prettier when she did it.

To continue with the spring theme I decided we should have some of the little animals born in spring - little chicks, bunnies and a little pony - all should be in the number. The set was beautiful and Mackie's gown was a full skirt, tight bodice breath of spring concoction that certainly defined spring.

In the song Mitzi is on the ground with her skirt spread wide all around her. I decided it would be great to spread the little chicks and bunnies all over the skirt with the little pony looking over her shoulder. It was quite pretty until Mitzi started to get a little giggly during the song. Half way through the song something happened that made her just burst out laughing. What we couldn't see was all these little creatures were crapping all over her beautiful Bob Mackie dress. Fortunately all the scooting around activity of the little animals distracted from their pooping so it wasn't obvious on camera. When we had finished taping the number there was only one thing that could be done with Mitzi's beautiful dress - burn it. It should be said that I don't think the chicks' actions in any way related to what they thought of Bob's work.

Bob Mackie and I have had good times talking about all the shows we've done and all the celebrities we have worked with. We agree Mitzi remains a favorite. I am happy to see Bob progress in his work to become one of the most sought after designers in the business. Bravo, Bob!

Left: Mitzi introduces Tony at The Paley Center for Media - an event celebrating Mitzi's TV specials: Mitzi Gaynor... Razzle Dazzle, The Special Years, Above right: Bob Mackie, Mitzi, and Tony, Lower right: Tony and Mitzi celebrate many years.

Years of working with Mitzi have been rewarded with a wonderful, enduring friendship. In the last stage show I did for her, I was so pleased to witness the triumph she experienced opening night on stage in San Francisco. Standing ovations are usually reserved for the end of the show. In Mitzi's case she broke that tradition. At the end of the first act she got a rousing standing ovation. Something I had never seen before and will always remember it.

Mitzi threw me a birthday party at her house not too long ago.

My last directing project was staging and lighting her recent one woman show *My Life Behind the Sequins*.

My hat's off to Rene Reyes and Shane Rosamonda, Mitzi's current managers and producers, who put together that show and have kept her in front of audiences over the last seven years, since the passing of her husband Jack in December 2006.

From my first introduction to Mitzi I believe the mold was formed for us to work together. This chapter contains only a portion of all our accomplishments. Our working together for so many years seemed simply something destined to be. Creating shows for her will keep me pumped up forever.

I can retire well satisfied.

Photos for this chapter were graciously provided from the private collection of Mitzi Gaynor/ Green Isle, Inc."

GREEN ISLE

April 7, 1993

Mr. Tony Charmoli

Dear Tony:

For years and years Mitzi and I have had the great joy of telling everyone we know what a pro you are, what a friend you are, and how many times you have come forward in our need. Clearly I've done as much as I thought I could to extol the Charmoli virtue. Now you've completely reversed me. In other words, I've got to start over. Whatever I thought you were and whatever Mitzi believes you are is true completely. We just owe you more appreciation. I don't mean to cover a fine feeling with a bunch of bilge, but Tony, you're out of this world. We both know it. We love you and love the idea of knowing you further. Thanks for your kindness.

Very Sincerely,

Jack Bean

JRB:ck

GREEN ISLE ENTERPRISES INC

Chapter 20

The Christmas Party

My annual Christmas party blossomed into a huge holiday affair when I began inviting the *Star Search* winners to come and show off their talent at my party. Sam Riddle our producer emceed the show and his son Scott took care of the music tracks.

The house was mostly just decorated with a Christmas tree in the living room till Robert came to work for us. He is a master and decorates every room in the house and the exterior as well. Bravos and cheers are always extended to Robert for his fabulous décor. The living room is always a standout masterpiece, the staircase and foyer entrance always draw exclamations from arriving guests. And there were a lot of extraordinary guests who passed through that foyer. Some were quite famous and some were not - but they all were interesting.

The show was done in my living room and I had speakers placed throughout the house for those who couldn't squeeze in. One year, the room was packed and some celebrities wound up sitting on the floor. Sam Riddle came out and did his usual warm up and introduced Margaret Cho as the current winner in comedy. Margaret came out and scored. She got big applause, but on her exit I could see she was visibly shaken.

I checked on her in the next room, "Margaret what's the matter? They loved you."

Margaret Cho

She replied, "Oh my God Tony! I just love Shirley MacLaine and there she was sitting on the floor right in front of me! I had her laughing! Oh! I just can't believe it. I'll remember this forever."

I said, "Welcome to Hollywood, Margaret, and Merry Christmas!"

As the party developed into an annual event, it grew until I had to hire a caterer and double the kitchen help, hire bar tenders, waiters, parking attendants, and of course the sound system with a microphone so *Star Search* winners could perform and be heard throughout the house. The party guest list expanded year after year but only *Star Search* winners performed - with the exception of my old friend Gisele McKenzie from my *Hit Parade* days who would lead everybody in Christmas carols later in the evening.

Debbie Reynolds always arrived with her assistant carrying her usual two bottles of wine. She'd announce, "I always bring my own wine. I drink only cheap wine, because you can't get a buzz on expensive wine." It was easy to see it really worked for her. She'd frequently sit with Phyllis Diller out in the garden or in the living room, holding court with whoever gathered around them and there were many. She was a hoot at the party. And Phyllis and Debbie together meant you never knew what would come out of their mouths. More than a few guests came away giggling from hearing their rapport.

One evening I was greeting Carol Channing and her husband, Charles Lowe, at the front door. Carol looked great in a long fur coat and white fur cap. Seconds later, Shirley MacLaine arrived. Seeing Carol's coat she cried, "Carol you're wearing a fur coat???" Shirley didn't believe in wearing fur.

Carol immediately smiled, shrugged, and dropped her arms to her sides letting the fur coat slide to the floor. She was wearing what looked like men's long white winter underwear and stayed that way for the entire evening. Even Shirley had to laugh.

The whole buzz that Christmas party was, "Did you see Carol, did you see Carol?" It was the damndest funny thing you could imagine. Carol doesn't drink alcohol at all and has always been quite health conscious. She will bring her own bottled water to every event and will bring her own disposable utensils to dinner parties.

Johnny Mathis lives just up the street and would stop in some years for a bit. Johnny is actually a little shy around big groups, so he rarely stayed long. He was constantly

Charles Lowe & Carol Channing

smothered with well-wishers, and a lot of celebrities find that a mixed blessing. It is exciting and validating but at the same time it makes it a little hard to relax. He missed a few years in a row, but when the last party came around I sent him a note to let him know it would be my last big Christmas party. He came and had a good time. These days I sometimes see him driving by when I am on my daily walk. We always wave. It's nice to have him as a neighbor. I think he plays golf in the mornings.

A lot of celebrities work through the holiday season since it is a popular time of year to get bookings, especially on a Saturday night. So, attendance often varied with everyone's schedules. And even celebrities have to bring home the bacon - or tofu as the case may be.

Johnny Mathis and Tony

It was at one of my Christmas parties that Tennille of "Captain & Tennille", a vegetarian, accidentally ate beef pate that she hadn't realized was beef. She liked it till she found out what it was - then she did not feel well at all and had to lie down upstairs. I suppose it has to be tough for vegetarians having to guess what is on the buffet table.

Betty White was a perennial at my annual Christmas parties and in all the years missed only one and that was because she was doing a book signing in Georgia. She did call however, to tell me she would have to miss this one. Of course everybody asked about her. I should have put up a sign saying Betty won't be here tonight!

One year, a young friend of mine who was a grammar school teacher, told Betty that one of the little girls in his class was a big fan of hers, and that the little girl had written her a letter. He handed her the letter and she stuffed it right down into her cleavage "so it wouldn't get lost". Betty being a comedienne, of course milked the moment - a funny lady even when she is not trying. The little girl was delighted when Betty wrote to her some time later. Not all evening gowns come with pockets - so at times down the cleavage is the dependable way to go!

It's amazing and pleasing to me to see the acclaim suddenly and profusely being heaped on Betty. Fortunately we met and became friends a long time ago and still remain good friends. I had the good fortune of attending her huge 90th Birthday celebration as

Tony, Betty White & Michael Feinstein

the guest of John Shaffner and Joe Stewart who did the magnificent job of decorating that huge ballroom in the old Biltmore Hotel. And the birthday cake was particularly delicious! An added plus was catching up with Carol Burnett and Mary Tyler Moore. Betty's sudden popularity has put a crimp on how often I see her. I'm thrilled with her success, but I do miss our visits together.

One year Eddie from Le Dome restaurant called to say his wife was coming to the party. What a pleasant surprise. She, being Swedish, arrived with six or eight young Swedish girls all dressed in white wearing a wreath of flaming candles on their heads walking single file while singing Swedish Christmas carols. They carefully walked through all the rooms full of guests who always made room for them to pass through and into the garden and around the pool for all the guests to see, then exited to their waiting limo. It was a remarkable and unforgettable Swedish tradition, which worked very well, in an Italian-Danish household.

Mitzi always attracted a group and would end up in the library, which has always been a comfortable room near the Christmas tree. And of course Bob Mackie was a frequent guest. Bob and I were good friends long before he started designing for Mitzi. I remember at one of my Christmas parties, Bob arrived and stepped down into the living room and right there was Paul Rose's mother Hortense.

I said "Hortense, this is Bob Mackie. He dresses Judy Garland."

She replied, "You make all of Judy Garland's clothes?"

With a big smile Bob replied "Yes, I do."

Hortense growled, "Awful, just awful."

Bob turned to me and asked, "Who's your friend?" I said, "Paul Rose's mother."

He replied, "Oh of course, it figures."

Carol Lawrence always appeared in a knockout outfit. Each year she seemed to top herself. Sometimes she'd be off working but it was always a pleasure when she could make it. She's another one who works a lot over the holidays.

Above left: Lisa Kirk; Right: Bob Mackie & Maria Pogee;

Opposite page: Top left: Mitzi Gaynor and Carol Channing; Top right: Michelle Lee, Tony, Boots, Barbara Eden; Middle left: Tom Troupe and Carole Cook; Middle: Carol Channing and John Epperson (Lypsinka); Middle right: Tony and John Bailey; Bottom right: Barbara Lazaroff, Tony, Debbie Reynolds, and David Streets; Bottom right: Carol Lawrence

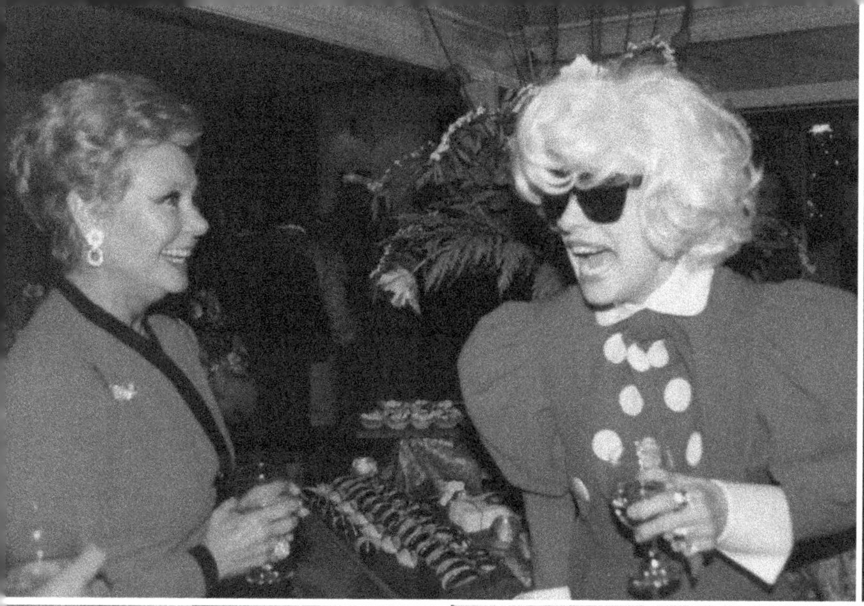
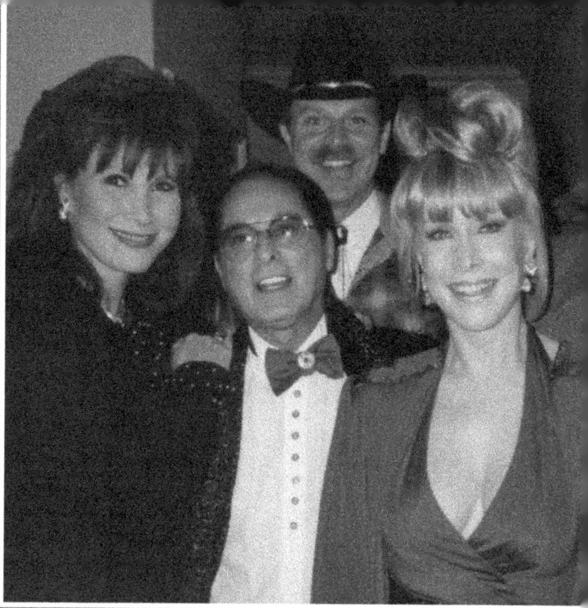
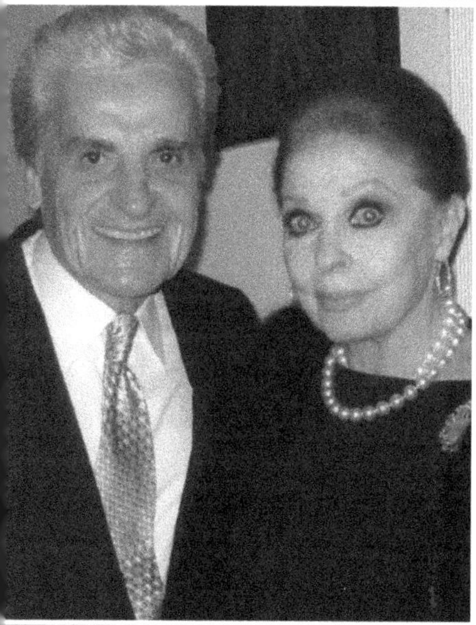
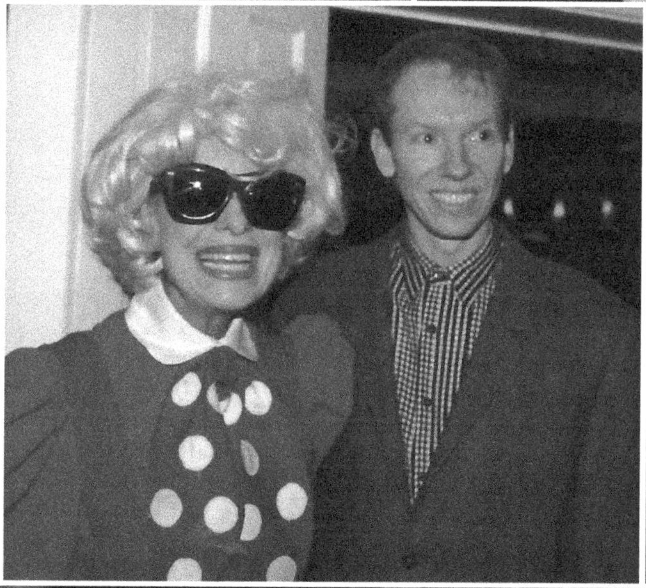
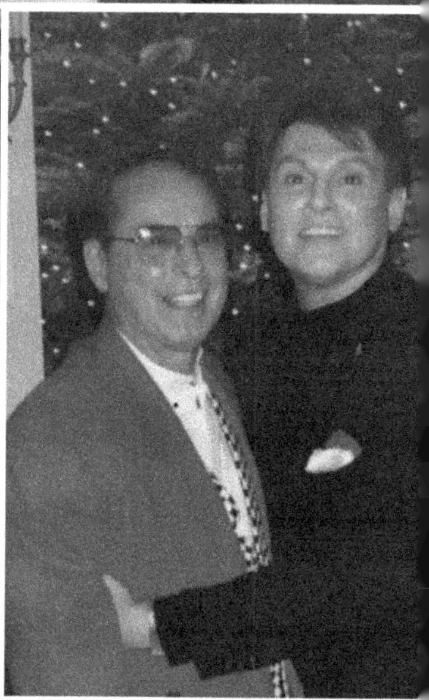
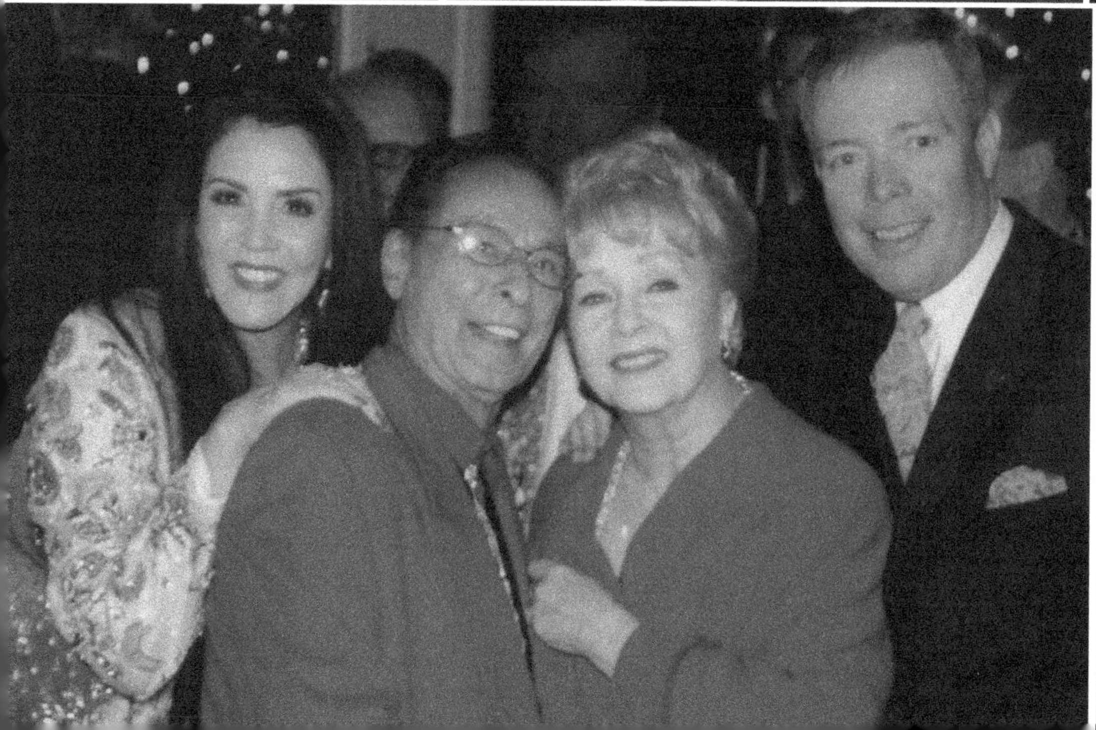
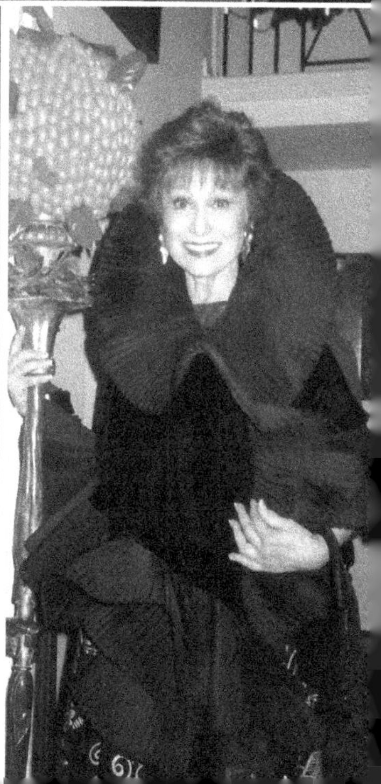

Above left: Nanette Fabray and Tony; Above right: Will, Rebecca Wright and husband, George De La Pena (who played Nijinsky in the film), and Tony; Left: Frances Taylor was a favorite dancer of Tony's, and whose marriage to Miles Davis is now chronicled in the film **Miles Ahead** *directed by Don Cheadle; Bottom left: Stephanie Powers and Tony; Bottom right: Dick Sargent, unidentified guest, and Rip Taylor.*

Opposite page: Top right: Tony Martin and Cyd Charisse; Top Left: Rip Taylor, Betty White, Phyllis Diller, and unidentified guest; Middle left: Tony and Sid Krofft; Middle right: Billie Hayes (Witchipoo & Mammy Yokum), Tony, and producer Bob Finkel; Bottom left: Tad Tadlock, Shirley MacLaine, Kip Grimm; Bottom right: Juliet Prowse and Dick Beard (Tony's longtime assistant and one third of The Cabots)

Christmas Party photos by Barbara Lazaroff, Kip Grimm, Eric Underwood, and other guests.

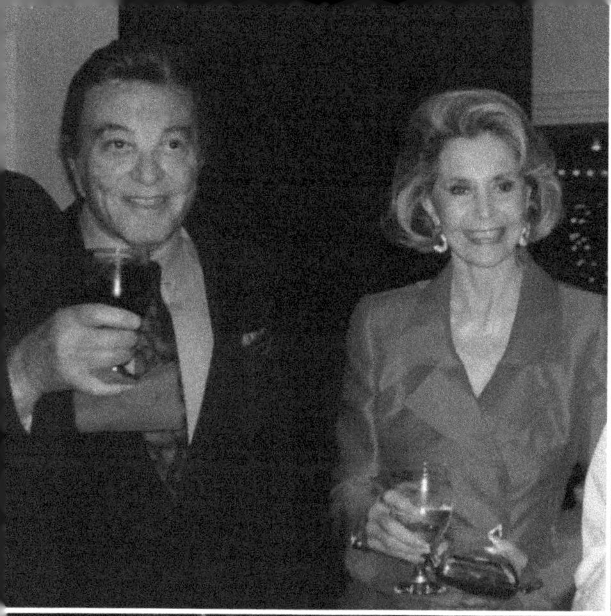
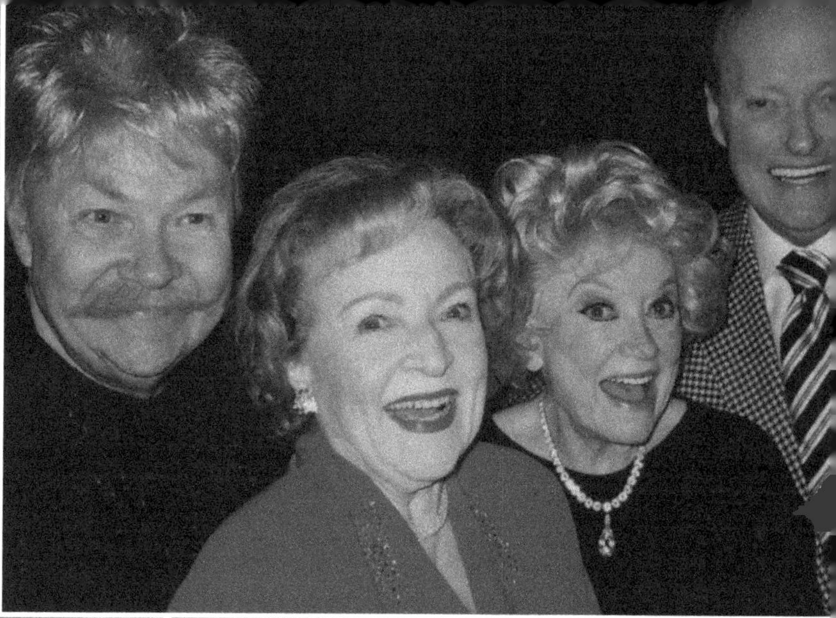
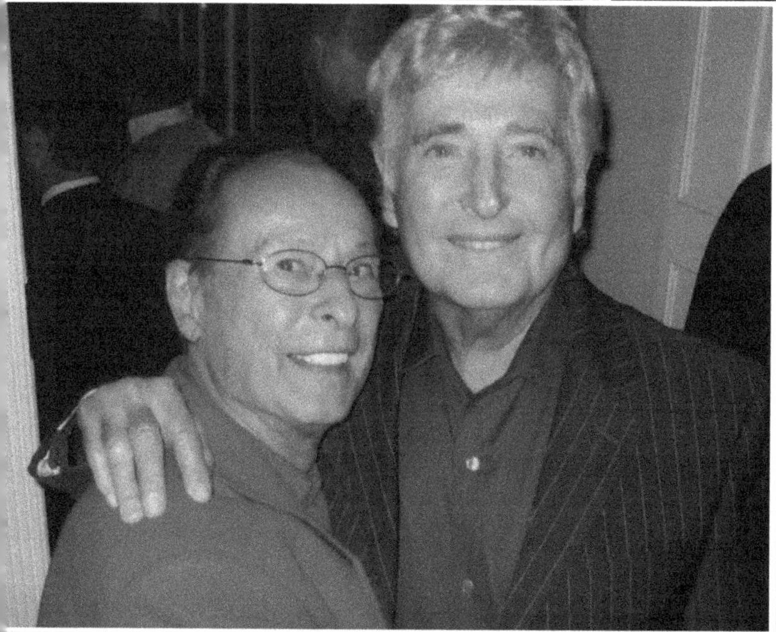
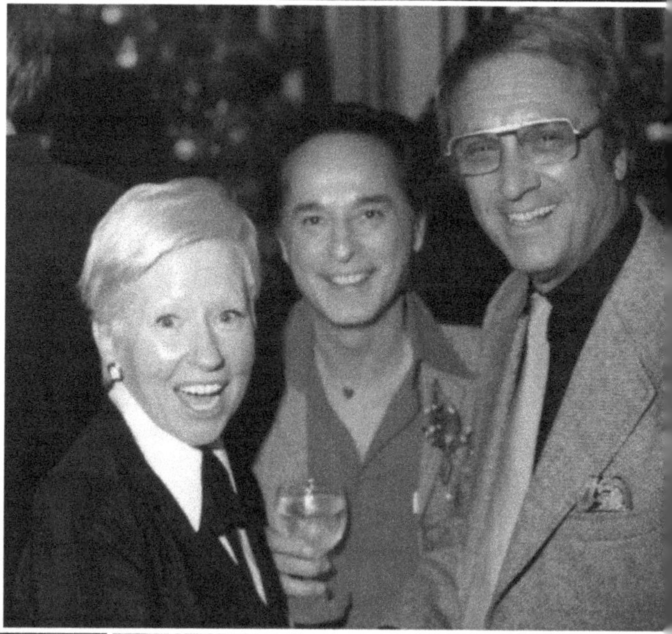
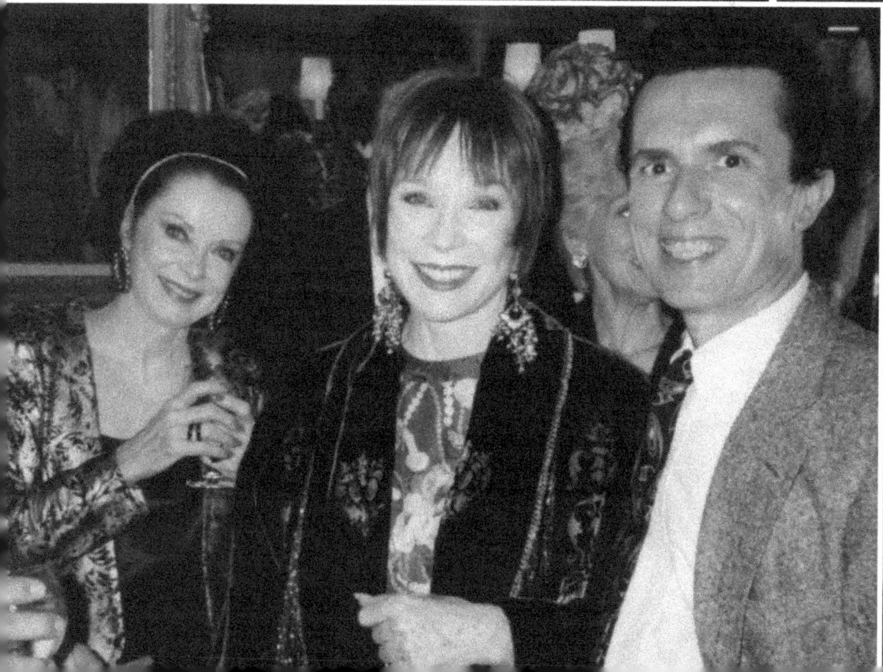
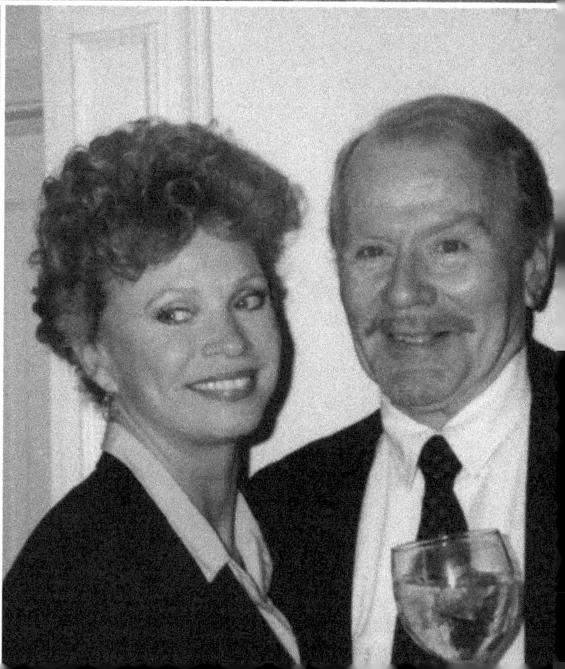

Above left: Phyllis Gehrig and Tony- Phyllis was Tony's dance partner in New York at the old YMHA Sunday shows; Above right: Tony's sisters- Claire, Nell, and Alvina on the far right, Tony's grand niece Lisa (between Nell and Al) and Bud Holden behind them all. Below left: Greg Gorman and friend with Tony; Below right: Marty Allen & Gretchen Wyler.

*Opposite page: Top left: John Epperson (Lypsinka), Rip Taylor, Debbie Reynolds, and Tony; Top right: Barry Manilow; Middle left: John Shaffner, Tony, and Joe Stewart; Middle right: Gisele MacKenzie, Mitzi Gaynor, and Tony; Bottom left: Tony with Broadway Babies Carol Lawrence and Raquel Welch; Bottom right: Jane Kean from Broadway's **Ankles Aweigh**.*

Christmas Party photos by Barbara Lazaroff, Kip Grimm, Eric Underwood, and assorted other guests.

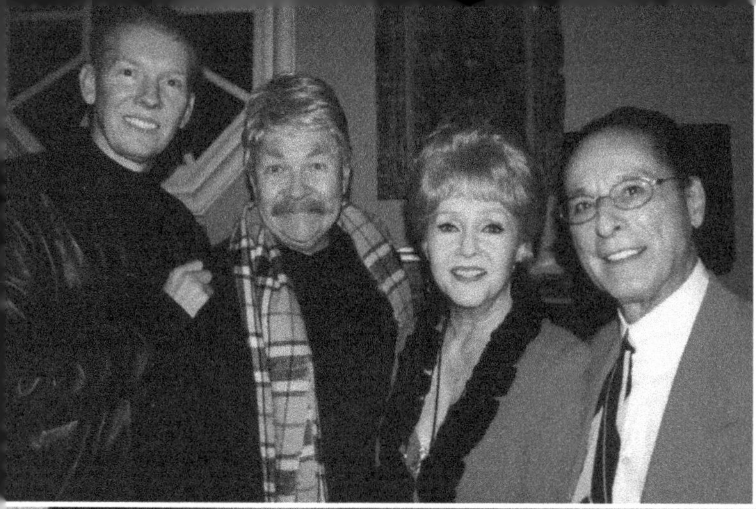
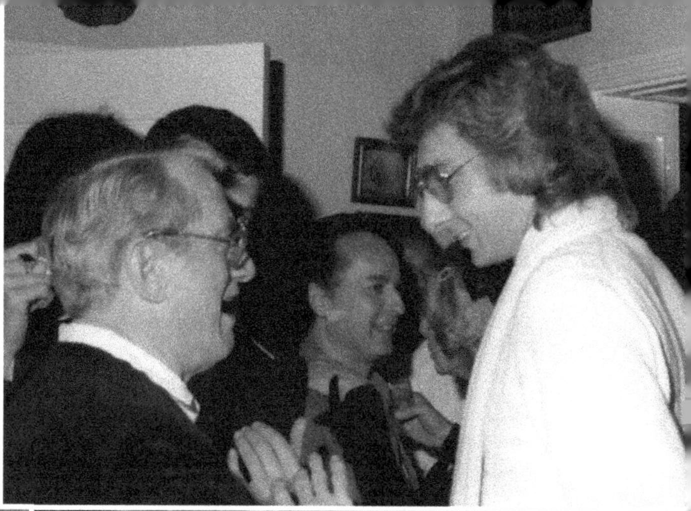
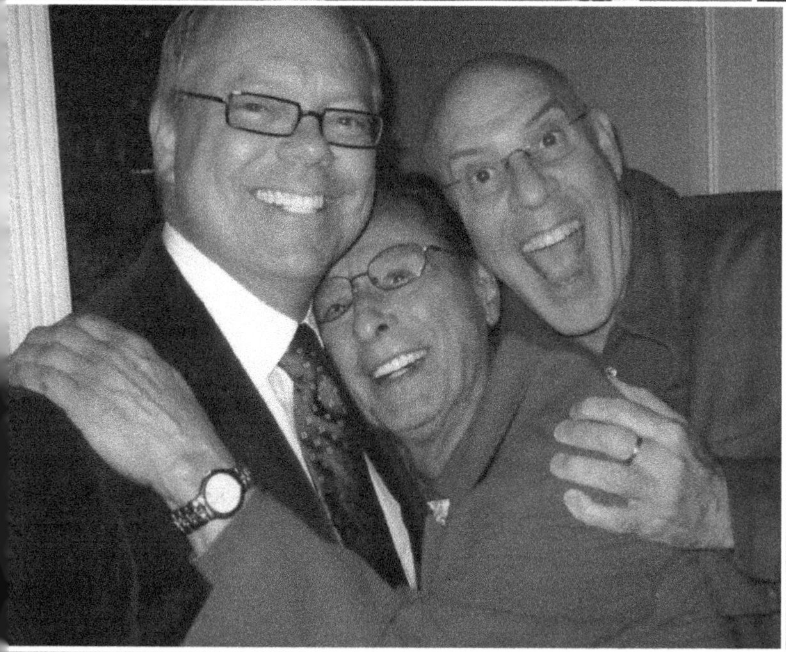
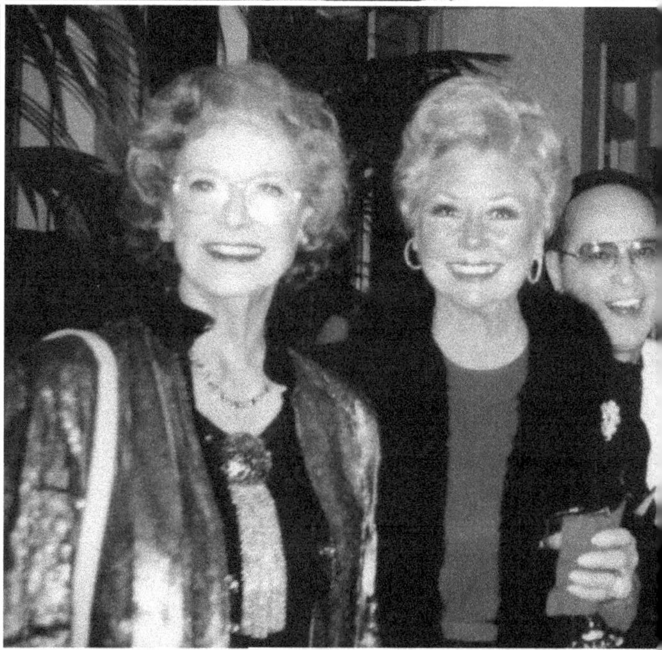
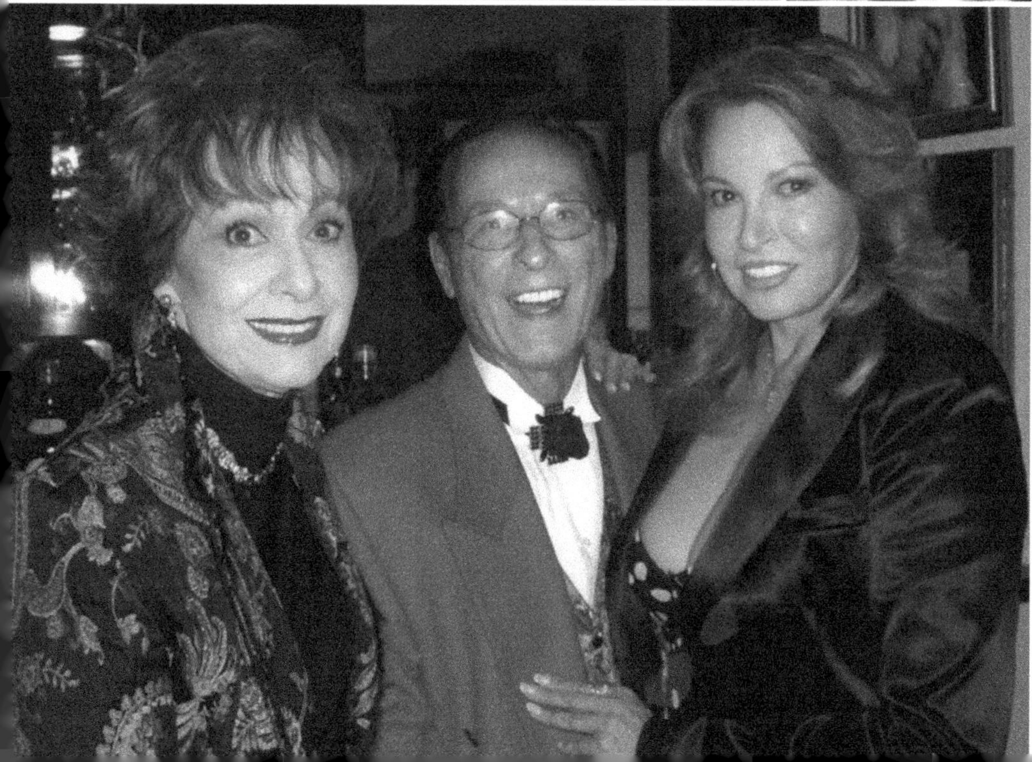
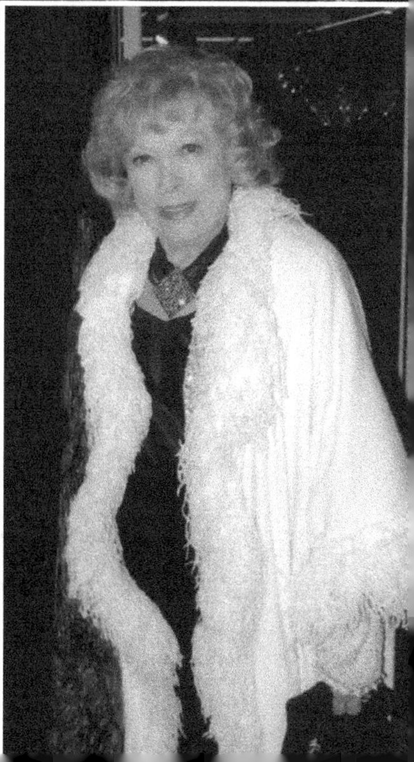

Left: Scotty Bowers of Full Service fame;   Right: Tony's niece Dorothy, Will, and Tony's sister Claire

Nanette Fabray was always full of her funny observations. So many interesting people came through over the years. Raquel Welch, Paul Reubens (Pee Wee Herman), Sid Krofft, John Epperson (Lypsinka), Stephanie Powers (when she was not at her wild life preserve in Africa), Carole Cook and her husband Tom Troupe... so many folks.

The prerequisite to be invited to my party had less to do with celebrity and much more to do with just being interesting. Guests' most frequent complaint was that there were so many unique people to talk to, you could not get across a room because of the number of conversations you would get involved with along the way.

Barbara Lazaroff always sparkled in some new outfit and always took hundreds of pictures. Many of the photos I have of my Christmas parties come from Barbara.

But, all things come to an end eventually. Guests started bringing extra uninvited friends, one brought as many as seven extra people none of whom I knew. When you figure the caterer counts heads and many uninvited guests are added to their guest list, and several guests do this, it shoots up the head count and expense quite dearly. It spoils it for everybody else. One film critic went into the kitchen and ordered a "take out" bag of food to take home with him. Really. So, finally it seemed time to say "this is the last one" and it was.

One lady called to ask when I was doing my next party and when I told her I wasn't going to give one she remarked, "Oh but you must. It's the only excuse I have for buying a new dress!" You see even the economy suffers!

Tony and Santa share a holiday hug; Opposite bottom: Claire, Tony, Dorothy's husband Nick, Dorothy, Seated: Nell, and Al

Long time friends: Barry Rogers, Jordan Randall, Paul Manchester, David Streets, Eric Underwood

We had some grand times at Christmas here in this house - but these years I keep it much smaller and more intimate. It is certainly easier on me as a host. At the big parties, I'd have to station myself in the entry to greet people and with all the going and coming I'd find myself standing in the same spot all evening. Small evenings allow me to sit down and actually have conversations! A different sort of good time.

On Christmas Eve, Will and I usually gave a holiday party for family and close friends. Scotty Bowers has been our bartender for years and everybody bursts into big cheers when they see him. And my sisters love him. Even since the success of his book, he still graciously pours our drinks each year. After cocktails and dinner we all retire to the living room in anticipation of Santa Claus' arrival. My niece Dorothy's husband Nick starts up with "Here comes Santa Claus" on his saxophone with David Streets at the piano. Santa is always a member of the family or a guest who has snuck off to get into costume. We have a variety of Santa costumes from skimpy to grande. It is always a surprise to see what comes down the steps. It is good to have a time of year that reminds us to stay in touch with our friends, and I hope big parties or small that I continue to see and hear from all these wonderful people who have made my life such an interesting journey.

Tony Charmoli has won three Primetime Emmy Awards for choreography; **Your Hit Parade** *(1955),* **Mitzi...A Tribute to the American Housewife** *(1974), and* **Gypsy in My Soul** *(1976). As a director, he has been nominated for six Primetime Emmys and five DGA Awards, winning the Guild's honors in 1977 for* **Gypsy in My Soul** *and in 1980 for* **John Denver and the Muppets: A Christmas Together.**

Thankfulness

Will and I had a marvelous journey together. We stuck together through war and tough times and we discovered more great adventures than I could ever recount here. I couldn't have done what I have done, without him. Will did a wonderful job managing my career and letting me focus on the creative tasks. He created a home that was always a home.

We only had one big argument in all those years which ended in him walking out the door shouting, "And I'm never coming back!" then punctuated it with a big slam. Just a little bit later, I was in bed in the darkness and I heard him enter and climb into bed.

"That was a short trip," I said. We both just started giggling. I have no idea what the fight was about. It is long forgotten. But I remember the good times.

In 1999, Will had been struggling with a long battle with cancer. I was in Hawaii directing a TV special at the time when I got a call on September 3rd from the hospital in Los Angeles.

Will and I talked on the phone. His last words to me were, "You gave me a good life. You gave me a great life. I just can't pull through this one. Don't worry about me. I'll be fine. This is goodbye. - I love you. - Oh Tony."

Will passed away before I got back to Los Angeles. I miss him more than I can say. But I am happy to have many dear friends who fill some of the void.

Whoever thinks show business is easy, doesn't have a clue as to what he is talking about. The talent and artistry of the professional just makes it look easy. Some are born with talent, others are taught. Being born the ninth into a family of immigrant parents in the snow and cold of northern Minnesota has its advantages. It gives you strength to work hard to find a better way of making life worth living.

Fortunately for me my path took me through many ways of working with some of our top talents who greatly enriched my life and my career. I had the fortune of being honored with many award nominations and was given three Emmy's by the Television Academy, and two Director trophies by the Directors Guild of America. I guess I fulfilled a dream. I know my family was proud, and especially dear Will was extremely proud.

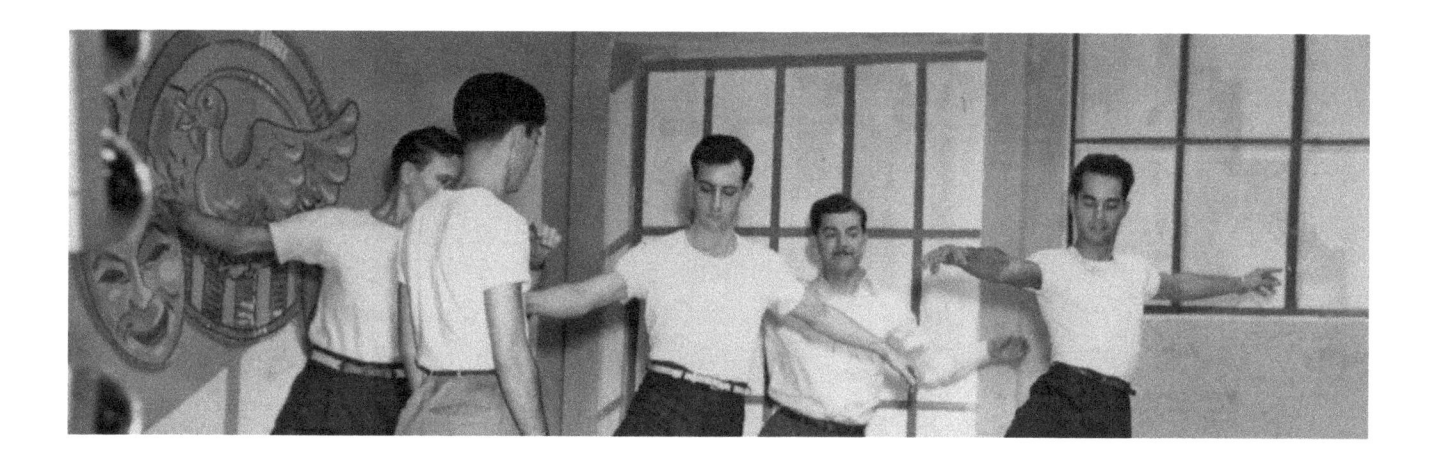

I wish to extend a wagon load of gratitude to all the dancers, actors, camera operators, lighting directors, costume designers, music conductors and arrangers, writers, stage managers, technicians and celebrities, who have made my work possible and enjoyed throughout the world. If anybody has been left out I believe I can safely say we can blame it on my age – 94!

I wish to thank my neighbor and friend, Greg Gorman, for his generous offer to photograph me for this book. He has created portraits of many of the most successful people in the world and I am touched that he would offer to do one of me as a gift. Wow. It knocked my socks off when he made the offer and I was able to keep my clothes on during the shoot. He is such a gentleman. It is always a delight to run into you on my morning walks.

I am totally indebted to my friend Paul Manchester who insisted this book should be written, then took it upon himself to persuade me to get a computer at the age of 90 and start typing out my memories. He has done a masterful job in pulling it all together, scanning hundreds of photos, asking questions and looking up details and I've enjoyed the journey. If you enjoy the book, thank Paul.

Many years back, Will called my attention to an ad in the newspaper of a Robert Jowers announcing he was available for houseman duties. I replied to the ad and suggested we have a meeting. At this get together we found all parties to be very compatible and Robert was on the job within a week. Robert is still holding everything together. And he has an exceptional design sense! I've been lucky to have such a gifted person to decorate my house for the holidays each year. It is always new and different and wonderful. Even Ernestine has come back to a party and wholeheartedly endorsed her replacement.

Paul and me at a Christmas party

Robert Jowers

Will was right on the nose when he found Robert Jowers to run my household. Robert takes good care of me, my house, the gardeners, the pool man, and anything else that sets foot on this property. In a way, I feel Robert is another case of Will looking after me in his absence. Besides, Robert's cute little Affenpinscher named Rhoda will get after anyone who does anything to rock the boat.

And of course thanks to YOU if you are reading this! Without an audience we all would be out of work. So, my gratitude and very best wishes to each of you!

Tony

Tony Charmoli,
as photographed by
Greg Gorman

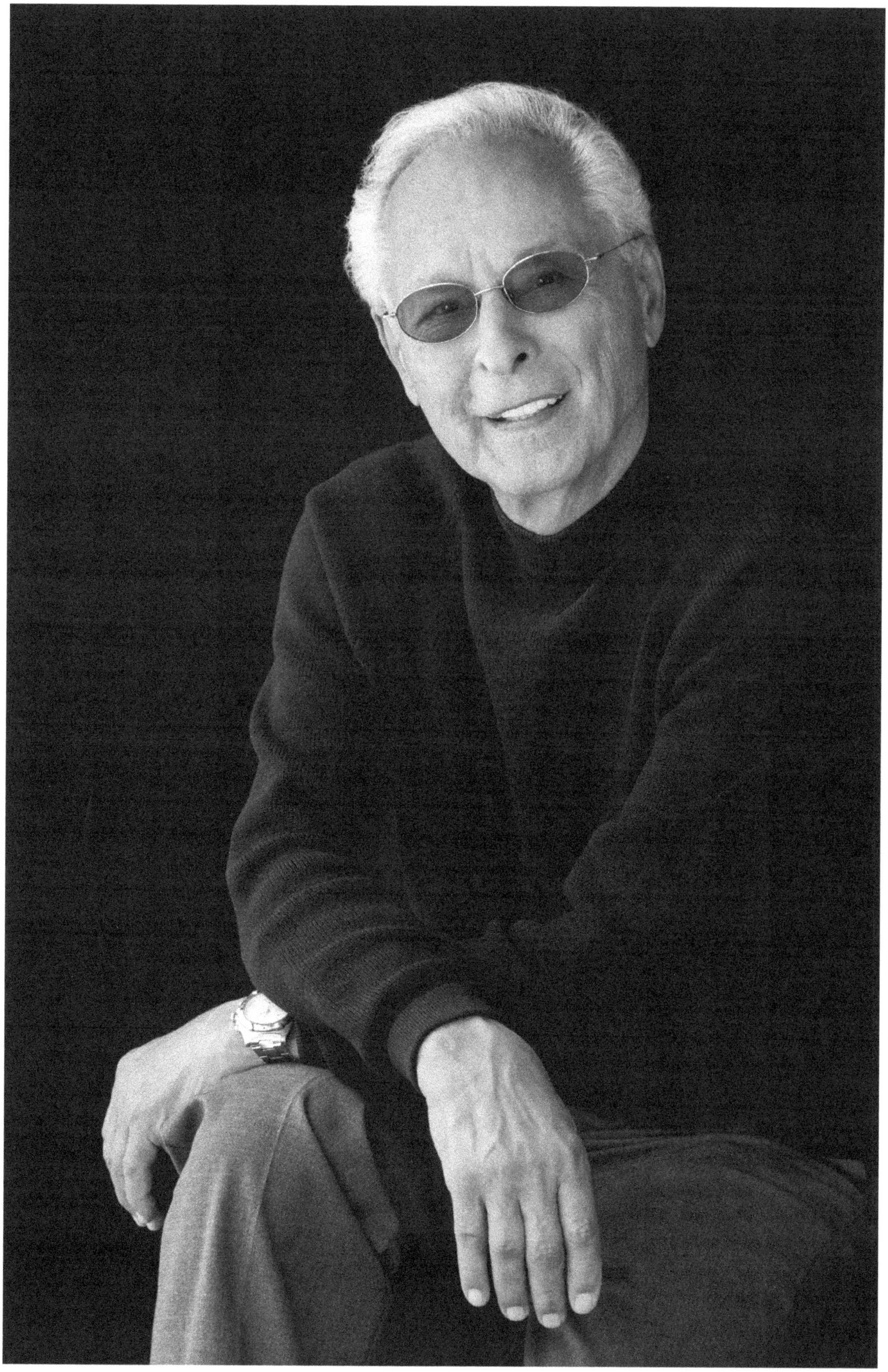

Tony's office

Index

A

Abdul, Paula 182
Adrian, Iris 114
Aguilera, Christina 244
Ailey, Alvin 182
Albee, Edward 202, 203
Alexander, Rod 77
Alice In Wonderland 83, 119, 206
Alice Through the Looking Glass 119
Allen, Marty 232, 233, 237, 276
Allen, Peter 156
All Star Super Bowl, The 175
Alridge, Alfreda 245, 258
American Theater Wing 42
America's Dance Honors 181
Andrews, Julie 45, 148, 157, 161, 174, 221
Anglund, Joan Walsh 115
Ankles Aweigh! 78, 80
Anthony Newley Show, The 156
Arden, Don 137, 138
Arms, Russell 67, 80, 83, 91
Arnett, Ray 171
Arthur, Bea 229
Astaire, Ava 101, 221
Astaire, Fred 101
Atkins, Chris 231
Atlantic City Holiday 85
Avant, Lance 126, 185

B

Bacall, Lauren 224, 232
Bailey, John 272
Bailey, Pearl 103
Baker, Josephine 63
Ballet Trockadero De Monte Carlo, Les 167
Ball, Lucille 122, 166
Balosni, Sal 73
Bankhead, Tallulah 48, 49
Banner, Bob 88, 109, 170, 179, 242
Barber, Gillian 83
Barnes, Billy 161
Barnett, Jackie 153, 154, 155
Barrymore, Ethel 80, 82
Baryshnikov, Mikhail 169, 218, 239
Bassey, Shirley 154
Bean, Jack 9, 259
Beard, Dick 98, 110, 137, 166
Beatty, Talley 47
Beatty, Warren 128
Bedeau, Fern 63, 75
Belle of the Klondike, The 78
Bell, Prince Rene Douala Manga 65
Bennett, Michael 188
Bergen, Polly 85
Beulah the Witch 84
Beyoncé 244
Bikel, Theodore 80
Bill Haley and his Comets 85
Birch, Peter 42
Blair, Janet 114
Bolero 72, 112, 126, 186, 187
Boleyn, Eleanor 71
Bondy, Sally 63
Bonshire, Forrest 54
Boone, Pat 85, 86
Bowers. Scotty 220, 279
Breaux, Marc 83, 132, 133
Brooks, Jim 140
Brooks, Jimmy 101
Brown, Kelly 102
Brunges, Hank 102
Bugaloos, The 191
Burnett, Carol 94, 272
Burns, David 52
Butler, John 62

C

Cabots, The 137, 138
Caesar, Sid 51, 174
Cantinflas 181
Captain & Tennille Show, The 169
Captain & Tennille, The 271
Carlos, Ernst 42
Carney, Art 103, 118
Carroll, Diahann 156
Carter, Jack 85, 86
Cartwright, Angela 115
Cartwright, Bruce 57
Cassity, Tyler 198, 217
Cave, The 260
Chakiris, George 182
Channing, Carol 80, 81, 83, 100, 103, 215, 270
Charisse, Cyd 108, 110, 182, 194, 274
Charles, Ray 67
Charnin, Martin 116
Chateau Marmont 27, 28, 81, 90, 100, 190
Cher 161, 162
Cher Show, The 161
Chevy Show, The 114
Cho, Margaret 244, 269, 270
Circus of the Stars 229, 238
Clark, Bobby 83
Clark, Dick 238, 246, 248
Clark, Roy 264
Clerk, Clive 205
Coca, Imogene 127
Cole, Jack 69, 78
Colgate Comedy Hour, The 89, 100
Collins, Dorothy 66, 70, 71, 89
Collins, Gary 236
Color Television 75
Conway, Tim 163
Cook, Carole 225, 272, 278
Cook, Don 221
Cosby, Bill 173
Crabbe, Gary 140
Craig, Brad 126
Craig, Bradford 183
Crawford, Joan 102
Crawford, Michael 182
Crosby, Bing 108

D

D'Amboise, Jacques 106
Dance Magazine 77, 78
Dance Theater of Harlem 182
Danny Kaye Show, The 113, 120, 125, 127, 136
Dateline II 84
Davis, Bette 119
Davis Jr., Sammy 173, 182
Day, Doris 163
Dean Martin Show, The 190
Dear Judas 50, 51
DeChiazza, Pepe 102
De La Pena, George 274
de Mille, Agnes 44
De Mola, Tina 132
Denver, John 163, 195
Desert Inn 144, 189
Dietrich, Marlene 144
Diller, Phyllis 221, 235, 270, 274
Dinah Shore Show, The 88, 90, 91, 93, 95, 106, 107, 112, 114, 148, 157, 242, 260
Dixie's Bar of Music 89
Domingo, Placido 180
Doris Day Today 163
Dorn, Geneve 57
Dragon, "Captain" Daryl 169
Drummy, Sam 256
Duane, Jerry 67
Duke Ellington Orchestra 153

Dumont, Margaret 114
Duncan, Sandy 170
Dunwiddie, Charlotte 65
Durante, Jimmy 119

E

Ebb, Fred 148, 225
Ed Sullivan Show, The 111
Eden, Barbara 272
Edwards, Blake 160
Edwards, Norman 185
Eileen Ford Models 161
Eisenhower, Dwight 38
Eisenhower, Mamie 38
Electric Light Orchestra, The 167
Electric Prunes, The 112
Emmy 45, 78, 167
Epperson, John 272, 276, 278
Evans, Bonnie 121
Evans, Dale 108
Evans, Maurice 83, 206

F

Fabray, Nanette 54, 55, 73, 99, 119, 222, 274, 278
Falana, Lola 170, 175
Fasnacht, Dixie 89
Feathertop 116
Feinstein, Michael 271
Ferrand, Louise 57
Field, Lorraine 186
Fields, Totie 194
Finkel, Bob 96
Fisher, Eddie 67, 128
Fisher, Nell 54
Fitzell, Roy 118, 121
Fitzgerald, Ella 153
Flatt, Ernie 259
Fol de Rol 194
Folies Bergère, The 142, 144
Follies 70
Fonda, Jane 180
Fonteyn, Margot 247
Ford, Betty 176, 182
Ford, Eileen 161
Ford, Gerald 176
Fosse, Bob 54, 69, 70, 174, 198
Franklin, Lydia 44
Frayer, John 126
Full Service 220

G

Gardner, Wilhemina 42

Garland, Judy 89, 122, 156, 190, 272
Gaynor, Mitzi 9, 207, 259, 272, 276
Geffen, David 163
Gehrig, Phyllis 44, 276
Gentry, Bobbie 151
Ghosts, Goblins and Kids 115
Giancolombo 134
Gielgud, John 62
Gold, Annabelle 52
Goldberg, Whoopie 234
Gorman, Greg 276, 283
Goulet, Robert 151
Grable, Betty 93
Graham, Martha 42, 44, 45, 174, 175, 182
Grant, Cary 125
Graziano, Rocky 85
Greenwood, Joan 80
Gregory, Jackie 113, 121
Greta Garbo 62
Grey, Dolores 73
Grey, Joel 148
Griffin, Merv 230, 231
Griffith, Andy 96
Grimes, Tammy 121
Grossman, Scott 254
Grove, Betty Ann 57
Grover Dale 102
Guardino, Harry 224
Gumm Sisters 122
Gyamarthy, Michel 142, 144
Gypsy In My Soul 128, 166, 167, 280

H

Hamilton, Joe 94
Hamilton, Peter 46
Hamlisch, Marvin 148
Handley, Alan 80, 119
Haney, Carol 95
Hanya Holm 30
Hargitay, Mickey 86
Harmon, Johnny 121, 149, 150
Harrah, Bill 152
Harrison, Ray 54
Harris, Sam 244
Harvey, Laurence 106, 107
Haydn, Richard 80
Hayes, Billie 193, 274
Helm, Eddie 186
Henderson, Charles 56
Henson, Jim 195
Hit Parade Dancers 231
Hit Parade Dancers, The 66, 69, 76
Hockney, David 163

Holden, Bud 91, 276
Holiday, Billie 46
Holloway, Stanley 148
Hollywood Forever 198, 217
Holm, Hanya 42, 48
Hope, Bob 175, 176, 262, 263
Horne, Lena 31
Hoving, Lucas 42, 46
Howard, Ron 114
H. R. Pufnstuf 191
Hudson, Rock 204
Hulouse, Jean 43, 44
Hunter, Tab 99
Hutchins, Aubrey 31
Hutton, Betty 97

I

I Believe in Miracles 125
Il Terrone Corre Sul Filo 132
Invitation to the Dance with Rudolf Nureyev 174
Irete, David 256

J

Jackson, Jerry 121
Jackson, Mahalia 99, 156
Jackson, Michael 182
Jacob's Pillow 24, 25, 28, 30, 31, 43
Jeffers, Robinson 50
Jillian, Ann 175
John Denver and the Muppets: A Christmas Together 195, 280
John, Elton 161, 162
Jones, Dean 99
Jones, Katie 245, 251, 258
Jones, Sally Mae Tucker 215
Jones, Shirley 164
Jones, Tom 161
Jourdan, Louis 98, 116
Joyce, Elaine 121
Julie Andrews Hour, The 158
Junger, Esther 50, 51

K

Kamali, Norma 227
Kaye, Danny 91, 120, 124, 125, 127, 221
Kaye, Nora 44
Kaye, Sylvia Fine 124, 178
Kazan, Elia 54
Kean, Betty and Jane 78, 80
Keane Brothers, The 108
Kean, Jane 276

Kelly, Gene 158, 159
Kelly, Patsy 114
Kennedy, Joe 63
Kermit the Frog 196
Kerrigan, Ed 186
Kessler, Alice and Ellen 136
Kessler Twins 136
Kettle, Tim 229, 238
Kidd, Michael 54, 55
Kids Are People 114
King and Mrs. Candle, The 80
King, John 186
Kip, Marty 256, 257
Kirkland, Gelsey 239
Kirk, Lisa 140, 272
Kitt, Eartha 100
Kraft, Martin 57
Krofft, Sid 112, 190, 194, 274, 278
Kuhlman, Kathryn 125
Kukla and Ollie 84

L

Lanchester, Elsa 83, 84
Lang, Pearl 44
Lansbury, Angela 158
Lanson, Snooky 66, 67
Larson, Richard 152
Laughs and Other Events 148
Lawrence, Carol 149, 150, 272, 276
Lawrence, Steve 118
Lazaroff, Barbara 216, 272, 278
Leek, Ora 47
Lee, Michelle 272
Le Gallienne, Eva 83, 119
Lemmon, Jack 178
Lewis, Sheri 126
Liberace 170, 178, 190, 197
Lido 137
Lidsville 192
Lillie, Bea 95
Lily Sold Out 178
Limon, Jose 42
Lindquist, John 28
Lippincott, Gertrude 39, 42, 44
Lipton, Peggy 175
Little, Rich 164
Lone, Bob 110, 149
Loren, Sophia 136
Loring, Estelle 57
Louganis, Greg 238
Lou Rawls Parade of Stars 173
Love Wagon, The 49
Loved One, The 197, 198
Love Life 54, 55, 57, 58, 59

Lowe, Charles 81, 270
Lynde, Paul 165
Lypsinka 276, 278

M

MacDonnell, Kyle 51
Mackenzie Gallery 205
MacKenzie, Gisele 66, 89, 90, 270, 276
Mackie, Bob 122, 162, 186, 250, 266, 267, 272
MacLaine, Shirley 69, 94, 128, 166, 167, 182, 239, 270, 274
Magnani, Anna 137
Make Mine Manhattan 51, 54, 69
Manilow, Barry 261, 276
Mann, Anita 108
Manning, Irene 80
Mansfield, Jayne 85, 86, 87
Marcos, Imelda 252
Mareno, Gilda 132, 133, 136
Margaret, Ann 182
Marsh, John 116
Martin, Nancy 121
Martin, Tony 274
Marx, Groucho 156
Mason, Sally 121, 127
Mathers, Jerry 115
Mathis, Johnny 180, 204, 205, 270, 271
Mayfair, Mitzi 56, 57
McCaffrey, Dusty 68
McIver Ewing, Blake 243
McKenzie Gallery 221
McKenzie, Richard 221
McMahon, Ed 242, 243
Menefee, Pete 252, 254
Menteer, Gary 121, 127
Merman, Ethel 83, 96, 225
Mickey Mouse 182
Middleton, Ray 54
Midler, Bette 161
Millis, Nanon 75
Minnelli, Liza 156, 182
Miss Dixie 89, 90, 246
Miss Piggy 195, 196
Miss Teen USA 245, 246
Miss Universe 85, 245, 247
Miss Universe Pageant 253
Miss USA Pageant 245
Mitchell, Arthur 182
Mitzi and a Cast of Thousands 260
Mitzi and a Hundred Guys! 262
Mitzi... A Tribute to the American Housewife 261
Mitzi Gaynor... Razzle Dazzle, The

Special Years 267
Mitzi Roaring in the Twenties! 264
Mitzi... Zings into Spring 265
Mobley, Mary Ann 237
Mondavi, Robert 213
Montand, Yves 101
Montano, Robert 182
Montgomery, George 96
Moore, Mary Tyler 125, 272
Moorhead, Agnes 119
Mordente, Tony 102
Mordoh, Mark 183, 186
Morris, Carole 85
Mr Universe 86
Mumaw, Barton 26, 30
Muppets, The 195
Musical Comedy Tonight 178
Myerberg, Michael 51
My Fair Lady 148

N

Navarro, Nicholas 121, 126, 185, 186, 222
NBC 80, 84
NBC Comedy Hour, The 84
NBC Sunday Spectacular 85
Nellie Bly 114
Nelson, Ricky 194
Nesbitt, Cathleen 116, 171
Newley, Anthony 156
Newman, Paul 90
New York City Ballet 58
Nicholas Brothers 182
Niles, Mary Ann 69, 70, 86
North, Jay 115
Nureyev, Rudolf 45, 174, 175
Nureyev, Rudolph 218
Nutcracker, The 218, 239

O

O'Brian, Hugh 116
O'Conner, Donald 108
O'Connor, Donald 159
O'Donnell, Rosie 244
O'Hara, Maureen 95
Olson, Merlin 175
Olympic Gala 180
O'Neal, Tatum 162
Onofrio, Michael 245, 257, 258
Ortega, Kenny 182

P

Pageant, Bob 42

289

Painter, Walter 182
Palance, Jack 119
Palmer, Lili 206
Palmer, Marina 57
Panama Canal 36
Paone, Remigio 132, 133, 135
Papermill Playhouse 49
Parks, Bert 57
Paul Lynde Comedy Hour, The 165
Pee Wee Herman 278
Perkins, Tony 100
Persian Room, The 140, 141, 150, 155
Phil the Fiddler 51
Pippin, Don 48
Platova, Helene 42, 58
Pogee, Maria 272
Pointer Sisters, The 173
Ponti, Carlo 136
Portia Nelson 204
Poupées de Paris, Les 190
Powell, Eleanor 145, 146
Powell, Jane 116, 231
Presley, Elvis 185
Priborsky, Richard 145
Prowse, Juliet 126, 142, 165, 171, 182, 183, 184, 185, 186, 188, 189, 221, 229, 274

R

Raitt, John 104
Rathbone, Basil 80, 82, 83
Raye, Martha 191
Reagan, Gordon 203, 214
Reams, Lee Roy 121, 126, 225
Redgrave, Lynn 238
Reilly, Charles Nelson 192
Reiner, Carl 264
Reinking, Ann 174
Reubens, Paul 278
Reynolds, Burt 108
Reynolds, Debbie 198, 199, 200, 223, 228, 270, 272
Richardson, Tony 197
Rickles, Don 175
Riddle, Sam 242, 269
Rimes, LeAnn 244
Rip Taylor 236, 274
Ritchard, Cyril 80, 96
Rivera, Chita 101, 102, 166, 182
Robbins, Jerome 58, 72, 80, 182, 247
Robinson, Mable 186
Rock, Chris 244
Rodgers, Mary 116
Rogers, Ginger 83, 100, 101

Rogers, Roy 108
Rogers, Wayne 264
Rooney, Mickey 173, 194
Rose, Paul 207, 208, 259, 272
Rowlf the Dog 195
Rush, Jerry 140
Russian Ballet 218

S

Sabella, Frank 137
Salerno, Enrico Maria 136
Sanders, Marion 137
Sargent, Dick 274
Schlatter, George 107, 114, 163, 167
Schroeder, Ricky 233
Scott, Raymond 70
Shaffner, John 206, 218, 243, 272, 276
Sharr, Jules 111, 151
Shawn Dancers 25, 34
Shawn, Ted 24, 26, 28
Shelley Winters 199, 200
Sherman, Lee 52, 56
Shields, Brooke 231
Shields, Robert 194
Shore, Dinah 88, 89, 90, 91, 92, 95, 99, 100, 101, 102, 103, 108, 157, 158, 221
Showboat 43
Sid & Marty Krofft 191, 193, 194
Simmons, Richard 235
Sinatra, Frank 92, 183, 184
Skirit, Queen of Thailand 250, 251, 253
Skylarks, The 94, 109
Smith, Sid 258
Smothers Brothers 119
Smuin, Michael 182
Sondheim, Stephen 70
Sonja Haney 264
Sothern, Ann 194
Spears, Britney 244
Sporn, Michael 225
Stanley Simmons 57, 58
Starr, Kay 98
Star Search 218, 242, 244, 269
St. Denis, Ruth 26, 27, 28
Stephanie Powers 221, 274, 278
Steve Allen Show, The 77
Stevens, Tony 182
Stewart, Joe 206, 218, 243, 272, 276
Stivers, Bob 229, 230
Stivers, Bunny 229, 238
Stone, Sharon 244
Stop The Music 56, 57, 58, 62, 66
Streets, David 279

Streisand, Barbra 105
Sullivan, Ed 55
Sumac, Yma 194
Svengali and the Blonde 80, 81
Swayze, Patrick 182
Swenson, Swen 174, 194, 198

T

Tadlock, Tad 231, 245
Tahse, Martin 148, 207
Talbot, Lyle 114
Taming of the Shrew, The 206
Taranto, Nino 132, 135
Tate, Charles 43
Taylor, Frances 274
Teague, Scooter 140
Ted Shawn School 24
Television Test 46
Temple, Shirley 104
Templeton, Paul 203, 214
Tennille, Toni 169, 271
Terry, Walter 25, 30
Terry, Walter 48, 51
Thomas, Danny 99
Thomas, Kurt 181
Thompson, Kay 104, 105
Thorson, Scott 171
Tillstrum, Burr 83, 84
Timberlake, Justin 244
Tomlin, Lily 178
Tony Charmoli Dancers 84
Traubel, Helen 156
Traveling Saleslady, The 83
Trelease, Bobbie 72
Trilby 80, 81
Tropicana 142, 173
Troupe, Tom 272, 278
Tryon, Tom 205
Tune, Tommy 182
Turner, Lana 98, 235

U

Underwood, Eric 212, 279

V

Vaccaro, Brenda 165
Vartan, Sylvie 138
Verdon, Gwen 78, 95, 104, 118, 120
Verdy, Violette 106
Vosburg, George 231

W

Webb, Dan 256
Weidman, Charles 42, 44, 46, 76, 132
Welch, Raquel 162, 172, 226, 276, 278
Wells, Bob 140
Westbrook, Frank 44
West, Mae 64, 87
What's The Matter With Helen? 198
Where Do We Go From Here? 167
White, Betty 127, 231, 232, 271, 274
White, Onna 182
Whitmore, Dean 116
Wilde, Cornel 114
Wilder, Mark 101
Williams, Tennessee 220
Wilson, Clive 205
Wilson, Eileen 66
Wilson, Flip 161, 162
Wilson, Lester 182
Winters, Jonathan 85, 197
Woman of the Year 48, 200, 224, 227, 228
Wright, Rebecca 274
Wyler, Gretchen 276
Wylie, June 245

Y

Your Hit Parade 60, 62, 65, 66, 72, 73, 75, 78, 88, 101, 138, 259

Z

Zeffirelli, Franco 136
Zimmerman, Harry 99

CPSIA information can be obtained
at www.ICGtesting.com
Printed in the USA
LVHW070956160919
631202LV00013B/67/P